ANATOMY of a SCANDAL

**An Investigation
Into the Campaign
to Undermine the
Clinton Presidency**

James D. Retter

GENERAL PUBLISHING GROUP
Los Angeles

Publisher: W. Quay Hays
Editorial Director: Peter L. Hoffman
Editor: Dianne Woo
Editorial Assistance: Steve Baeck, Dana Stibor, Marvin J. Wolf
Production: Gus Dawson

Copyright © 1998 by James D. Retter

For information:
General Publishing Group. Inc.
2701 Ocean Park Boulevard, Suite 140
Santa Monica, CA 90405

Library of Congress Cataloging-in-Publication Data
Retter, James D.
    Anatomy of a scandal : an investigation into the campaign to
undermine the Clinton presidency / by James D. Retter.
        p.   cm.
    Includes index.
    ISBN 1-57544-063-6 (hc)
    1. United States--Politics and government--1993- 2. Mass media-
-Political aspects--United States. 3. Press and politics--United
States. 4. Hate--Political aspects--United States.
5. Conservatism--United States--History--20th century. 6. Clinton,
Bill, 1946- --Public opinion. 7. Clinton, Hillary Rodham--Public
opinion. I. Title.
E885.R48   1998
302.23'0973'09045--DC21   97-26020
                                                           CIP

Printed in the USA by RR Donnelley & Sons Company
10 9 8 7 6 5 4 3 2 1

General Publishing Group
Los Angeles

For my wife, Judy,
and my sons, Steve and Matt

ACKNOWLEDGMENTS

My heartfelt gratitude to publisher Quay Hays for his patience, guidance, and support. I would also like to thank Lester Kauffman for his invaluable assistance, Carolyn Chriss for her tireless research, and Hisashi Yamamoto for his many kindnesses. Finally, I want to express my sincere appreciation to the following people: Jonathan Alter, Ronnie Anderson, Steve Baeck, Paul Begala, Chris Bell, Rob Boston, John Brady, Jonathan Broder, Willie Bryan, Paul Colford, Mary Ann Collins, Joe Conason, Harry Crocker, David Crowe, L.J. Davis, Steven Edwards, David Eichenbaum, Ambrose Evans-Pritchard, Al Franken, Dominic Friesen, Cynthia Frost, John Fund, Judy Gaddy, Laurie Garrett, Mike Gauldin, Lamar Goering, Chris Hansen, Phil Hartman, Blake Hendrix, Peter Hoffman, John Hudges, Michael Isikoff, Cliff Jackson, Manuel Johnson, John B. Judis, Dick Kaplan, Mickey Kaus, Carl Kirkland, Joe Klein, Frank Luntz, Deborah Mathis, Pat Matrisciana, Larry Nichols, Grover Norquist, Jim Porter, Randy Raley, William C. Rempel, Carrie Rengers, Lori Rick, Tommy Robertson, Rick Sanders, Richard Schenkman, Edward Spannaus, Dana Stibor, Steve Talbot, Scott Thompson, Murray Waas, Randy Wright, and Buddy Young. Special thanks to Gene Lyons, Bill Simmons, and Max Brantley.

TABLE OF CONTENTS

INTRODUCTION

One hundred years from now, Americans will look back at the way Bill Clinton has been treated as modern-day Salem witch trials.
— Joe Klein

I got involved with this book because of Rush Limbaugh. In 1992, when I first heard his radio show, he was calling Bill Clinton a draft-dodging coward. In the intervening years there has been a nonstop barrage of salacious attacks against the president of the United States. Limbaugh is far from alone.

On a typical day, talk radio blankets the morning airwaves with anti-Clinton invective hot enough to melt plastic. By afternoon, the television talking heads take over. "It's time to break out the baseball bats," says one. Another says the president is a "spider closed in a cereal box in 1992, and now when we open the box, out comes this big ugly thing. We should have listened to the scratchings six years ago." Then its on to late-night, and a continuing series of one-liners from Leno, Letterman, and Maher. For Bill Clinton, it's just another day as president. Tomorrow will be no different.

For the first time in history, it was ruled that a sitting president could be taken to court in a civil case. The vehicle for this unprecedented event began as a tale about sex in a hotel room and ended up in a courtroom in downtown Little Rock. Yet, given the money and partisans involved, there was almost an air of the inevitable about it.

There are also some questions which beg to be answered. Are the president's accusers prepared to receive the same scrutiny into their financial and private lives that has been demanded of the Clintons? Will the press pursue such an examination with the same, unremitting zeal? And is any of this good for the country?

It's a new world. The Information Age is upon us and with it comes an insatiable need to produce news. Gone are the lines that once divided the "trashy" tabloid media from the "respectable" mainstream press. Allegations of sometimes murky origins are reported in rapid bursts, resulting in the "New Journalism" that is driven less by cautious fact-checking and more by the rush to deadlines. How much of what is reported is reliable?

The global community thinks the United States has gone crazy. We are on top of the world—crime is down, unemployment is at its lowest level in decades, the economy is surging, and there is peace in the land. Yet, we seem to be trying our mightiest to rip apart the heart of our republic—the office of the presidency. Why is Bill Clinton under such assault? Is it simply that politics is dirtier than ever?

Columnist William Safire suggests that this may not be the case. In a March 30, 1997, column for the *New York Times*, he wrote about a problem Thomas Jefferson had with a "scurrilous" journalist named James Callender. "Out of the goodness of his heart," Jefferson had given Callender some money over the years, and then, Safire wrote, Callender began "hinting that Jefferson had passed him the funds to keep him quiet about his earlier support of Jefferson's anti-Federalist cause, which had encouraged the journalist to attack Alexander Hamilton and even to cast aspersions on President Washington."

But Safire neglected to note that Callender's "attack" on Hamilton was that he was having an adulterous affair.

Moreover, Callender's reportage effectively ended Hamilton's political career and introduced the young republic to the grimy world of sex and politics.

When it comes to the mix of money, "scurrilous journalists," and politicians, I have learned two things: one is that, inevitably, things are never as simple as they seem; and two, beware of someone who gives money to a smear artist to destroy a rival and then claims it was "...out of the goodness of his heart."

Regarding Joe Klein's comment comparing Bill Clinton's treatment to the Salem witch trials, it should be noted that Klein is the author of *Primary Colors*. Still, it is a point worth exploring. An examination of Bill Clinton's many and varied detractors is not only about fairness, it's about time.

James D. Retter
March 28, 1998

A SCANDAL

Sex hung in the air like cheap perfume...

It was a like a scene in a dime-store paperback, complete with purple prose: A shapely young lady from the wrong side of the tracks finds herself alone in a hotel room with a powerful, attractive older man whose intention is sex. That much she knew. She also knew he was married, and for a smart girl, the situation was pregnant with possibilities. For he was a man seemingly destined to end up as president of the United States. He moved to touch her, and from that moment, the nobody from the wrong side of the tracks became a very important young lady who had the power to end the man's presidential aspirations.

The scene in the hotel room took place in Philadelphia in 1791. George Washington was president; the man in question was his esteemed secretary of the Treasury, Alexander Hamilton; The lady was Maria Reynolds; and the ensuing scandal rocked the young nation and very possibly changed the course of its history.

*　　*　　*　　*　　*

What is known about Reynolds is that on a hot summer day in July 1791, she appeared in Hamilton's office. It was late in the day and she was the last visitor to see him. No sooner had the door closed behind her than she broke down, sobbing that she had been abandoned by her husband, James Reynolds, and she was penniless with nowhere to turn. Believing Maria to be an innocent and the husband a cad, Hamilton made arrangements to stop by her hotel to give her some money. They began an affair and later, when Hamilton tried to break it off, Maria threatened suicide and hired as her lawyer Hamilton's nemesis Aaron Burr.

Eventually, Maria moved to New York and, with Burr's help, divorced her accommodating husband. Hamilton assuaged himself that what had happened was a personal indiscretion, a moral lapse answerable to his conscience and his wife but of concern to no one else. Time passed, and the election of 1796 loomed. His affair seemed all but forgotten.

A surprise visit by James Monroe and a delegation of congressmen made it clear that it was not. Confronting Hamilton, they accused him of using public money to pay blackmail to one James Reynolds. Hamilton was given until the following day to prove his innocence. He did so by turning over letters from Maria and drafts from his personal account showing that the money paid to Reynolds was his own and not from the U.S. Treasury. Assuring Hamilton that they were satisfied, the delegation took the documents and departed.

The documents, however, were leaked to a smear artist named James Callender. He revealed the affair and the charge of stealing from the Treasury in his book, *The History of the United States for 1796*. Hamilton faced an impossible dilemma: To clear his public reputation, he had to admit to the affair. He wrote a pamphlet in which he did so it and published bank drafts that showed the money he paid Reynolds came from his personal account. In so doing he went from being an accused adulterer to a confessed one—an admission that devastated his wife and family and shocked his supporters.

Callender then shifted into second gear. Intending to remove any vestige of influence Hamilton still had within his Federalist Party, Callender denounced Hamilton's confession. It was, he thundered, a lie, proffered under the guise of coming clean. Hamilton had never had an affair; to hide a vast embezzlement scheme, he had shamefully sacrificed the reputation of a virtuous woman.

There was no need for Hamilton to say anything more on the Reynolds affair. America's first morality casualty was convinced that Burr had hired Reynolds to ruin him, and that his other nemesis, Thomas Jefferson, had engaged a smear artist to remove him as a presidential rival. The truth may never be known, but the fact is that Alexander Hamilton was politically dead, done in by a series of inexorable events that all started with a lady in a hotel room.

*　　*　　*　　*　　*

On April 29, 1994, on TV's *700 Club*, Paula Corbin Jones held the audience spellbound as she told of her encounter with President Clinton when he was governor of Arkansas. She explained that she had been working the registration desk at a state-sponsored conference at the Excelsior Hotel in Little Rock. A state trooper named Danny Ferguson approached and said that the governor wanted to meet her in his hotel room. The governor introduced himself and welcomed her inside. According to Paula, no sooner was the door closed than he started loosening his tie and commenting that her boss was a good friend. Suddenly, he leaned over and pulled her toward him.

When Jones had revealed the rest of the details of her sordid claim, the *700 Club* reporter Dale Hurd was moved to observe that "Paula's story has the potential to bring down the Clinton presidency." Pat Robertson, the show's host, commented that "These things are mounting up, more and more and more and more and sooner or later, the American people are going to demand that they get the truth on these things."

*   *   *   *   *

From Maria Reynolds and Alexander Hamilton to Paula Jones and Bill Clinton, sex and politics have been a volatile mixture from the country's beginning—even moreso when we examine the two ladies in question to see exactly who they are, how they came to be compromised in hotel rooms, and if they were mere innocents or part of a conspiracy to use sex and scandal to destroy political opponents.

SETTING
THE STAGE

Gennifer Flowers

January 1992

He was reading *Penthouse* "for the articles," when something jumped out at him. A woman claimed that while lounging around a hotel pool in Little Rock, then-Governor Bill Clinton tried to pick her up. Granted, the alleged incident was said to have taken place in 1984, and the woman in question was a self-described "rock groupie," but it had a certain appeal, an appeal most readers would surely have missed. But Dick Kaplan wasn't just any reader. He was the editor of the *Star*, and this tidbit, with its suggestion of randiness in high places, was the stuff tabloids are made of—especially since Clinton was now a presidential candidate. He would have to send someone to Little Rock to snoop around, but if something was there, it would be a small price to pay for the next sex-and-politics scandal.

Kaplan called Chris Bell at his home in Atlanta and told him to get on the next flight to Little Rock.

A stringer by trade, Bell's job was to check things out before sending in the big guns. All he had to go on was an eight-year-old *Penthouse* clipping that suggested Clinton might like the ladies. One of his first stops was the governor's mansion, where a reception was in process. He walked in and eventually met Clinton, and the two struck up a spirited conversation. "You can tell if someone's for real," Bell said. "He was. I liked him a lot." Unfortunately for Clinton, Bell was about to encounter a man named Larry Nichols.

Standard practice in such scouting matters is to stop by the courthouse to check on pending lawsuits. Bell paid the clerk for a copy of a suit Larry Nichols had filed against Clinton, and he excitedly called Kaplan at the *Star*'s offices in Tarrytown, New York. The lawsuit named five women as Clinton's alleged mistresses. It was almost too good to be true.

Writer Steven Edwards was sent to join Bell. Together, they set out to find the women and get their stories, systematically going down the list. Of the five, only a couple still lived in Little Rock. One was Gennifer Flowers. Finding her proved a challenge, as she had been out of circulation for a while and had an unlisted number. Bell and Edwards began making the rounds, going to nightclubs where Flowers had been known to sing. Finally, a woman said she knew her and might know how to contact her. Not wanting to take any chances, Bell slipped the contact a $100 bill. A few moments later, Flowers was on the phone talking to Edwards. Bell's job was done. He left the next morning.

When Edwards met Flowers, it seems she had already decided to come forward about her alleged affair with Bill Clinton. She had even secretly tape recorded conversations with Clinton to help bolster her claim. But she wanted to go public in the *Washington Post*. Edwards had to convince her to go with the *Star*. "I had a helluva time persuading her to go with us," Edwards told the author. "I told her that, unlike the *Star*, the *Post* would pay nothing. In the end she went with us—money was the deciding factor."

Once she agreed, the *Star*'s New York editors took over. Flowers got a lawyer, and arrangements were made to immediately fly her and her attorney to New York, where final negotiations took place. Flowers' secretly recorded tapes were an important element and the *Star* wanted to hear them before offering a dollar amount. Once Flowers, her lawyer, and the tapes left for New York, Edwards was free to sit down with Larry Nichols to hear about his lawsuit and his problems with Bill Clinton.

*   *   *   *   *

In 1990 Larry Nichols had filed a lawsuit naming me as one of Bill's lovers.
— Gennifer Flowers at her press conference, January 29, 1992

For Associated Press (AP) reporter Bill Simmons,[1] the assignment was nothing particularly unusual. An anonymous tip to the bureau's Little Rock offices claimed that a recently hired state employee was misusing state monies, and there was something about phone calls and Contras. It was worth looking into, but Simmons had no way of knowing that what he eventually reported would be the catalyst that propelled both the ubiquitous *Clinton Chronicles* narrator, Larry Nichols, and Miss Gennifer Flowers into the spotlight. His report in the *Arkansas Democrat-Gazette*, went as follows:

Sunday, September 11, 1988

ARKANSANS FINANCED CONTRA CALLS

Simmons reported that Nichols, while marketing director of the Arkansas Development Finance Agency, made 408 domestic and overseas calls from his office telephone to Contra leaders, at a cost of more than $820. Furthermore, he made 392 calls to one Durrell Glascock in Alexandria, Virginia, at a cost of $414. (Glascock was a consultant to Clinton's 1986 Republican challenger, Frank White, who produced a pro-Contra video in which Nichols appeared.)

When confronted, Nichols said that every call to the Contras was authorized by his boss, ADFA Director Wooten Epes. On a trade mission with then-Governor Clinton to South Korea, Epes told the reporter that, "not only did I not authorize them, I didn't know about them." Epes vowed to investigate upon his return.

Nichols continued that his contacts with the Contras paved the way for contact with then-Representative Jack Kemp to discuss mortgage revenue bonds. But Kemp's public relations aide, Marcie Robinson, said that Nichols spoke with a Kemp aide about the Contras. "That aide doesn't know anything about bonds," she said. "He wouldn't know what to say about them. They talked strictly about Contra matters."

Tuesday, September 13

EMPLOYEE SHOULD PAY FOR CONTRA CALLS, CLINTON SAYS

Clinton was asked about the calls, and thought that Nichols "should at least pay back the state and possibly be suspended," adding that he was concerned at the number of calls made when Nichols should have been working on bond issues. "It looks to me like he could hardly have been doing anything else," Clinton said. For his part, Nichols told the AP, "I keep digging a hole. You got everything down and put out the article. I feel the article is wrong, but I'd just as soon not say no more."

Wednesday, September 14

EMPLOYEE RESIGNS OVER CALLS, ALLEGES 'HATCHET JOB'

Larry Nichols resigned, saying he was forced to do so "because of an unfair news story, based on lies." He added that he had "not used Arkansas taxpayers' dollars to assist the Nicaraguan revolutionary movement," and complained about the "knee-jerk liberal reaction from Governor Clinton," who had made "unfair and inaccurate accusations." Nichols had held the job for less than six months.

Saturday, September 17

FORMER STATE WORKER FACES THEFT CHARGES IN 2 COUNTIES

The Associated Press reported that Larry Nichols was facing felony theft charges in two Arkansas counties. The charge was "theft by deception," and it involved two separate electronics companies. The state police had investigated and turned their findings over to the prosecuting attorney's office for review. The maximum penalty for the charge is a prison term of 10 years and a $10,000 fine.

Monday, September 18

EMPLOYEE WHO CALLED CONTRAS SAYS HE EMBARRASSED CLINTON

In an interview, Nichols said that he lost his job because he was an embarrassment to Governor Clinton. "I guess my knowing the Contras poses a problem for Bill Clinton," he said. "I can say I've been destroyed, my family's been destroyed for doing my job," Nichols said. He maintained that he was calling the Contras in an attempt to use their influence with conservative members of Congress to win support for mortgage revenue bonds. "I used the Contras to support Arkansas taxpayers," he said.

*   *   *   *   *

How Larry Nichols came to be responsible for Gennifer Flowers was still a couple of years away and the road would take some remarkable twists and turns. But he would increasingly come to blame Bill Clinton for all his woes. That part of the saga had just begun.

October 1990

> This is the largest scandal ever perpetrated on the taxpayers of the state of Arkansas.
> —Larry Nichols' lawsuit

Stating that he was wrongfully fired from his $22,500-a-year job with the ADFA and claiming that he was being made a "scapegoat," Nichols filed a libel lawsuit asking for $3 million in damages. In the lawsuit Nichols named his boss, Wooten Epes, and Bill Clinton as defendants. The "scandal" he referred to involved Clinton who, he claimed, used the ADFA's funds for "improper pur-poses"—suggesting that Clinton had five mistresses on which he spent the agency's money. One of the women named was Gennifer Flowers.

To announce the lawsuit, Nichols held a press con-ference on the Capitol steps. His claim of being wrongfully fired was old news. The new news was about Clinton's alleged mistresses. When the reporters asked for proof, Nichols produced nothing. With nothing substantial to report, the story of Nichols' lawsuit appeared on the back pages and little if any mention was given to his claim of "improper purposes." However, copies of his lawsuit were freely available at the campaign headquarters of Clinton's 1990 Republican challenger, Sheffield Nelson. There, the "largest scandal ever perpetrated on the taxpayers of Arkansas" was not given short shrift.

*　　*　　*　　*　　*

January 24, 1992

Bill Simmons was more than a little surprised. As the reporter who broke the story of Larry Nichols' Contra phone calls nearly four years ago, he assumed Nichols carried a grudge. After all, things had not gone well for Nichols: he'd declared bankruptcy, lost his house, and was in trouble with the law over bad checks. However, the *Star* tabloid had just hit the newsstands, and splashed across the front page was the story of Nichols and his claim that Clinton used public money to support five mis-tresses. Yet, here was Nichols on the phone, offering an "exclusive," saying that "the feud with Clinton was over." It was an apparent retraction of what he'd stated in the *Star*. Nichols read the following statement:

It is time to call the fight I have with Bill Clinton over. I want to tell everybody what I did to try to destroy Governor Clinton. I set out to destroy him for what I believed happened to me. I believe I was wrongfully fired from my job. Nobody has wanted to listen to me. All I ever wanted was a fair and honest hearing about what really happened. I want my family to know that I didn't do the things I've been accused of.

This has gone far enough. I never intended it to go this far. I hoped all along that the governor and I could sit down and talk it out. But it just kept getting bigger and bigger.

My family was hurt. And unfortunately, no one can make an ass out of himself better that I can, so I've got to be the one that corrects it and stops it. There's a big difference between what I set out to do and what happened.

The media has [sic] made a circus out of this thing and now it's gone way too far. When the *Star* article first came out, several women called asking if I was willing to pay them to say they had an affair with Bill Clinton.

This is crazy. One London newspaper is offering a half million dollars for a story. There are people out there now who are going to try to cash in.

I apologize to the women who I named in the suit. I brought them into the public's eye and I shouldn't have done that. The least significant parts of my case were those concerning the rumors. I have allowed the media to use me and my case to attack Clinton's personal life.

There were rumors when I started this suit and I guess there will be rumors now that it is over. But it is over. I am dropping the suit.

In trying to destroy Clinton, I was only hurting myself. If the American people understand why I did this, that I went for the jugular in my lawsuit, and that it was wrong, then they'll see that there's not a whole lot of difference between me and what the reporters are doing today.

Larry Nichols
January 25, 1992

Clinton's campaign issued a statement responding to Nichols' announcement:

I respect Larry Nichols for having the courage to come forward to set the record straight. It takes a strong man to admit he's wrong. I know this hasn't been easy for Larry and I am sorry for any hardships that his family has been through in this ordeal.

I know Larry Nichols feels he got wronged when he lost his job. But, as he said, the whole country has been wronged because that incident has been twisted around and blown up and turned into an issue in this campaign.

I don't think Larry ever meant for that to happen, and now he wants to put this whole thing behind him. I hope we'll all be able to put this behind us and get back to talking about the serious issues in this campaign.

Bill Clinton
January 26, 1992

It was, however, far from over, and no one knew that better than Buddy Young. For 10 years he had been the head of Clinton's security detail. Nichols contacted him and said that he wanted a face-to-face meeting with Clinton and that he wanted money. It was not the first time this subject had come up. Two days before the 1990 gubernatorial election Nichols had offered to drop the suit for $150,000 and a house. Nichols' offer was rejected then, and Young went to great lengths to make Nichols understand that money would not be forthcoming this time either.

Nichols said he understood, agreed to put his statement in writing, and it was released to Bill Simmons and the press on January 26. A week later Nichols filed papers to dismiss the suit. In so doing, the judge made Nichols sign a brief order stating that he could not refile the case or raise any additional claims. Nichols told Simmons that he didn't receive money for dismissing the suit. But he never said he hadn't asked.

The meeting with Clinton was arranged and took place on February 27. Nichols made his case that his ADFA/Contra calls were authorized and his firing unjust. Clinton told him that he would look into the matter. Subsequently, on March 12, Nichols met with Clinton's chief of staff, Bill Bowen, and State Department of Finance and Administration head Jim Pledger. At the meeting Nichols said he wanted $200,000. He was again told he would get nothing, so Nichols announced that he was "going another round" with Clinton.

Nichols began talking to national media organizations about alleged wrongdoing involving Clinton and ADFA loans. He was asked about drug and gun smuggling at Mena Airport, which allegedly occurred in the '80s to support the Contras. "I didn't know anything," he told Simmons.

That, however, was before producer Pat Matrisciana came to Little Rock and offered to put Larry Nichols in an anti-Clinton video called *Circle of Power*, soon to be followed by the *Clinton Chronicles*. Suddenly, Larry Nichols knew a great deal about Mena Airport, smuggled drugs, and Bill Clinton's personal life.

May 16, 1992

NICHOLS' SUIT SEEKS OUSTER OF CLINTON
—Arkansas Democrat-Gazette

Nichols filed another lawsuit against Governor Clinton, this time seeking to force his resignation. Contending that Clinton broke a public promise to complete his term as governor, he asked that Clinton repay the salary he'd earned since announcing his candidacy for president. Further, Nichols brought sex into the mix, by claiming that Clinton used a state vehicle and state employees for several "illicit" meetings with women.

Simmons felt the people of Arkansas pretty much knew the saga of Larry Nichols. Simmons had interviewed the people named in the allegations and ran down each of the charges, but nothing checked out. All the while, Simmons was becoming the authority on Larry Nichols. Anyone who wanted to know about Nichols would, of necessity, come to him first. He had files jammed with years of articles, interviews, and facts. Yet, when the *Star* reporters came to Little Rock and made Larry Nichols and his lawsuit(s) against Bill Clinton their primary feature, they never talked to Simmons.

THE TABLOID HITS THE STANDS

STAR EXCLUSIVE

DEM FRONT-RUNNER HAD AFFAIR WITH MISS AMERICA AND AT LEAST FOUR OTHER BEAUTIES...

January 28, 1992

The *Star*'s banner headline looked bad. It showed photos of a swimsuit-clad beauty contestant and various attractive women surrounding a large family picture of Bill, Hillary, and Chelsea Clinton. At the top of the article was a picture of Larry Nichols, identifying him as "Clinton's accuser." As for the five women, one was reported to be an unpaid member of Clinton's staff who "...Nichols says became pregnant and had to have an abortion." The remaining four had previously denied the two-year-old charge and two of them had threatened a lawsuit. One who filed a lawsuit was Suzie Whitacre, identified as Clinton's spokesperson. Subsequently, the *Star* would print a retraction, stating that "...she was not Clinton's lover." The other woman who had threatened legal action was Gennifer Flowers.

It had occurred a year earlier after a talk-show host on Little Rock's KBIS radio station allowed a caller to read the names of the women in Larry Nichols' earlier lawsuit. At that time, Flowers was ready to swear under oath that Nichols' claim was false. A letter from Flowers' lawyer to KBIS president Phillip Johnson, read as follows:

> On October 16, 1990, a radio announcer employed by KBIS and acting within the scope of his duties as a "talk-show host" caused to be

published a portion of a press release which wrongfully and untruthfully alleged an affair between my client, Gennifer Flowers, and Bill Clinton, governor of the state of Arkansas.

This defamation has not only caused my client great emotional and physical distress, but it has resulted in her inability to find gainful employment.

I have been instructed to file a legal action in this matter unless you are willing to compensate Ms. Flowers for her losses. I will, however, refrain from filing such lawsuit for two weeks; however, if we have not begun a meaningful discussion about Ms. Flowers' compensation at the end of that two-week period from the date of this letter, we will immediately commence litigation. Please contact me at my office.

The letter was dated January 30, 1991, and was signed by Robert M. McHenry, of the Little Rock law firm of McHenry, Choate and Mitchell. (See Appendix A.) The *Star* knew nothing about this. They only knew what Larry Nichols told them. Their exposé ran in three installments. The first one was on the sex life of Bill Clinton—according to Nichols.

EPISODE ONE
January 28, 1992

LARRY NICHOLS NAMES CLINTON'S EXTRAMARITAL LOVERS

"Just four years ago," the *Star* reminded everyone, "Gary Hart had to throw in the towel after being caught in sexual escapades with Donna Rice. Now, a *Star* investigation reveals that former Clinton aide Larry Nichols has filed a lawsuit claiming that the 45-year-old politician had extramarital affairs with..."

Flowers was described in the story as "a thirty-something singer." Her agent, Jim Porter, was quoted as saying she "is very attractive and well-endowed. I got her a job singing backup with Roy Clark. She toured with his show." Unlike the others, Flowers responded. "Contacted by the *Star*, Gennifer, now employed by the state's security services, wouldn't discuss the matter. 'I'm afraid of the repercussions if I talk about it,' she said in a halting voice." The account of her response was, of course, a ruse. Reporter Steven Edwards admitted, "We took a bit of dramatic license," for Flowers was already at the *Star*'s headquarters in New York. There, she and her attorney had come to terms and, under the watchful eye of editor Dick Kaplan, she was telling her tale of sex with Clinton to writer Mary Ann Collins for a reported $150,000.

How Nichols knew what he knew was explained: "Nichols told the *Star* that he began to tail the governor in January 1989, in the hopes of catching him with women. 'I wanted to confirm what I'd heard. Several times I saw him coming out of the governor's mansion jogging. He'd go for about half a block and a state police car would be behind him. As soon as he was out of sight of the mansion, he'd get into the car to go to an apartment complex nearby. He'd be in there for about 45 minutes, then come out, get into a police car, and be dropped a block from the mansion and run back in.'"

The apartment complex Nichols referred to was the Quapaw Towers. Gennifer Flowers lived there. A corroborating witness to Nichols' claims was the Quapaw's manager, John Kauffman. The *Star* quoted him as saying: "A couple of years ago we had trouble with the governor's car being parked out front. He'd arrive late in the evening and park in the unloading zone. The governor would get out, go into the complex, and stay from one to four hours. He visited 10 to 20 times. His driver would stay in the car." Kauffman said that he was told by tenants that "Clinton was visiting Gennifer Flowers."

The *Star* did state that Nichols was "fired after making allegedly unauthorized phone calls." Clinton, he claimed, "wanted him ousted because he had documented evidence of a slush fund to bankroll the governor's bid for the presidency and his illicit romances."

The *Star* did not ask for evidence of the "slush fund," nor was any supplied. All of the evidence supplied to support the *Star*'s banner headline was Nichols' word that "several times" he'd seen Clinton being ferried to the Quapaw Towers and the manager's complaint that the governor's car was parked out front. But the following week's issue would provide a firsthand witness.

EPISODE TWO
February 4, 1992

MY 12-YEAR AFFAIR WITH BILL CLINTON
Dems' Front-Runner Lied to America,
Says His Former Lover

Mistress Tells All:
We Were Lovers From 1977 to 1989

It was more than sex. Gennifer Flowers was in love. "He said he wished he could spend more time with me—but as time went on, I knew my chances of marrying him were slighter. I told myself that intellectually and physically I was fulfilled." As to why no one ever saw them together, Flowers stated: "In 12 years, we'd never had dinner out together or gone out like a regular couple...."

He just wouldn't risk being seen with me." Once, however, she was to sing at the governor's mansion, and, she said, Clinton tried to pull her into the men's bathroom.

They met in the fall of 1977 after Flowers had been hired by Little Rock's KARK-TV. "I was sent to the airport to get an interview with him. He was then the attorney general." One thing led to another, she said, and before long they were lovers. Flowers' career as a reporter made it quite stressful. "Bill treated our relationship as if he were bulletproof, but it made me very nervous. Just before the end of my first year, I quit."

But Flowers just couldn't give him up. "Sex was wonderful with Bill. He introduced me to things I'd never done before, like oral sex.... In the beginning, he'd talk about leaving Hillary for me, and I wanted so much for that to happen." In 1979 Flowers auditioned for the job touring with Roy Clark. But after a year of living on the road, she decided she'd had enough, left Clark, and moved to Dallas. However, in 1986, she moved back to Little Rock and into the Quapaw Towers. "We quickly fell back into our old routine," she said. There, she tried to break it off with Clinton. She reported that he cried when she told him that the affair was over.

Meanwhile, Flowers had started a serious relationship with "a stockbroker" and was thinking about marriage. The relationship ended when Nichols' lawsuit named her as one of Clinton's mistresses. She began to lose bookings. "When the *Star* discovered the Nichols lawsuit and wrote about it, I knew the wisest thing for me was to come clean.... For 12 years I lived a lie, and although I've no idea what's ahead for me, I'll be able to take off my dark glasses and face the world."

To add credence to her claim, Flowers offered the tapes—portions of which were transcribed—in the same issue of the tabloid.

NOW THE STAR REVEALS THE BILL CLINTON LOVE TAPES

Again, the image on the cover looked bad. Above a photo of Flowers holding a phone was a larger one of Clinton also holding a phone. Readers were told that the tapes were made between December 1990 and January 1991. A four-page excerpt of the audio transcripts made available by the *Star* did indeed prove that the two had spoken. Almost immediately copies of the audio were made publicly available by right-wing outfits like Citizens United.

Almost as damning in the article was Flowers' claim that Clinton got her a state job. She defiantly claimed:

I WON'T GO TO JAIL FOR BILL CLINTON
He Got Me a State Job—And I Won't Lie for Him.

"I won't stand in front of a judge and lie about the job. I will not perjure myself," she said. Apparently concerned that someone was going to ask her to do so, Flowers said that for her to get the $17,500-a-year position as an administrative assistant with the Arkansas Appeals Tribunal they had to "kick a supervisor upstairs, and deny promotion to the woman recommended to take her place, and then re-classify the job to an outsider [Flowers]."

Flowers told the *Star* that she "was not making enough money with her singing career and asked Clinton, 'Any chance of a job?' A few days later, he called back and told me to get in touch with an aide.... At the end of February (1991), [the aide] called me to say there was a job as a historical guide." Flowers went for an interview but didn't get the job. She said she complained to Clinton, "I didn't get it, Bill. They've already picked someone else!"

The following March she was sent for another interview. This time she was offered the position with the Arkansas Appeals Tribunal and it was this job that she claimed was such a payoff that she feared going to jail.

EPISODE THREE—TWO YEARS LATER
January 4, 1994

GENNIFER FLOWERS: "I'M FURIOUS, BILL CHEATED ON ME TOO!"

A little more than two years after her last appearance in *Star* magazine, Gennifer Flowers was back, claiming to be "horrified and bitterly upset." David Brock's article in the *American Spectator* had hit the stands the previous month. In it, Arkansas state troopers Roger Perry and Larry Patterson claimed that Clinton "ran rampant sexually while governor" and had six other mistresses. "People might think this strange, but I honestly believed I was the only one. To hear to the contrary leaves me in total shock," Flowers said.

Seemingly hurt that Clinton had denied their affair, she said, "I had tapes verifying my relationship with Bill. Legitimate proof." Clinton, she said, had implied that the tapes had been tampered with. "They never had," Flowers said. "I had 62 minutes of tapes, and the American public has only heard eight minutes worth. I know what's on those tapes." Still, she found kind words for the troopers. "At last we have people with enough guts to come forward in public and verify my thing with Bill.... These troopers have gone on the record and confirmed what I told *Star* readers."

Someone else who had praise for the troopers was the *American Spectator* writer Brock. He was quoted as saying that "the troopers' tales seriously call into question the truth of Clinton's statements during the Gennifer Flowers controversy. They also raise issues about Bill Clinton's judgment. What we have here is kind of an issue of corruption. This kind of behavior, at least at this scale, breeds an environment of lying and cover-ups."

Gennifer Flowers became the opening salvo fired into Bill Clinton's character. Yet, for all the din, some basic questions remain unanswered: Who is Gennifer Flowers, and was she telling the truth?

*　*　*　*　*

PRESENTING MISS GENNIFER FLOWERS

From the beginning her credibility was in question. When the story of her affair with Clinton first broke, one of her résumé claims stated that she attended the University of Arkansas at Fayetteville. Reporters checked and found no record of her. However, after school officials were supplied with the name Eura Gean, it was discovered that Flowers had indeed been registered for the 1968–69 school year.

On the same résumé, she claimed to have a nursing degree from the University of Arkansas. Yet there is no such degree for Eura Gean-Geannie-Gennifer Flowers. Nor is there any truth to her claims that she was Miss Teenage America (or Miss American Teenager), attended the elite Hockaday Girls School in Dallas, was a member of the Delta Delta Delta sorority, or that she had a twin named Genevieve.

What is known is that she was born in 1950, the only child of Gene and Mary Flowers. Her father was a crop duster, stunt pilot, and county GOP chairman who often served as a pilot for Republican Governor Winthrop Rockefeller. Her mother was a beautician, and their home was in Brinkley, Arkansas.

Flowers was always determined to make it big in show business. She left college after one year, printed business cards, and started down the circuitous road to fame and fortune. Her singing engagements eventually led her to places like the Flaming Arrow lounge, which was located in Little Rock's Quapaw Towers, where she lived. It was her love life, however, that brought her fame, as well as an unprecedented exploration into the character and private life of a presidential candidate.

*　　*　　*　　*　　*

I was sent to the airport to get an interview with him. He was then the attorney general.
　　　　—Gennifer Flowers, *Star* magazine

Someone who knew Flowers at KARK-TV was Deborah Mathis, then the station's political reporter. She was remembered fondly by Flowers: "When I started work as a news reporter with KARK-TV in 1977, I knew very little about the business. Only one person at the station was helpful to me, another reporter, Deborah Mathis." Today, Mathis is the Washington correspondent for Gannet News Service. She was also accused by Larry Nichols as being one of Clinton's lovers, something the sometimes bawdy Mathis denies: "Hell, if I'd slept with that fat white boy, he'd still be smiling."

An item Flowers stated in the *Star* has Mathis seeing red: "When I went out on stories, Bill made the other reporters wait until I got the interview first, and it became a bone of contention. The job began to get too stressful. Bill didn't try to hide his feelings for me..."

"I would bet my life that Gennifer was never sent out to interview Bill Clinton or cover any of his press conferences," Mathis told the author. "Firstly, she didn't know a thing about politics and, secondly, as the most junior reporter, she would never be assigned to cover them."

> *Bill treated our relationship as if he were bulletproof, but it made me very nervous. Just before the end of my first year, I quit.*
> —Gennifer Flowers, *Star* magazine

Flowers said she was invited to audition for country star Roy Clark's touring show, where she beat out hundreds of girls for a spot as a backup singer. Her agent, Jim Porter, contends that it was Roy Clark, not nervousness over her alleged affair with Bill Clinton, that caused Flowers to quit KARK-TV. After the *Star* hit the newsstands, Porter made news when he contradicted Flowers.

> Flowers, a Little Rock singer, has claimed she worked as an opening act for comedian Rich Little. She made the claim in an old publicity flier and in a 1987 newspaper article. But her former agent, Jim Porter, said late Friday that he had no knowledge of her doing any such work.
>
> —*Arkansas Democrat-Gazette*, February 28, 1992

"I did make that statement," Porter said. "I wanted to be certain I was correct, so I called Rich Little's manager. He said he was with Little wherever he performed and he had never heard of Gennifer Flowers until this broke on Clinton. She was never an opening act for Rich Little." In an interview with the author:

Retter: How long did you represent her?

Porter: I terminated my agreement with her at the end of 1991, so on and off it was 14 years. I got her the job at KARK-TV, which resulted in her very short run as a news reporter.

Retter: What happened? Why did she leave it?

Porter: Gennifer never had a job very long. A friend with the Roy Clark show called and said they were looking for a backup female vocalist— one with a good figure and charisma—and I said I have a lady that might be interested. Gennifer went to Tulsa for the audition and competed with 200 other women. She ended up getting it. Of course, she was one of three backup singers, but I think that is why she left KARK-TV.[2]

Retter: Why did she leave Roy Clark's show?

Porter: She didn't last but a few months. They were in Vegas, and the road manager for Roy Clark called me and asked if I'd heard anything from Gennifer. I said, "No, what's going on?" He said she hadn't showed up for the last two nights, and they were afraid something had happened to her. Finally, she called me. Turned out she met a man in Vegas and just left the show.

Then, I didn't hear from her for the longest time, until she called me from Fort Worth to ask me—of all the audacity—would I call Roy Clark and make up some story about her being kidnapped! She wanted back in his show. I told her that if she wanted to talk to Roy and give him that cock-and-bull story, that was up to her, but I wasn't doing it!

She stayed in Dallas for some time working as a restaurant hostess. And then she came back to Little Rock and said she wanted to get started again. So I took her on again and got her playing with a band, and stayed on representing her until the end of 1991.

Retter: Why did you stop representing her?

Porter: She would spend as little as five or ten minutes out of a 45-minute set on the stage with the band. The rest of the time she was out flitting around with the crowd. These people had paid to hear Gennifer Flowers perform on the stage, not just the band play. That was when I decided it was not doing my business any good to have that kind of a reputation. So I terminated her.

Retter: Did she ever mention having an affair with Bill Clinton?

Porter: No.

Retter: Did she ever mention other men?

Porter: She had been having an affair with a married businessman in this area named Bill. It's my opinion that for publicity purposes she utilized him and turned him into an affair with Bill Clinton.

Retter: Gennifer gives the impression that she was true-blue to Clinton and was devastated to learn he was alleged to have had other affairs.

Porter: I would dispute that. Gennifer liked men and was always going out with one man or another.

Retter: Have you ever discussed this before?

Porter: No. When the *Star* story broke, I was

assaulted by the media. I was offered money to go on various programs—I declined all of it. After the comment about Rich Little, I issued a statement saying I was no longer her agent, and at no time had she told me she was having an affair with Bill Clinton.

Retter: Did you also represent Larry Nichols?

Porter: Yes. I get all the greats.

*　　*　　*　　*　　*

THE STATE JOB

Next to the tapes, the state job is the cornerstone of Flowers' story—her offer of proof that indeed she had had an affair with Bill Clinton. According to what she told the *Star*, she got her post as an administrative assistant because Clinton:

　a) had his people kick a supervisor upstairs;
　b) denied a promotion to the woman recommended to take her place; and
　c) reclassified the job to give it to an outsider.

Flowers said that "a few days" after asking Clinton for help she received an application. "At the end of February 1991 [Clinton aide Judy Gaddy] called me to say there was a job as a historical guide." Flowers went for the interview but didn't get the job. Furious, she said she complained to Clinton. "By March I'd heard from the aide [Judy] again." Flowers interviewed for a second job and got it.

According to the *Star*, the job required public relations experience, supervisory experience, proficiency in computer systems, and the ability to train other personnel. "To make space for me, they promoted the longtime unit supervisor, Clara Clark. She had recommended a secretary, Charlette Perry, to take her place."

This may have looked bad for Clinton, but there was a paper trail that showed why there was no date given for Flowers' initial request for help in finding a job. The first time Flowers contacted Clinton's office about a job was in 1986, not 1991. It was after she had moved back to Little Rock from Texas. Yet, while supposedly in the middle of their "passionate affair," she sent a handwritten note to Clinton at the governor's mansion, which read as follows:

> I certainly enjoyed speaking with you by phone! Enclosed, please find a business résumé and an entertainer's résumé. Anything you can do is much appreciated.
> —Thanks, Gennifer.

A January 27, 1986, letter from Judy Gaddy acknowledged receiving Flowers' résumé. (See Appendix A.) There was no follow-up by either Flowers or the governor's office.

Then, four years later, in September 1990, Flowers called Clinton at his office and again requested help in finding a job. Clinton referred the matter to his staff. Flowers made repeated calls to Clinton's staff during September, October, and November of that year. She was sent public notices of job openings. On February 23, 1991, Flowers sent the following note to Clinton:

> Since we've been unable to connect by phone, I thought I should drop you a note. Judy [Gaddy] had not been very successful in the job hunting area. I've been to one interview at Arkansas Historical Heritage. It only pays $15,200 a year, but, as of yet, I haven't been

offered the position. When I asked Judy if there were any more prospects, she said "no." It took her three weeks to come up with that one.

Bill, I've tried to explain my financial situation to you and how badly I need a job. Enclosed is some correspondence that will be of interest to you. Unfortunately, it looks like I will have to pursue the lawsuit to, hopefully, get some money to live on, until I can get employment.

Please, be in touch.

—Gennifer

The correspondence Flowers was referring to was a copy of her lawyer's letter threatening to sue radio station KBIS for identifying her on-air as Bill Clinton's lover. (See Appendix A.)

*   *   *   *   *

According to Judy Gaddy, Flowers' complaints about her were justified. "Between 30 to 50 job requests came in every month," Gaddy told the author. "They're passed on to me. The fact is Gennifer Flowers was treated like everybody else who asked for help. She got no special treatment.

"That job at the Historical Society was an appointment—you didn't need the merit test for it. If anything special was being done, wouldn't that have been the time to do it?" Gaddy asks.

Flowers' next interview required the merit exam. She had to take it just like all the other applicants. Furthermore, far from the "few days" that she told the *Star*, it had actually taken from September 1990 until June 1991—10 months from the time she first contacted Clinton's office—for her to be interviewed for two jobs. One she didn't get, one she did.

The Boss

I called Bill and said to him: "This job will be fine. I just want to make sure the same thing won't happen again—that it will be given to someone else."
"No problem," he replied.

—Gennifer Flowers, *Star* magazine

Actually, if then-Governor Clinton "got" Flowers the state job she was applying for, it required a somewhat elaborate conspiracy. First, the job had to be publicly posted for a period of 60 days, and all candidates who applied had to be merit-tested and referred by the testing agency. After evaluations, Flowers was one of a dozen referred for an interview as an administrative assistant to Randy Wright, who spoke with the author.

Retter: Were you told to hire Gennifer Flowers?

Wright: No. Of the 10 candidates sent over, some were incredibly qualified. I offered the job to the first one, but by the time I got back to her, she had already taken a job somewhere else. Gennifer tested fairly high because she had worked for the state before—it's like being a veteran. I was impressed that she'd run her own business and had worked at KARK-TV. She said she knew computers—that was a big plus.

Retter: Flowers claims that "to make space for me they promoted the longtime unit supervisor, Clara Clark."

Wright: That's not correct. Clara had taken another job. She's the one who left. The job description was changed from unit supervisor to administrative assistant.

Retter: What about Flowers' claim that Charlette Perry was recommended for the job and that she filed a grievance?

Wright: Charlette was the only in-house secretary to apply for the job and would have filed against whoever got it. She was a good worker, but she'd quit once before over a fight with someone and was brought back. Clara was her friend, but why should she tell me who should replace her as my administrator? Besides, Charlette knew nothing about computers.

Retter: How long was Flowers employed?

Wright: Six, maybe seven months. At first things went well. She wasn't afraid to discipline staff. The whole department was converting to computers—I knew nothing about them—which is why I wanted someone who did. On her application and in her interview, Gennifer said she was proficient. Yet, the little bit I was learning from a computer class about basic terminology, she didn't know. I got suspicious and checked her computer references. They were phony, and I confronted her about it.

Retter: Did she quit or was she fired?

Wright: The day after I counseled her, she said her grandmother in New York was sick and she wanted to go see her. I remember this because my birthday was on a Friday. She had left to see her grandmother on Tuesday. The last scene I have of Gennifer was the day she left for New York. She was in the hall walking away from me.

I said, "See you," and she raised her right hand and wiggled her fingers. That weekend the *Star* came out.

Retter: Did she ever mention Bill Clinton?

Wright: She asked if I knew she was one of the women named in the Larry Nichols lawsuit as having had an affair with Clinton. When I told her I didn't, she said it was all bullshit anyway. That was the only time Clinton's name came up, which is surprising, because Gennifer liked to talk. Sometimes it was strange. She said she spelled Gennifer with a 'G' instead of a 'J' out of memory for her dead twin sister, Genevieve. She liked to talk about sex. Once, she walked into my office and made a comment about oral sex while I was talking to someone from outside the office staff. I went out after her and said that was terribly inappropriate. Sometimes her stories were bizarre. Gennifer used to live in Dallas and claimed that she and a girlfriend used to go to bars, pick up married men, and then blackmail them. You never knew when she was telling the truth, but keeping quiet about seeing Bill Clinton? You couldn't get her to stop talking about men and her sex life.

It turns out that Gennifer had previously held a state job. Actually, she'd had two. On July 1, 1971, she was hired as a clerk stenographer for the Department of Corrections. On February 16, 1972, Flowers was hired to be the personal assistant to the deputy director of the office of accounting in the Department of Finance and Administration. Her supervisor was John Hale, whose brother David Hale eventually became one of the witnesses against Clinton in the Whitewater investigation. These facts have never been reported, nor does Flowers acknowledge these jobs in her book *Passion and Betrayal*.

∗   ∗   ∗   ∗   ∗

THE TAPES

I had tapes verifying my relationship with Bill. Legitimate proof...
—Gennifer Flowers, *Star* magazine

"As a woman, I had to fight a hundred times over for credibility on this. I even had to produce the tapes," said Flowers. The tapes did prove that Clinton talked with her. But whose case did they prove? As reported in the January 29, 1992, *Star* magazine:

Dial tone. Dialing sounds. Ringing.

Voice: Governor's mansion, Roger Creek.

Flowers: Is Bill Clinton in please?

Voice: Ma'am, he's with some people right now. May I ask who's calling?

Flowers: This is Gennifer Flowers, I'm returning his call.

Voice: Gennifer Fowler?

Flowers: FLOWERS!

Voice: Hang on just a second.

What this excerpt and further information culled from the tape showed is that Gennifer's name was not recognized, Clinton had a sore throat, and Gennifer was going to see her mother.

The *Star* said that the tapes were made by Flowers between December 1990 and January 1992. They were released in three formats: transcripts in the *Star*, transcripts handed out to the press, and on audiocassette. A comparison of the different formats shows some discrepancies. For example, the transcription in *Star* differs from the audiocassette and the press transcript as follows:

Voice: Governor's mansion, Roger Creek, can I help you?

Flowers: Is Bill Clinton in, please?

Voice: Ma'am, he's with some people right now. May I ask who's calling?

Flowers: This is Gennifer Flowers, I'm returning his call.

Voice: Hang on.

Gennifer Fowler is gone. Gennifer Flowers, however, is put right through. The sore throat and visit with her mother remain the same. Both versions mistakenly identify the person answering the phone as Roger Creek, when it was actually a trooper named Roger Perry.

Another tape ends suggestively. In a summary the *Star* reported that "Clinton tells her to call him back after 11 P.M. at home—the governor's mansion." The transcript, however, reads:

Clinton: Why don't you just call me tonight after 11. I'll try to get [state trooper] Carl Kirkland on the phone. Call me at the mansion. I'll be home.

If a later call took place, there is no tape of it. Why did Clinton want trooper Kirkland on the line? Might it have had something to do with a burglary Flowers said happened in her apartment but hadn't reported to the police? Kirkland, a veteran state trooper who has served under four governors, told the author that he has no idea. "I've never met Flowers and don't remember her calls." However, when the trooper is left out of the transcript the tape conversation goes from being a mystery to being suggestive.

In other discrepancies, the transcripts have Clinton saying, "...we have to watch as we go along," and they have them using words of endearment, "Good-bye, Baby" though neither is on the audiotape. Flowers does bring up sex , saying she was going to tell reporters that he "ate good pussy." After Clinton says "what," Flowers repeats her flattering oral sex comment, to which the transcripts record his response as:

Clinton: ("Garbled.")

I thought they'd look into it. But, you know, I just think a crazy person like Larry Nichols is not enough to get a story on television with names in it.
            —Bill Clinton, Gennifer Flowers' tapes
            Star magazine

Bill Clinton was concerned. Ever since Larry Nichols filed his lawsuit in October 1990, naming Flowers as the governor's lover, there had been questions. Something the tapes don't show and that Flowers would later reveal is that she called Clinton to tell him that she had been offered $50,000 and a job in California to say the affair had occurred.

Well, it's like I told you, if I leave a message, it's important. I won't call you unless something like this has gone on. So just get back to me, because, like I said, I'm not good at this and may need advice.
—Gennifer Flowers, Gennifer Flowers' tapes

There was no way to determine whether Flowers' claim that Republicans were offering money was the topic of the tape, which begins in the middle of a conversation and ends with Clinton yawning. "Well," Flowers says, "same to you."

Another tape that shows how seriously Clinton took the situation abruptly begins with Clinton suggesting, "...like I told you before when I called you, is to have an on-file affidavit explaining that you were approached by a Republican and asked to do it." Flowers seems unsure and then asks, "Are you going to run? Can you tell me that?" Clinton responds: "I want to. I wonder if I'm going to be blown out of the water with this. I don't see how they can...if they don't have pictures."

Another time Flowers asks a question dripping with irony: "But why would they waste their money and time coming down here unless someone showed them some interest?" Clinton responds: "They're gonna run this Larry Nichols thing down, they're gonna try to goad people up, you know, but if everybody kinda hangs tough, they're just not going to do anything. They can't... They can't run a story like this unless somebody said, 'Yeah, I did it with him.'"

Specific dates were a problem for Flowers. When her story first surfaced, she said that the affair began "in 1979 or 1980" at the Excelsior Hotel in Little Rock. The hotel wasn't built until 1982. It was the last time and date she ever offered. The tapes were no different. There is no indication as to when or where a conversation is taking place. Futher, they're chopped, random, and full of talk about politics, not sex.

*   *   *   *   *

I had 62 minutes of tapes and the American public has only heard eight minutes worth. I know what's on those tapes.
—Gennifer Flowers, *Star* magazine

When the *Star* broke Flowers' story, its editor, Dick Kaplan, said it was hard news. "This isn't Martians walking on Earth. It isn't chickens with two heads. It isn't 'Elvis is alive.' It's real journalistic inquiry into the integrity of a major presidential candidate," Kaplan said in the *Star*. He added that there would be two parts. "The upcoming one is even more damaging," to Clinton's presidential campaign, he said.[3]

Hard news, however, requires something more than gossip. If a presidential candidate was to be knocked out of the race by sex, some witnesses were necessary. In Flowers' case, there were three: her mother, her best friend, and the Quapaw Towers' manager. Flowers' mother, Mary, had remarried and was living in Minnesota. She told the *Star* that she knew about her daughter's affair with Clinton. However, after the story broke, a Little Rock reporter tried to contact her and was told that "she was too ill to talk."

Lauren Kirk was identified as Flowers' "best pal for 10 years," whom she told about Clinton. "Every time he'd come into town, she'd get all excited." The town was Dallas, where Flowers and Kirk were living. Kirk told the *Star* that Clinton used to visit her friend often. What she didn't say was that—even though she lived with Flowers—she'd never personally seen or met Clinton.

Lastly, there was the manager of the Quapaw Towers, John Kauffman. He was quoted as saying that Clinton's car was seen out in front of the building "between 10 and 20 times," and that he "was told by tenants Clinton was visiting Gennifer Flowers." Kauffman categorically denied the quote to both AP reporter Bill Simmons and the author.

* * * * *

I'm not David Brock, believe me...
   —Dick Kaplan, Editor, *Star* magazine

To prove his statement, Dick Kaplan tells how he is motivated solely by story and not politics. "When George Bush was accused of having an affair," he told the author, "the *Star* used every resource known to get ahold of the woman. We spent a lot of money and failed—she was too well hid. No one could find her."

> **Retter:** In the copy of the [tape] transcript that was released to the press there are some key omissions. How could that have happened?
>
> **Kaplan:** We had it transcribed by a transcription service. At first, we tried to do it ourselves, but we're not equipped for that sort of thing, so we sent it out to a professional transcription service. We were so concerned about security that we had someone sit there the whole time it was being transcribed. If there was something left out it was unknown to me.
>
> **Retter:** In the version for the *Star*, a trooper's failure to recognize Flowers' name when she called the governor's mansion is omitted.

Kaplan: I have no knowledge of that. It has never been pointed out before.

Retter: Was there one specific time or place Flowers gives when she was with Clinton that could be checked out?

Kaplan: We tried to check it out, we did the best we could. If people didn't believe her, she would have come and gone. But she didn't—people do believe her. I believe her.

Retter: Why was there no pillow talk? No, 'weren't we lucky no one saw us together?' Nothing intimate?

Kaplan: We interviewed Gennifer exhaustively. Do I wish there was a photograph? Yes. Do I wish there was pillow talk on the tapes? Yes. Was there? No. The only sexual allusion was made by her. Do I think they had a sexual relationship? Yes. Did that particularly matter to me? Not really. What mattered to me was he gave her a state job.

Retter: How were the tape excerpts chosen?

Kaplan: I heard the complete tapes over and over again—and gave eight minutes of extracts—that was the best of what there was.

Retter: Was there any pillow talk on the tapes that weren't excerpted?

Kaplan: No.

Retter: Did it seem odd that there was not one note or picture to support Flowers' claims?

Kaplan: Yes it did. But it was hard to get around the tapes and the details she brought to the plate. Journalism in a hurry means we tried to check it out, we did the best we could. I'm glad Clinton won—I wouldn't have wanted to have been the one to torpedo his campaign. I'm glad it ran when it did. A few months later and it would have been a different story. Now, would I run the story again? I would.

Retter: Do you believe Paula Jones?

Kaplan: No.

Retter: So it is possible to go after the president and have it go all the way to the Supreme Court, based on a lie?

Kaplan: You bet.

Retter: Did it ever occur to you that Gennifer was lying?

Kaplan: When I saw her in *Penthouse*, I was appalled. It wasn't the nudity—she talks about her mother telling her to call her vagina her "precious." And the way she talks about the president! I told her I thought she'd gone too far. I knew she'd done it to cash in—she got three to four times what she got from the *Star*. Did it occur to me that she'd done the one for us to cash in, too? Yes it did.

*　　*　　*　　*　　*

CHARACTER AND PENTHOUSE

Gennifer, do you think that a person should be disqualified from the White House just because he's had an affair?

—*Star* press conference

I would have to think about that very carefully before I would vote for someone who'd had an extramarital affair.
—Gennifer Flowers, *Penthouse* magazine

Never mind that on the tapes Flowers was heard to coo, "Oh, I'd love to see you be president. I think that would be wonderful." She'd obviously changed her mind, and the public was left to decide about a candidate whose national name recognition, at the time, was barely 50 percent.

Two people who might have helped the voters are Buddy Young and Tommy Robinson. As the head of the state's troopers and security for the governor, Young knew Clinton. "I was with him around the clock for days at a time," he said. "I never saw him with Gennifer Flowers or even alone in a room with another woman."

He also knew troopers Roger Perry and Larry Patterson and of their charges that Clinton was a reckless womanizer. "They're a couple of guys who loved to run women. Do I think they used Clinton's name to pick up women? Yes." As to the notion that Clinton confided in them about his womanizing, Young says, "Bullshit! Bill Clinton was too smart to trust a couple of characters like Perry and Patterson with anything that could hurt him politically."

Young's objectivity, however, is questionable. After Clinton became president, Young became a regional director for the Federal Emergency Management Administration. He stands accused of being an "insider" who knows to keep his mouth shut. Someone who doesn't have that problem is Tommy Robinson, who, it can be safely said, is no fan of Bill Clinton's.

During Clinton's first term in 1979, Robinson was appointed to head the Public Safety Department. Overseeing the state police guarding the governor 24 hours a day, Robinson said he knew Clinton as well as anyone. Clinton, he said, had no affair with Flowers. "I would have known about it. I don't like the way the guy governs, but I'm not going to do a hatchet job."

After one term Robinson left to run for sheriff, eventually becoming a Republican and winning a seat in Congress. It was his congressional aide who Larry Nichols was calling about the Contras. When Nichols went to Honduras, it was with Robinson. Today, however, Robinson calls Nichols a "nutcase—he's a guy with an ax to grind after he got fired from his state job." As for Nichols' claim that he saw Clinton going to the Quapaw Towers, "They had a bar downstairs and a bunch of legislators lived there— hell, you could say the same thing about me—I used to go to the Quapaw Towers, too!" He said there are so many things to say about Bill Clinton—"like he's a draft dodger running the military—but that he was a reckless womanizer? I saw nothing. The guy wanted to be president—he's not stupid. [Clinton's Republican opponent] Sheffield Nelson spread rumors of Clinton's womanizing during the 1990 campaign, and kept it up after he lost. The real story is, 'Why did he [Nelson] orchestrate this?'" Robinson asked.

* * * * *

I know he lied.
I just wanted to make his asshole pucker.
　　　　—Bill Clinton, Gennifer Flowers' tape
　　　　　Penthouse, December 1992

Nine months after her appearance in the *Star,* Flowers appeared in a *Penthouse* pictorial. For a reported $600,000 she was offering new tapes, new claims, and a new Gennifer Flowers.

The object of Clinton's above tirade was his 1990

Republican opponent, Sheffield Nelson. Just prior to the quote the *Star* tells the reader: "On one tape Clinton says he'd long suspected a dirty trick—a trick that failed—courtesy of rival Sheffield Nelson, who denied it." The context and "trick that failed" was never alluded to.

At another point in the article Clinton says: "[Sheffield] Nelson called me and he said, 'I want you to know we didn't have anything to do with that.'"

Clinton said he didn't buy it. He told Flowers: "[Nelson] was calling people off the street, trying to get people to say I'd slept with them."

The subject of their conversations is the women Clinton is accused of having affairs with—one of whom was allegedly Flowers. Her response would be revealing, especially with Clinton angrily denying the charges, calling the man he feels guilty of spreading the tales a liar. But Flowers said nothing. At another point Clinton discusses how Flowers "might turn double agent and attempt to entrap the local Republicans who had approached her with a reported $50,000 offer to go public." He suggests that she sign an affidavit that would detail any GOP dirty tricks. Flowers' response:

"Well, it's like I told you, if I leave a message, it's important. I won't call you unless something like this has gone on. So get back to me, because like I said, I'm not good at this and may need advice." It is impossible to say for certain what "important" information Flowers was referring to because the tape excerpt starts in the middle of the conversation.

This begs the question, why were excerpts purporting to show more than they deliver promoted first by *Star* and then by *Penthouse*? In what context were the quotes given? What was on the remaining 56 minutes?

It was up to *Star* and *Penthouse* to decide what was newsworthy and incriminating. The answer lies in the "complete and unedited" tapes of Gennifer Flowers, which were offered for sale by "The Gennifer Flowers Company."

But it is important to understand that the tapes are not complete and they are edited. In her introduction, Flowers says the first tape was recorded in December 1990, just after Larry Nichols had named her and four other women in his lawsuit against Clinton.

Clinton tells Flowers how she "got on the [Nichols'] list":

Flowers: Well, I hope that they'll just leave everything alone.

Clinton: I think they will. I think this suit will be dismissed now. So, I don't think you have to worry about that.

Flowers: Well, I'm, you know, I'm actively looking for a job and I don't need all that. And I know you sure as hell don't need it, but...

Clinton: ...I'll tell you exactly what happened. The way you got into that is when you were living at Quapaw Tower and the watchman alleged that I came to your apartment.

Flowers: Yeah, I remember that.

Clinton: That was the sole basis of it. And that son of a bitch, whoever that scumbag is, told it all over town.

Flowers: Well, that was probably (name deleted). I don't know his first name, but he's been there for a long time. He's a real gossip.

Clinton: Yeah, he burned your ass on a bunch of stuff. He talked about you real bad.

Flowers: Well, they do that down there, though. They're like a bunch of little old people.

The lawsuit is very much on Clinton's mind. He says that "10,000 copies" have been mailed out and that Sheffield Nelson is behind it. "That's why he called and started to cover his ass. He thinks I'm (inaudible) and that I'm gonna come after his ass then."

Tape two, recorded in September 1991, also begins in mid-conversation. Flowers tells Clinton that some Republicans are willing to pay her $50,000 to admit to an affair, and Clinton asks her to sign an affidavit. "I wish I was guilty of all this stuff with you," Clinton says. The lawsuit continues to worry him. "It's awful. You know, I go along for a day or two and then I hear this stuff. It just takes all the energy out of me."

> **Flowers:** ...My theory is, because I've been a news reporter, if it were me and I looked at [Larry Nichols' list of five women], I would pick Gennifer Flowers out as being one of the most vulnerable for a couple reasons; one, is that I'm not married.
>
> **Clinton:** So, you have less incentive to be quiet.
>
> **Flowers:** And two, I'm an entertainer.
>
> **Clinton:** Yeah.
>
> **Flowers:** And, most of the time entertainers, you know, it's publicity.
>
> **Clinton:** Yeah.
>
> **Flowers:** Even if it's bad, it's publicity.
>
> **Clinton:** Yeah.
>
> **Flowers:** See. So, if it were me looking at that list, I'd go after me too.
>
> **Clinton:** Yeah.
>
> **Flowers:** So if, you know, they may be doing the same.

Clinton: That's why they're calling you and Lencola [Sullivan, former Miss Arkansas], I guess.

Flowers: Is she an entertainer?

Clinton: Yep, and she's single.

Flowers: Oh really? Oh, I didn't know that! Well...

Clinton: She was going with Stevie Wonder all during this alleged time.

Flowers: Where does she live now?

Clinton: New York.

Flowers: Well, of course, again, see she's not here in Little Rock either.

Clinton: Yeah. It's hardly handy.

Flowers: Uh huh. Well, anyway...

Clinton: I don't even know how, I mean, that's what I'm telling you. This whole thing's been a mystery to me. I don't know how [Nichols] got the list.

Flowers: Well...

Clinton: The night watchman, that's who did it to us.

Flowers: Oh, the guy at Quapaw Tower?

Clinton: Yeah.

Flowers: Oh, (name deleted)? I know. And he was such an old toot. I tell you.

Clinton: He really monitored you bad, anyway.

Flowers: Well, everybody always does. I wish sometimes some of the things they say I do, sound so good, I wish I'd done them.

Clinton: I know.

The date of the fourth and last tape is given as December 1991. Flowers says that her apartment has been broken into.

> **Clinton:** That is so weird. I mean, that break-in, but I wouldn't put it past them. The Republicans are really sort of frightened of this whole deal. I mean they've made no secret of the fact that they think I'm the only guy that can beat Bush. And that...
>
> **Flowers:** Oh, Bush isn't doing real well right now in the popularity ball game.
>
> **Clinton:** No. He's down. Well, he's so out of it, Gennifer. He's a nice enough guy.
>
> **Flowers:** Oh, I don't like him.
>
> **Clinton:** He basically doesn't have a clue about what the hell's going on; what ordinary people's lives are like, you know. He just doesn't have a clue. He has no idea how awful it is for them.

Flowers goes on to say that she has a "little company" called Concepts Plus, that "does jingles..."

It is clear is that Bill Clinton was more passionate when the subject was Sheffield Nelson than when it was Gennifer Flowers. Someone who is not surprised by this is John Hudges.

*   *   *   *   *

Nelson's press secretary, John Hudges, was once a friend of Flowers'; they'd worked together at a Little Rock television station, where he was assignment editor and she did a brief stint as reporter in 1977–78.
—Penthouse magazine, May 1992

David Brock wrote that it was Hudges who brought Flowers to the *Star* reporters. Hudges said that while he and Flowers were working together at KARK-TV she "...discussed her relationship with Clinton as early as 1977 and several times afterward."

Lest there be any doubt about where Hudges stands today, he bristles: "As governor, Clinton sat there, keeping the chair warm until he ran for president. We have the worst roads, the worst bridges, the worst child care..." Hudges spoke about Flowers, Clinton, and Nelson in an interview with the author.

Retter: How did you know Flowers and Sheffield?

Hudges: I worked at KARK while she was there, and in 1990 I was Sheffield's press secretary.

Retter: Describe the relationship between Clinton and Nelson.

Hudges: They hated each other. The only time Sheffield called Clinton, it was to grovel because pressure was on him to apologize or explain something.

Retter: David Brock wrote that you brought the *Star* reporters to Flowers.

Hudges: That's not true. In the '86 campaign I told several reporters that "If you ask Gennifer Flowers, she's going to tell you a story about Bill Clinton." Right before the Democratic primary I said the same thing to some reporters. I think she's telling the truth, and I still do.

Retter: She told you she was having an affair with Clinton?

Hudges: What she said was that he'd sneak up to her place—she was living at the Georgetown apartments. At first I told her I didn't believe it, but she said it so often that eventually I did.

Retter: So you came forward in *Penthouse*. She said you exaggerated.

Hudges: Yes, it was strange—Gennifer said I was exaggerating my knowledge of the affair. I thought, "Hells bells, girl, I was backing up your story!" I stepped forward and said she told me this, and she goes, 'Oh, he's exaggerating.' I thought, what the hell is she doing? Does she think Bill is going to call sometime in the future and say, "Thanks for covering my ass?" That tells a lot about her. Now, when I look back on it, she was a pretty good bullshitter.

Retter: Had you ever heard about the $50,000 offer from the Republicans?

Hudges: No, but frankly I wouldn't doubt it.

Retter: Did she tell you that she taped other men?

Hudges: Yeah, she told me that a lot.

Retter: Did she say why she was taping them?

Hudges: She used to say, "Men are the dumbest things in the world." She told me, "I'll always have some ammunition."

*　*　*　*　*

THE BEST FRIEND

She's been my best pal for 10 years, and it saddens me to see Bill Clinton running for president and blatantly lying about his affair with

Gennifer. I've been telling her to come out with this for years, but she wouldn't—she didn't want to wreck his career.
—Lauren Kirk, *Star* magazine, January 29, 1992

Lauren Kirk was Flowers' most compelling witness. "Back in 1984," she told the *Star*, "she told me she was involved with someone named Bill who was breaking her heart." Two years later, Kirk was told that "Bill" was in fact Clinton. "Every time he'd come into town, she'd get all excited, and when he left, she'd be very depressed."

Yet, if the *Star* knew that Kirk had never seen nor met Clinton, it didn't report it. Nor did it inform readers that Kirk and Flowers were roommates living in Dallas and that both were hostesses at a nightclub. The *Star* reported that Flowers said: "Bill called to tell me he was going to announce his candidacy for president and warned me again that our relationship would be scrutinized."

No tapes exist to support this version. What does exist is one in which Clinton asks Flowers to sign an affidavit swearing that she'd been approached by Republicans and offered money. Flowers then asks, "Well, are you going to run? Can you tell me that?"

Lauren Kirk would soon paint a different portrait of her "best pal for 10 years."

* * * * *

She said, "It's tempting, but I'm going to wait until after he's nominated. It will be worth a lot more."
—Lauren Kirk, *Penthouse* magazine, December 1992

After she claimed that in 1992, a state Republican offered her $50,000 and a job in California to go public about her alleged affair with Clinton, Flowers phoned Kirk and said she was going to hold out. "Clinton," Kirk said in the *Penthouse* story, "has been planned out like a military campaign. Flowers is using it as a springboard because she never made it as a singer....She intends to become famous at all costs—and this was the perfect avenue."

According to Kirk, Clinton wasn't Flowers' only victim. Flowers knew how to get a man hooked. Kirk said, "She'd say, 'Okay, today I'll go down on him at a red light, or strip in his office and fuck him on the floor'— things the average woman just doesn't generally do." There was a pattern, according to Kirk—the men were powerful, rich, and married. The latter had a certain advantage. Kirk describes a "Dixie mogul" who Flowers got "hooked" on her; she then struck with him a deal for money. "She picked up souvenirs" at his mansion and then told him, "now we wouldn't want your wife to know who took them." *Penthouse* reported that friends were enlisted to secretly photograph her with the man in public.

Remarkably, it is a story that Flowers doesn't deny. *Penthouse* went on, "She pitched an ex-Dallas sugar daddy for a Porsche, then dropped the geezer cold when he gave to charity and not to her. As Gennifer Flowers likes to say, 'You've got to pay to play.'"

*   *   *   *   *

Years later, Gennifer Flowers was questioned by President Clinton's lawyers in preparation for the Paula Jones trial. The following is what she revealed about her "best friend" for 10 years:

Question: Do you have a former roommate

whose name is Kirk?

Flowers: I do not.

Question: You have no roommate that you recall the last name was Kirk?

Flowers: No.

Question: First name was Kirk?

Flowers: No.

Question: Do you have a friend whose name is Kirk?

Flowers: Not a friend, no.

Question: Would you call her an acquaintance?

Flowers: Yes. I would call him an acquaintance.

Question: Him an acquaintance. I apologize. What is his full name?

Flowers: We don't know his full name. He's a (deleted).

Question: And that is the same individual who's referenced in the *Penthouse* magazine December 1992 issue?

Flowers: That's correct.

Subsequent to questions about the "offer from Republicans":

Question: At your press conference held in January of 1992 in New York City, you stated that you were approached by the Republican party and asked to publicly confirm that you had an affair with Mr. Clinton, and at that press conference were you referencing the approach made by [Ron] Fuller?

Flowers: I was.

Question: Isn't it true that you elected not to go public with the story when Mr. Fuller approached you because you thought you could get more money from the stories after Mr. Clinton declared his candidacy for president?

Flowers: That is not true.

Question: Did you ever tell anyone that?

Flowers: I don't recall ever telling anyone that.

Question: Do you deny making that statement?

Flowers: I do not recall ever making that statement.

Flowers described Ron Fuller as a friend she knew socially. "He was a Republican," she said. "He had held Republican office." What Flowers didn't say was contained in a January 30, 1992, article in the *Arkansas Democrat-Gazette*. The article reports that Flowers "worked for Republican Ron Fuller's 1990 state senate campaign." It was reported that Flowers, "was hoping he would get elected so he could get her a job, a source said." She reportedly made telephone calls, went door-to-door, and sang at a fund-raiser.

"Fuller said he was not the local Republican that Flowers said approached her several months ago. 'You guys are obviously trying to establish Republican connections with Ms. Flowers.'" The paper reported that Fuller served in the state house from 1985 to 1989, and was President Bush's 1988 campaign co-finance chairman in Arkansas. Federal Election Commission records show Flowers donated $1000 to Fuller's campaign.

*   *   *   *   *

TICK, TICK, TICK

The Clintons on *60 Minutes*

Guests: **Governor and Mrs. Clinton**
Airdate: **January 26, 1996**
Correspondent: Steve Kroft

Kroft: It's been quite a week for Arkansas Governor Bill Clinton. On Monday his picture was on the cover of *Time* magazine, anointed by the press as the front-runner for the Democratic presidential nomination. Six days later, he's trying to salvage his campaign. His problem—long-rumored allegations of marital infidelity—finally surfaced in a supermarket tabloid, and last week they were picked up and reprinted by the mainstream press.... Who is Gennifer Flowers? You know her?

Clinton: Oh yeah.

Kroft: How do you know her? How would you describe your relationship?

Clinton: Very limited—friendly but limited. I met her in the late '70s when I was attorney general. She was one of a number of young people who were working for the television stations around Little Rock...

Kroft: Was she a friend, an acquaintance?

Clinton: She was an acquaintance. I would say, a friendly acquaintance. When this story, this rumor, got started in the middle of 1990 and she was contacted and told about it, she was so upset and called back; she said, "I haven't seen you for more than 10 minutes in 10 years." She would call from time to time when she was upset or thought she was really being hurt by the rumors, and I would call her back. I'd call her back at the office, or I'd call her back at the house, and Hillary knew when I was calling her back. I think once I called her when we were together, so there's nothing out of the ordinary there.

Kroft: She's alleging—and has described in some detail in the supermarket tabloid—what she calls a 12-year affair with you.

Clinton: That allegation is false.

Mrs. Clinton: When this woman first got caught up in these charges—as I felt about all of these women—that they had just been minding their own business, and they got hit by a meteor and it was no fault of their own. I met with two of them to reassure them. They were friends of ours; I felt terrible about what was happening to them. You know, Bill talked to this woman (Flowers) every time she called distraught, saying her life was going to be ruined, and he'd get off the phone and tell me that she said sort of wacky things which we thought were attributable to the fact that she was terrified.

Clinton: It was only when money came up, when the tabloid went down there offering people money to say that they had been involved with me, that she changed her story. There's a recession on, times are tough, and I think you can expect more of these stories as long as they're down there handing out money....

Kroft: You've said that your marriage has had problems, that you've had difficulties. What do

you mean by that? Does that mean you were separated? Does that mean you had communication
problems? Does that mean you contemplated
divorce? Does it mean adultery?

Clinton: I'm not prepared, tonight, to say that any
married couple should ever discuss that with
anyone but themselves.... I have acknowledged
wrongdoing. I have acknowledged causing pain in
my marriage. I have said things to you tonight...
that no American politician ever has. I think most
Americans who are watching this tonight, they'll
know what we're saying, they'll get it, and they'll
feel we've been more than candid.

*The Clintons were nervous, but you could also
sense they were really up for it, particularly
Hillary.... The interview was either going to
make 'em or break 'em. And clearly, it made
them. Everybody comes up to me and says if
you hadn't done that* 60 Minutes *interview, he
never would have become president.*

—Steve Kroft

*   *   *   *   *

The significance of Gennifer Flowers is not her claim of
having sex with men in high places. Rather, her case proved
that an unexamined claim could start with a tabloid and
end up a conclusion without ever having to pass through
scrutiny. She successfully laid a foundation for the character assault on Bill Clinton that would be equally embraced
by the right wing and the popular culture, softening his
image so that each future attempt to defame his character
would be taken a bit more seriously than the one before.

Where is Gennifer Flowers today? As of December 1997, her name was on a Website, which reads:

Hi—I'm GENNIFER FLOWERS—former lover of PRESIDENT BILL CLINTON, and I have 100s of the most beautiful CO-EDs, MODELS, and X-RATED STARS for you to MEET, SEE, and TALK TO, right from the privacy of your own PC.

PRESIDENTIAL-QUALITY CYBERSEX!
RIGHT HERE ! RIGHT NOW !

Connect with real, live, gorgeous nymphs waiting to give you HEAD of State Treatment!

For $4.95 per minute, Flowers promises the viewer that there are "hot and horny presidential-quality sluts waiting for you!"

*   *   *   *   *

From the author's interview with Larry Nichols—the man who "discovered" Gennifer Flowers and set the stage for all that followed:

> **Retter:** Did you know Gennifer Flowers before the *Star* article?
>
> **Nichols:** Of course. I knew her quite well. I played guitar in a band, and we had the same agent.
>
> **Retter:** How do you explain the discrepancies in her story about her affair with Bill Clinton?
>
> **Nichols:** The problem was she put in all that crap about being in love and it being a 12-year affair.

Retter: Did you know that she had tapes of her conversations with Clinton?

Nichols: Everybody knew she had tapes.

Retter: Did you tell the *Star* that she had tapes?

Nichols: Can't say.

Retter: Did she ever talk to you about the tapes and ask what she should do with them?

Nichols: Can't say. Like I said, everybody knew she had them. Clinton was a fool for talking to her. She taped other men, too.

Retter: There is no pillow talk on the tapes. Did Flowers ask you to punch them up—to splice in some sex talk?

Nichols: Why would she come to me to doctor the tapes?[4]

Retter: Did you get money from the *Star* for your story?

Nichols: I gave it back. I didn't want it to seem like I was doing it for money.

Retter: Why did you drop your lawsuit against Clinton and then later refile it?

Nichols: I had done what I intended to do. I knew Clinton was running for president, so all I had to do was keep the court case alive, then the media would come in and take it.

---

1. Simmons is now with the *Arkansas Democrat-Gazette*.

2. Flowers was employed at KARK-TV for six months, from July 1977 to February 1978.

3. Associated Press, January 25, 1992.

4. In a January 28, 1992, interview, Nichols complained that the controversy from the *Star* articles was affecting his business, which he said was "recording commercial jingles."

TAKING THE PRESIDENT TO TRIAL

Paula Jones

Alexander Hamilton could attest that, with sex and politics, honesty is not always a good career move. But the Maria Reynolds affair showed that, with a strange lady in a hotel room, prudence dictates knowing the literal route taken by the lady to the room, and the political route taken afterward. Revealed also is the inestimable value of someone like James Callender; for what good is a scandal without a smear artist to spread it around? In the case of Paula Corbin Jones, such an examination might shed some light on both the veracity of her claim and the role played by those who helped a 24-year-old haul the reputation of a sitting president to the Supreme Court and nearly take him to trial.

> *All I want is my reputation back.*
> —Paula Jones
> *60 Minutes*, March 16, 1997

Born in 1967 in the sleepy mill town of Lonoke,

Arkansas, Paula Corbin Jones grew up poor. Her father Bobby Gene worked as a laborer in a shirt factory, where he brought home leftover fabric for his wife, Delmer, to sew into dresses for Paula and her two older sisters, Lydia and Charlotte.

Bobby Gene and Delmer were strict. Church was three times a week and Bobby—a lay preacher of the fundamentalist Nazarene denomination—traveled on weekends to nearby towns to deliver fire–and–brimstone sermons. Dressed in their homemade smocks and bonnets, Paula and her sisters often accompanied him. Television was forbidden; the outside world was a fearsome place. "Her father was very strict, the mother followed the father, and he ruled the house," recalled Gwen Standridge. Married to Paula's cousin, she stayed close friends with Paula throughout her childhood. "Paula was never allowed to socialize with friends of her own age unless it was church affiliation or family," she said. "As she grew up and realized there was a lot more to it than that, she wanted to be a lot more worldly than Christianly."

Paula's world changed dramatically when her father died of a heart attack in 1985. "The day he died, boy, those skirts went up ten inches," a classmate told *People* magazine. "The dresses got shorter and the tops got lower." Another told the *London Daily Mirror*, "she went from a Plain Jane to a really pretty young woman. Soon there was boys' cars parked outside there all night."

Never much interested in academics, Paula cut classes until, in despair, her mother transferred her to a school for troubled students in nearby Carlisle. Upon graduation, she became the first girl in her family to get a high school diploma. Setting her sights on becoming a secretary, she enrolled in Little Rock's now-defunct Capital City Community College. She dropped out six months later.

In 1985, 19-year-old Paula began dating a 31-year-old bond trader named Mike Turner. Although she lived with her mother, Paula had no difficulty staying the night at Mike's house. He told *Penthouse* magazine that she sent cards that he's kept. One read, "I miss every inch of you. But I miss some inches more than others." Another thanked him for "letting me sleep my drunk off over here."

Over a two-year period, they saw each other once or twice a week, but neither expected the other to be faithful. "The little boys liked her too much," Mike said. "She had them worked into a frenzy. She'd say, 'So-and-so who I'm going out with heard I was going out with an older guy, and they said they were coming to beat your ass.'"

Turner said that Paula loved sex and boldly stripped for his camera wearing only scanty panties. "She was proud of the pictures," her sister Charlotte said. Charlotte, however, was not, and could not understand how—given the strict upbringing both sisters had had—Paula could so easily display the X-rated pictures to her family. Eventually, Turner would sell the photos to *Penthouse*.

In December 1986, a candle tipped over, setting the Corbin home ablaze and burning it to the ground. There was no insurance. Paula, Lydia, and her mother moved into a crowded house trailer with sister Charlotte and her husband, Mark Brown.

Brown first met Paula when she was 16 and he'd begun dating Charlotte. He told the *London Daily Mirror* that Paula enjoyed dressing provocatively and flirting with men. "Hot damn, I'd have probably propositioned her myself." He said that over the years she came to consider him a father figure and confided her private life to him. Brown was "shocked at the number of men she counted as lovers. He estimates she'd been to bed with 15 different men before she was 17." He added that, "Paula was hitting one right after another."

As for jobs, the January 1998 issue of *I.F. Magazine* states that after high school, Jones had a spotty work record prior to working for the state. Citing interrogatories, it states that Jones worked two years for Paul Shoes before quitting, and then "...went to work for J.B. Transport, but was fired after less than a year because the company was dissatisfied with her performance. She lost her next job at Dillard's Department Store where she was fired after one year for being late to work too often. A four-month stint ended with Hertz Rental Car when she was fired again. She claimed she quit her next job at Crown Rental because another employee was 'physically violent.' Another four-to-five-month job at Pest Master ended again with her firing. She next quit a job at Holliday's Fashions because she found the commute too long."

In December 1989, while she was working as a clerk for Pest Master Exterminators, Paula met Steve Jones, an aspiring actor working as a ticket agent for Northwest Airlines. The *London Daily Mirror* later reported that she quickly fell for his Presleyesque looks and started calling his answering machine just to hear his voice. Soon they were living together in Valonia, 45 miles north of Little Rock.

Paula was hired in March 1991 as a document examiner by the Arkansas Industrial Development Commission (AIDC). An entry-level job, it paid $10,000 a year. Barely two months into the job, she was assigned to work the registration desk at the Excelsior Hotel, where AIDC was sponsoring the third annual Governor's Quality Management Conference and Bill Clinton was to deliver a speech. By this time, Paula was engaged to Steve Jones.

The date of the conference was May 8, 1991, and whatever did or did not happen in a hotel room that day between Paula Corbin Jones and Bill Clinton lay dormant for nearly three years. In 1992, Bill Clinton was elected president. Paula and Steve Jones married and—after his employer, Northwest Airlines, transferred him—moved to California in February 1993. Months passed. Nothing out of the ordinary happened until Paula returned to Little Rock for a visit in January 1994, where she met with a friend who had a copy of a certain magazine.

The conservative, right-wing *American Spectator* had hit the stands with an article by David Brock, called, "His Cheatin' Heart: Living With the Clintons." At the time, Brock was the self-proclaimed attack dog of the right who had boasted that "I kill liberals for a living." The article quoted four Arkansas state troopers—Roger Perry, Larry Patterson, Ronnie Anderson, and Danny Ferguson—who had guarded then-Governor Clinton. They described, among other things, an encounter between Clinton and a woman named Paula in a hotel room. It stated that:

> One of the troopers told the story of how Clinton had eyed a woman at a reception at the Excelsior Hotel in downtown Little Rock. According to the trooper, who told the story to both [troopers] Roger Perry and Larry Patterson as well, Clinton asked him to approach the woman, whom the trooper remembered only as Paula, tell her how attractive the governor thought she was, and take her to a room in the hotel where Clinton would be waiting.... [Afterward] The trooper said Paula told bim she was available to be Clinton's regular girlfriend.

The story, which prominently featured troopers Perry and Patterson's accounts of Clinton's sexual adventures, was promptly dubbed "Troopergate" and it sparked a media frenzy. On December 19, 1993, CNN began round-the-clock coverage. ABC and NBC jumped on the bandwagon the following day as did the *Los Angeles Times*, which featured its own interviews with Roger Perry and Larry Patterson, the two most vocal troopers.

Paula, however, heard about it for the first time that January from her friend in Little Rock. As she listened to the account, she felt that the article implied she had had sex with Clinton. A short time later, Jones happened to be at a Little Rock restaurant when Danny Ferguson approached her and spoke about the situation. Each would have their own version of what was discussed in that encounter, but what is certain is that shortly there-after, Jones retained a Little Rock attorney by the name of Danny Traylor with the intention of suing President Bill Clinton. Until then, Traylor's practice had been virtually limited to real estate and tax matters.

Danny Traylor soon did something he would live to regret—he contacted a Little Rock businessman whom he knew had connections to the White House with an offer to settle the case. The man was George Cook, and he signed an affidavit stating that Traylor admitted that "his case was weak," but that it could "embarrass the presi-dent" if he did not pay to keep Jones quiet. Cook's state-ment also said that Traylor wanted Clinton to use his influence to get Steve Jones an acting job in California.

Traylor does not contest this account and has openly worried that he may be liable for a charge of attempted extortion. However, Traylor has never com-mented as to whether Paula and Steve Jones knew of his overture; Paula has said she did not.

Danny Traylor felt he needed some help and approached another Little Rock attorney, Cliff Jackson, who was representing troopers Roger Perry and Larry Patterson with their stories about Clinton and sex. Although Jackson had gone to Oxford, where he and

Clinton knew each other, he had "turned" on his former friend. When the two troopers told their stories at a press conference before the Conservative Political Action Conference (CPAC) in Washington on February 11, 1994, Jackson offered the forum to Paula.

Jackson contacted *Washington Post* reporter Mike Isikoff, and offered him an exclusive on Paula's story. He told the author that he selected Isikoff because, "I thought he would be fair." After the press conference, Jackson took Isikoff to meet with Paula at her hotel room. (Curiously, in a March 16, 1997, edition of *60 Minutes*, Ed Bradley reports that Isikoff met with Paula the day after the convention and convinced her to give the *Post* an exclusive. There is no mention of the role played by Jackson.)

Danny Traylor, however, watched the press conference in horror. Linked with the troopers' charges and CPAC, Paula telling her story in a room full of Clinton-haters was a public relations disaster. Her charges received scant national coverage. As for Isikoff's interview with Paula, the editors at the *Post* did not find her credible and initially refused to run the story without corroboration. Isikoff, enraged and then suspended, finally left the paper for a job at *Newsweek*.

Danny Traylor knew the case was in trouble and put out another call for help. Gilbert Davis, a trial attorney from Fairfax, Virginia, and Joseph Cammarata were the first to respond. The hand-off from Danny Traylor to Davis-Cammarata marked a major escalation in Paula's legal case.

Meanwhile, Jones started making appearances. On the April 29, 1994, *700 Club*, viewers were warned that Jones' interview "contains graphic descriptions that are offensive to all of us, but especially for your children." Haltingly Jones said that after she was in the hotel room for three or four minutes, Clinton "...just leaned over as I was speaking. You know, we were talking and he pulled my hand and tried to walk me up towards him and I said no. I said, 'No,' and I'm not going to do this—I just did not want to be there, so I refused. And then I walked over and he followed me over to the middle of the room and he leaned up against a wingback chair and he started telling me that he liked the way my curves were and how my hair went down the middle of my back and I thought it was really strange. I did.

"And it happened so quick. He got up and it seemed like he was trying to kiss me on my neck—I pushed him away. I did not let him. I said, 'I need to go.' That's when I said the first time, 'I need to be leaving.' And he kind of made it sound like it was okay, you know, that I could stay there. Maybe he wouldn't bother me again, so we continued to talk some more and I had walked over to the couch on the other side of the room to get away from him and I sat down on the far end of the couch. And before I know it, he was sitting down beside me and he had exposed himself. He unzipped and he dropped his pants down. He was sitting right beside me on the couch. He asked me to 'kiss it' and I refused."

Show cohost Dale Hurd asked, "What are you trying to accomplish with this suit? What are you trying to make right?"

Jones answered, "Well, make right what was done wrong to me and let people know—you know, there's been—since this has come out, there's been lots of rumors of him, you know, being with other women and everything and I'm here to say that it is true and people need to know what their president has done in the past, and probably—who knows, he may still do it. But just because it's the president, everybody is sleeping on it and I don't think that's right."

Also interviewed was Paula's coworker, Pam Blackard, who said that Paula returned to the registration desk where the two were working "15 or 20 minutes" later. In recounting her episode with Clinton, Blackard said Paula expressed a "full range of emotions" that included "embarrassment, horror, grief, shame, fright, worry, and humiliation." Viewers were told that Blackard had signed an affidavit, as had another friend, Debra Ballentine, whom Paula rushed to see after leaving work early.

Paula repeated her story in the *Clinton Chronicles*, a videotape peddled by Jerry Falwell, and appeared on radio talk shows with Oliver North and Reed Irvine.

The statute of limitations had run out for a sexual harassment suit so Jones charged Clinton with intentionally inflicting emotional distress, violating her civil rights, and defaming her. The suit was filed in Pine Bluff, Arkansas, on May 6, 1994, and asked for $700,000 in compensatory and punitive damages. It was a week when South Africa inaugurated its first black president, yet virtually every newspaper, CNN's *Crossfire*, ABC's *Nightline*, the weekend talk shows, and all of talk radio were consumed with Paula and her story of sex in a hotel room.

That the case had come this far was a victory for the president's detractors and a bonanza for pundits. Talk-show hosts were having a field day. When Clinton insisted that his administration was the most scrutinized in history, David Letterman quipped, "Bill, if you're tired of scrutiny, quit dropping your pants!" When Clinton said he would expand Head Start, a program created to better prepare disadvantaged children for school, Jay Leno said this meant that "Now women in his hotel room will get a 20-minute head start."

Still, by a large margin the public didn't really believe Paula and her story. The more rabid members of the right wing had milked it for all it was worth. Her case was limping along and few predicted Paula would see victory. Then a writer by the name of Stuart Taylor published an article that caused a reconsideration of Paula and her ordeal in the hotel room with Bill Clinton.

In the November 1996 issue of the *American Lawyer*, Taylor wrote, "The evidence supporting Paula Jones's allegations of predatory, if not depraved, behavior by Bill Clinton is far stronger than the evidence supporting Anita Hill's allegations of far less serious conduct by Clarence Thomas." His evidence consisted of strongly corroborative statements by two of Jones' friends that had not been published before. These friends revealed that an extremely upset Paula had told one of them within 10 minutes of the event, and the other within 90 minutes, that Clinton had exposed himself and demanded oral sex after Jones had rebuffed his efforts to grope her. One was Pamela Blackard, Paula's coworker that day at the registration table. The other was Debra Ballentine, who had read the *American Spectator* article to Paula and had found her lawyer, Danny Traylor. Both had signed sworn affidavits for Jones in 1994.

They first told their stories in February 1994 in exclusive interviews to Michael Isikoff. But the *Washington Post* printed only sketchy accounts 11 weeks later. Their unpublished story is what comprised Taylor's "new" evidence and his admonishment that "all mainstream news reports and commentaries about Jones have ignored or downplayed the strength of her corroborating witnesses." He noted that "not a single one of the feminist groups that clamored for a Senate hearing for Anita Hill, and then for Clarence Thomas' head, had lifted a finger on behalf of Paula Jones." "Most striking," Taylor continued, "is the hypocrisy (or ignorance) and class bias of feminists and liberals—who proclaimed during the Hill–

Thomas uproar that 'women don't make these things up,' and that 'you just don't get it' if you presumed Thomas innocent until proven guilty."

Taylor excused Paula's right-wing appearances and lawyer Danny Traylor's initial interest in the potential money from her case as a combination of naiveté and misunderstanding—a country girl and a country lawyer in way over their heads. Suddenly, the press was taking a hard look at itself and another look at Paula. The "trailer trash" girl was on the cover of *Newsweek*; *60 Minutes* wanted an interview. Mea culpas were flying fast and furious—a sea-change occurred in the way the media looked at Paula and her lawsuit, which insisted that it proceed to trial while Bill Clinton was president.

Clinton's lawyer Bob Bennett, however, disagreed. He wrote that to allow a sitting president to be dragged into court to defend a civil suit was both unseemly and unconstitutional. If Paula Jones wanted her day in court, Bennett argued, she should wait until Clinton had finished his term in office. A May 20, 1994, *Los Angeles Times* editorial stated:

> The issue is not simply Bill Clinton and Paula Jones and their respective fates; the issue is the welfare of this nation, and whether this president—or any president—can govern effectively while he is the subject of a civil matter in the courts.... Only a fool would believe that Jones' action will be the last of such cases if it can be shown that you can seriously damage a president—if not bring about his removal from office—simply by filing a civil lawsuit.

U.S. District Judge Susan Webber Wright agreed and Paula Jones' motion was denied. Paula's lawyers, Davis and Cammarata, promptly began preparing an appeal that would be heard by the Supreme Court. Meanwhile, Paula's cause was getting some help from a right-wing network that had two things in common: an abiding hatred of the Clintons and funding from a reclusive 65-year-old billionaire named Richard Mellon Scaife.

Scaife's three nonprofit foundations dispersed almost $133 million between 1988 and 1994 to his political causes. In the March 19, 1998, *Rolling Stone*, Eric Schlosser notes that, "A number of right-wing organizations supported Jones. Accuracy in Media (financed by Scaife) placed ads in mainstream newspapers asking WHO IS PAULA JONES AND WHY IS THE MEDIA SUPPRESSING HER CHARGE OF SEXUAL HARASSMENT? The Landmark Legal Foundation (financed by Scaife) offered to assist her attorneys. Judicial Watch (financed by Scaife) subsequently challenged President Clinton's use of insurance payments to cover his own legal fees. And the Independent Woman's Forum (which received its first grant from Scaife that very year, in the amount of $100,000) consulted a private attorney named Kenneth W. Starr about some legal issues in the Paula Jones case."

Schlosser observed that, "Kenneth Starr had worked in the Justice Department during the Reagan Administration and had served as solicitor general under George Bush. He planned to write an amicus brief on behalf of Paula Jones, and he advised her attorneys on at least three separate occasions. But before Kenneth W. Starr could become immersed in the Paula Jones case, he was appointed independent counsel in the Whitewater investigation, a job that by law was meant to be free of any 'political conflict of interest.'"

On May 28, 1997, in a stunning decision, the Supreme Court ruled 9–0 that Paula Jones' lawsuit against

Clinton could proceed. For the first time in U.S. history, a sitting president would be going to trial in a civil case.

Still, behind-the-scenes settlement talks were under way. On August 5, 1997, at a late-night meeting 11 floors above the deserted streets of downtown Washington, they nearly succeeded. Davis and Cammarata were anxious to settle. They had been representing Jones for more than three years and had done hundreds of hours of work for which they had not been paid.

While Jones' legal fund had raised money, most of it had been used for expenses that the *Arkansas Democrat-Gazette* reported to include a $2800 home computer, an $800 excursion to a Nordstrom department store, beauty-salon appointments, and payments to a health spa and to a kennel that boarded Paula's dog, Mitzy. The newspaper also reported that the Paula Jones Legal Fund was a for-profit entity, one that was administered by Jones' new "spokesperson," Susan Carpenter-McMillan, and had raised an estimated $250,000—money that donors may have mistakenly believed was tax deductible and was being used to pay Jones' legal bills. Painfully, Davis and Cammarata knew that was not the case.

Someone who knew the details of the August 5 negotiations was Jeffrey Toobin. In a November 3, 1997, article in *The New Yorker*, he wrote that Clinton's lawyer, Bob Bennett, started the settlement talks by announcing that "This case is bullshit—we're wasting our time even talking to you." But Mitchell Ettinger, Bennett's partner at the law firm of Skadden, Arps, Slate, Meagher, and Flom, offered conciliatory words. "Maybe there's some way we can work this out," he said.

The gap was formidable. Jones was asking for $700,000 and an apology. Never, Bennett said. "If you want $10 and an apology, you're not going to get it." Toobin reported that "Jones' lawyers said that they would have to check with their client but that they thought they might have the outline of a deal: a $700,000 payment and a statement in which Clinton acknowledged no improper conduct by Jones, giving her a chance to accomplish her stated goal of 'clearing her name.' Cammarata and Ettinger went downstairs to Ettinger's office, where they sat at his word processor and typed up the mutually acceptable language for the statement. Close to midnight, the four men reconvened and agreed that progress had been made. Cammarata and Davis said they would call Paula for her approval in the morning."

Thinking ahead to the tidal wave of if-he-wasn't-guilty-why-did-he-settle criticism, Bennett tried some horse trading. Jones had signed a secret affidavit describing "distinguishing characteristics" in Clinton's genital area. Bennett said, "I gotta have the affidavit. I think it's horse-shit, and I want it." He believed, Toobin wrote, "that if he could prove that there were no 'characteristics' he could deny that his client had admitted to anything by settling."

Bennett tried an enticement for his adversaries to produce the affidavit. "We'll show you our best evidence," he promised. He thought that Jones' lawyers would want to see what he had on their client before they agreed to any settlement. However, it all came to nothing.

Davis and Cammarata proposed the settlement to Jones, who demanded an apology and turned it down. Toobin reported that Davis and Cammarata were furious with the obstinacy of their client, and they attributed it to the consuming presence in Jones' life of Susan Carpenter-McMillan. On September 8, 1997, attorneys Davis and Cammarata asked to be released as Paula Jones' counsel, citing "fundamental differences" and an unspec-ified situation in which "...the client persists in a course of conduct involving the lawyer's services that the lawyer reasonably believes is illegal or unjust."

They have never elaborated on exactly what might be "illegal or unjust" about Paula Jones' case.

That same day, on CNN's *Burden of Proof*, Carpenter-McMillan was asked why, after representing Paula Jones for three years and taking her case all the way to the Supreme Court and winning, the team of Davis and Cammarata was out. "What happened here?" Roger Cossack asked. "Was it Paula Jones who really lost confidence in the lawyers?" To which Carpenter-McMillan replied that the difference was over money. "You see, [Davis and Cammarata] claim they wanted to be on an hourly basis. So that's the piece of the puzzle that maybe the American public is missing." The lawyers, however, told Jeffrey Toobin that they agreed to keep their fee to one-third of the total, leaving the Joneses more than $400,000.

Susan Carpenter-McMillan described Paula Jones as the "little sister she never had." Toobin visited Carpenter-McMillan at her home near Pasadena, California, and overheard McMillan's side of their many phone conversations, reporting that it sounded like baby talk. "Hi, my Paula-poo," she begins, and concludes a conversation with "I dub-boo, I dub-boo, I dub-boo."

According to Carpenter-McMillan's business card, she is the "Media Spokes Woman" of "The Women's Coalition," which is bankrolled by her husband and, Toobin observes, "apparently consists only of her." Joe Conason reported that Carpenter-McMillan was asked what in fact The Women's Coalition actually did, and the answer was that "we went into comic-book stores to make sure that pornographic comic books weren't between Bambi and Barbie."

A former chief spokesperson of the Right to Life League of Southern California, Carpenter-McMillan was the kind of abortion foe who tolerated few exceptions to her 'pro-life' stand, not even in cases of rape or incest.

She fell out of favor with the antiabortion movement when it was revealed in the April 2, 1990, *Los Angeles Times* that she had had an abortion while in college. As for her relationship with Paula Jones, she is as much her alter ego as her friend. It was she who—barely five weeks after Davis and Cammarata's withdrawal from the case—announced that the search for Paula's new legal team was over and Paula's defense was now being funded by the Rutherford Institute.

Donovan Campbell Jr. became Paula Jones' new lead lawyer. A Dallas attorney, Campbell made his mark in Texas as the moving force behind efforts to uphold the state's 1974 law banning sodomy. Writing for the April 1998 *Penthouse*, Joe Conason said, "When gay rights organizations challenged that statute in 1993, Campbell led the legal team that defended it before the state Supreme Court. This struggle had occupied him for nearly a decade, beginning in 1983, when he represented a group of physicians who sought to reinstate the prohibition on sodomy after the law banning it had been found unconstitutional in federal court. The doctors argued that only by criminalizing homosexual activity would it be possible to prevent an AIDS epidemic."

Despite his long record of opposing civil rights for homosexuals, there was no hint of irony when Campbell said he was representing Jones because her case is "a very significant constitutional and civil-rights lawsuit. That's the type of work that my law firm does." Eyebrows were further raised when it became known that Campbell had been the secretary-general of the Rutherford Institute.

The Rutherford Institute calls itself the "ACLU of the right." Based in Virginia, it was founded in 1982 by John Whitehead, an attorney who had previously worked for Reverend Jerry Falwell's Moral Majority Legal Defense Fund. In fact, when Falwell disbanded the Moral Majority in 1989, he told reporters that its mission would be taken up by other groups, naming Rutherford specifically. Before taking on the Jones case, the institute had never handled a sexual harassment matter of any kind. Its focus was almost exclusively religious freedom cases, such as school prayer and those which, as Whitehead once outlined, "involve a religious person." This caused Barry Lynn, the executive director of Americans United for Separation of Church and State, to comment, "Unless Clinton-bashing has become a religion, I don't know why they are involved in this case."

Whitehead denies his involvement is driven by anti-Clinton bias. Yet, in an article he authored for the Rutherford Institute newsletter, he compared Clinton's health-care plan to fascism. He wrote:

> Clearly, the Clinton administration has been on the offensive against families since its inauguration. The Clintons will now decide who can provide medical care for our children, what the care will be, and when it will be provided. If a parent attempts to go against their decision, he or she may be sent to jail. Thus, this latest 'healthcare' provision is simply another insult to our God-given right to care for and nurture our children. These types of coercive government activities have not, of course, arisen in a vacuum. They have been congealing for years, but not until now has America had a president willing to force such ideologies into law and action.

In June 1995, the newsletter published articles promoting the *Clinton Chronicles*—a video which was distributed by Falwell accused Clinton of drug running and murder. On March 9, 1998, Whitehead was a guest on

C-SPAN. A caller asked him if it was appropriate for Ken Starr to 'wire' Monica Lewinsky. He responded by saying that the president is powerful and "sometimes a 'sting' operation is the only way to get the truth." On the same program, he said that he got involved with Paula Jones' case because, "I sat down with Paula, listened to her story, and believe she's telling the truth."

The rest of the country, however, will get to make up their own minds if the facts of *Jones* v. *Clinton* are ever presented at trial. Then, no longer will it be about what Jones or her spokesperson Susan Carpenter-McMillan have to say. Neither is it about the Rutherford Institute paying Jones' legal bills. If they win their appeal, a sitting president would be going to trial in a civil case. While that may be victory enough for some of Bill Clinton's enemies, the legal case is what matters.

THE LAWSUIT

On December 5, 1997, the Rutherford Institute filed an amended legal complaint in the *Paula Jones* v. *William Jefferson Clinton and Danny Ferguson* lawsuit. Civil action No. LR-C-94-290, filed with the Eastern District of Arkansas Western Division, demands a jury trial and states:

> Plaintiff Paula Jones, by counsel, brings this action to obtain redress for the deprivation and conspiracy to deprive Plaintiff of her federally protected rights as hereafter alleged and for the tort of outrage or intentional infliction of emotional distress.

Under "Facts," the reason is given as to why both Paula and Bill Clinton were at the Excelsior Hotel in Little Rock on May 8, 1991. Clinton was there because it was "The Third Annual Governor's Quality Management Conference," and he "...delivered a speech at the Conference on that day." Also on that day, Jones worked "...at the registration desk at the Conference along with Pamela Blackard, another AIDC employee."

Jones describes the following events:

9. "A man approached the registration desk and informed Jones and Pamela Blackard that he was Trooper Danny Ferguson, Bill Clinton's bodyguard...."

10. "At approximately 2:30 P.M. on that day, Ferguson reappeared at the registration desk, delivered a piece of paper to Jones with a four digit number written on it, and said: 'The Governor would like to meet with you in this suite number....'"

13. "Trooper Ferguson then escorted Jones to the floor of the hotel suite whose number had been written on the slip of paper Trooper Ferguson had given to Jones. The door was slightly ajar when she arrived at the suite."

15. "The room was furnished as a business suite, not for an overnight hotel guest. It contained a couch and chairs, but no bed."

Jones alleges that Clinton, "Took Jones' hand and pulled her toward him, so that their bodies were in close proximity," and while Paula "retreated," he "put his hand on Plaintiff's leg," in an attempt to "reach Plaintiff's pelvic area," while "attempting to kiss Jones on the neck, also without her consent."

21. "Plaintiff Jones exclaimed, 'What are you doing?' and escaped from Defendant Clinton's physical proximity by walking away from him. Jones tried to distract Defendant Clinton by chatting with him about his wife and her activities. Jones later took a seat at the end of the sofa nearest the door. Defendant Clinton asked Jones: 'Are you married?' She responded that she had a regular boyfriend. Defendant Clinton then approached the sofa and as he sat down he lowered his trousers and underwear exposing his erect penis and asked Jones to 'kiss it.'"

22. "There were distinguishing characteristics in Defendant Clinton's genital area that were obvious to Jones."

"Horrified," Paula "jumped" up from the couch, absolutely refused to engage in such conduct, and said, 'Look, I've got to go,' but not before Clinton said, "You are smart. Let's keep this between ourselves," and suggested that her boss call him if she had any trouble about being away from work.

28. "Jones was visibly shaken and upset when she returned to the registration desk. Pamela Blackard immediately asked her what was wrong. After a moment, during which Jones attempted to collect herself, she told Blackard much of what had happened. Blackard attempted to comfort Plaintiff."

29. "Jones thereafter left the Conference and went to the work place of her friend, Debra Ballentine, whom she told about the events."

Trooper Danny Ferguson is in a very strange position. On one hand, he's being sued by Jones for implying that she had sex with Bill Clinton. On the other, he is her 'offer of proof' that she was taken to see the then-governor in a room at the Excelsior Hotel that had no bed and was described by a representative for the hotel as a conference room.

In his answer to Paula's complaint, Ferguson states that:

> 7. "...after the speech given by Governor Clinton, Paula Corbin Jones did make several comments to defendant Danny Ferguson about how she found Governor Clinton to be "good looking" and about how she thought his hair was sexy, and which comments she asked defendant Ferguson to relay to the Governor."

> 11. "...Ferguson admits traveling in an elevator with Jones and pointing out a particular room of the hotel. He has no information as to whether the door was opened or closed."

> 14. "...when Paula Jones returned to the second floor, some 20 to 30 minutes later...she asked if the Governor had a girlfriend and Danny Ferguson answered negatively, and she then responded that she would be the Governor's girlfriend. Paula Corbin Jones did not appear to be upset in any way at this time."

> 16. "...Approximately a week or two after the aforesaid conference, Paula Jones came into the

Governor's office to deliver mail when Danny Ferguson was present. She motioned for him to follow her into the hall as she left and he did so. Once in the hall, she asked if the Governor had said anything about her and Ferguson replied in the negative. Jones then asked for a piece of paper and pen and wrote down her home phone number and told Ferguson to give it to Governor Clinton. She said to tell him that she was living with her boyfriend and that if the boyfriend answered, Governor Clinton should either hang up or say that he had a wrong number."

22. "...He does admit that the parties had a conversation at the Golden Corral Steak House in which Paula Corbin Jones inquired as to how much money Ferguson thought that she could make for herself by coming forward with her allegations..."

24. "...Ferguson avers that he was not outside the door to the hotel room."

As to how Ferguson's story about Paula came to exist in the first place, Jane Mayer has some thoughts. Writing in the July 7, 1997, issue of *The New Yorker* magazine, she points out that Ferguson broke away from the other Troopergate troopers after the redoubtable Cliff Jackson urged them not to wait on a book deal before telling their story to the press. Ferguson, however, "...still harbored hopes of making a fortune from his stories about Clinton."

Mayer revealed that Ferguson was expecting to fetch a "million dollars" for what he supposedly knew about Clinton's sex life and concluded that while it doesn't mean

Ferguson's account of the meeting with Paula Jones is false, it "...does suggest a previously unknown financial interest and an incentive for Ferguson to make his story as marketable as possible."

It gets even murkier. A sworn affidavit signed by fellow trooper Roger Perry reports on Ferguson's "chance meeting" with Jones at a Little Rock restaurant shortly before Jones filed her lawsuit. Perry states that "...[Ferguson] told her then, according to his conversation with me, that he would testify on her behalf if she did file suit against Clinton." The identical language is used in an affidavit signed by Larry Patterson. Both were signed on March 28, 1995.

Paula Jones' complaint also cites that she was—as a result of her refusal to have sex with Bill Clinton—denied pay raises and subjected to a hostile work environment. If this goes to trial, one person who can contest this claim is the person who was her direct supervisor, Clydine Pennington.

In her affidavit dated January 14, 1998, Pennington states that she interviewed Jones on February 5, 1991, for a position with AIDC as a document examiner. The primary duties were to "make daily trips between state agencies to deliver and retrieve interagency correspondence, and enter data relating to AIDC purchases." In the interview and on her application, Paula did not reveal that she'd been fired from any prior job.

Pennington notes that during Paula's two-year tenure with AIDC, she "received every merit increase and cost-of-living allowance for which she was eligible." Moreover, she was upgraded to a Secretary 1 classification with an increase in pay, and on her one-year anniversary received a satisfactory rating with a 2.5 percent pay raise. She would have been eligible for another merit increase on the second anniversary of her hire date, but resigned before them.

While Paula received "satisfactory" evaluations, Pennington states that she did "find it necessary to counsel (Jones) about job-related concerns such as accuracy, tardiness, excessive socializing in connection with her duties, excessive use of the phone for personal reasons, and the importance of wearing appropriate attire."

After the May 8, 1991, AIDC-sponsored Governor's Quality Management Conference at the Excelsior Hotel, Pennington observed that Jones "told me that she had met Governor Clinton" and was excited about it. She also "expressed a desire to obtain a position in the governor's office and expressed that desire on other occasions as well." At no time did Paula mention an unwanted sexual advance. Pennington would know, for—in addition to being Jones' supervisor—she was also a grievance officer.

Susan Carpenter-McMillan maintains that after maternity leave, Paula was demoted. Not so, according to Pennington, who can show that Paula returned to an equivalent position with the same rate of pay and benefits and reported to the same supervisor, Clydine Pennington. The only change was in the data entry responsibilities. Everything else was the same.

Pennington remembers Jones' last appearance at AIDC. After resigning to move to California, Paula came in to pick up her personal belongings. "She referred to me as a 'bitch,' and repeatedly stated that she was 'tired of this fucking place.' Because of the loud and vulgar nature of her conduct, I did not attempt to speak with Ms. Jones."

DISTINGUISHING CHARACTERISTICS

Jones claims it existed and was "...obvious to [her.]" 'It' has been identified as Peyronie's disease—which *The Medical Advisor*, published by Time-Life Books, describes as "fibrous plaques on the upper side of the penis that cause the shaft to thicken and often produce a bend during erection, which may be painful."

By definition, it is a condition that Jones could have witnessed only if Clinton had exposed himself in an aroused condition, as she alleges.

ITEM: *Rivera Live*

> Host: Geraldo Rivera
> Guests: Gennifer Flowers and law professor Paul
>   Rothstein
> Date: January 19, 1998

Rivera: Is it not a fact that you were never asked about the president's so-called "distinguishing characteristics" in his genitalia?

Flowers: That's right. I was not.

Rivera: You were never asked any questions?

Flowers: Not about that—no.

Rivera: About which way it turned or any marks on it?

Flowers: No, I was not.

Rivera: Were you specifically asked on your oath whether you and the president of the United States had a physical relationship?

Flowers: Yes, I was.

Rivera: And you answered in the affirmative?

Flowers: Yes, I did.

Rivera: OK. Now, Paul, doesn't it strike you as odd that they say the smoking gun—to use another phallic symbol—is "distinguishing characteristics," and here's a person who presumably is an eyewitness, not even asked.

Rothstein: It strikes me as odd. It strikes me that they were afraid they'd get the wrong answer, that is, the answer they did not want to get—that he did not have any physical deformities, and they were afraid of that. Now, maybe they knew from previous interviews with Ms. Flowers that she would say that, but even so, I think it raises an implication, when they don't ask, that they believe that he does not have that deformity and that that's what she would say.

Rivera: ...So you never saw anything that would in any way make the president of the United States seem different or abnormal or a deviation from average people?

Flowers: Absolutely not.

Also revealed was that Paula Jones' lawyers provided Gennifer Flowers with the questions they were going to ask her under oath before she was deposed.

ITEM: *The New Yorker* **magazine,** Jane Mayer, "Distinguishing Characteristics—Why the Paula Jones Story Changed Again," July 7, 1997.

In an interview with Paula Jones' Little Rock attorney Danny Traylor, Mayer wrote:

> "...Traylor added that Jones did not tell him that Clinton had shown her 'distinguishing characteristics' on his genitals. The first time he heard of this was after she went out to dinner with her (new) lead lawyers, Joseph Cammarata and

Gilbert K. Davis. It was elicited in their interviews with Ms. Jones when I was out of the room..."

In fact, Traylor first learned of it when he read the draft complaint, prepared by Paula's two new lawyers, almost four months after Paula had first retained him and told him her story.

PAULA'S DEMEANOR

Jones became horrified, jumped up from the couch, stated that she was 'not that kind of girl...' Jones was visibly shaken and upset when she returned to the registration desk...
   —Jones' first legal complaint that contains the phrase, "not that kind of girl."

"Horrified" and "shaken," Jones fled the room and told two witnesses: coworker Pam Blackard and her friend Debra Ballentine.

ITEM: *60 Minutes*

   Host: Ed Bradley
   Guests: Paula Jones and Danny Ferguson
   Date: March 16, 1997

Jones: I mean, this is almost like a mental rape. And I just started feeling guilty about what—I shouldn't have even went up there in the first place.

Ferguson: She's lying about being upset when she comes down.

Bradley: She wasn't upset?

Ferguson: No, sir.

Bradley: She say anything to you?

Ferguson: Yes. She said, 'Does the governor have a girlfriend?' And I said, 'No.' She said, 'Well, I'll be his girlfriend if he wants one.'

Jones: Now why would I say that? If it went so well in that room, why wouldn't I tell the governor myself? Why would I go hunt down his bodyguard or whatever to tell him that I wanted to be his girlfriend? Now isn't that kind of stupid?

*　　*　　*　　*　　*

Someone who is expected to testify as to Paula's demeanor is Carol Phillips, who was a receptionist at the governor's mansion. She and Jones became friends—going to lunch an average of three times a week—and kept no secrets from each other. They met the day after the conference at the Excelsior Hotel. "In a happy and excited manner," Phillips states in her affidavit, dated June 27, 1994, "she told me that she had met Mr. Clinton at the conference." In describing the meeting, Paula "did not make reference to any sexual advances by Mr. Clinton." On the contrary, she described him as "gentle," "nice," and "sweet." Phillips continues that, "given the nature of our relationship, I am sure that had anything improper occurred between the governor and Paula that she would have told me. "It was," Phillips concluded, "totally innocent." Moreover, Phillips states that after Paula met Clinton, she "stayed longer during her daily visits," and "often asked whether Mr. Clinton was in." Jones added her signature to a group birthday card from Clinton's staff.

Another witness will be Cherry Duckett, who was deputy director of the AIDC, and attended the event.

"I spoke to Ms. Jones after the conference. She appeared happy and told me that she had been able to meet and speak with Governor Clinton. She was clearly excited about it." Jones also said that she wanted to work at other AIDC-sponsored events.

Paula Jones' sister Charlotte Brown can be added to the list of witnesses who will testify that whatever happened in the hotel room that fateful day with Bill Clinton, it did not cause "emotional distress" to Paula Jones.

On March 11, 1998, Geraldo Rivera's guest on *Rivera Live* was Paula's sister, Charlotte Brown. Rivera introduced Brown saying, "...I found out today, [Paula] stopped by Charlotte's home on May 8, 1991, shortly after the alleged incident with Bill Clinton that started this whole mess." Charlotte answered that during the visit, Paula "was her normal self...nothing odd about her actions or behavior whatsoever."

> **Rivera:** So when we saw her crying, for instance, when she said she wanted to get back her good name, do you think she was faking it?
>
> **Charlotte:** That had to have been. If she had been sexually harassed, if this had happened like she claims, she would have been upset with me that day. She would have been crying then. She wouldn't have hid it from me because her and me were close. She would have told me.
>
> **Rivera:** She said she wanted to get back her good name. I don't mean to insult you, your family, or your sister, but did Paula have a good name? You know what I mean? Was she a loose woman? *Penthouse* magazine's on the stand and there's

her, nude with this boyfriend. What was her reputation?

Charlotte: She liked men. She enjoyed men. And she would dress very provocative. She went out with a lot of men.

The truth, according to Paula Jones, begins on the afternoon of May 8, 1991, at Little Rock's Excelsior Hotel.
> —Ed Bradley
> *60 Minutes*, March 16, 1997

10. "At approximately 2:30 P.M. on that day..."
> —Paula Jones'
> legal complaint

One person who remembers things differently is the man who was then-Governor Clinton's press secretary, Mike Gauldin. Rather than the afternoon, he recalls that Clinton was at the Excelsior Hotel in the morning. Gauldin spoke with the author:

Retter: Were you with him on May 8, 1991, at the Excelsior Hotel?

Gauldin: No. If I'd expected it to be covered by the press I'd have been there.

Retter: What do you recall about the schedule for that day?

Gauldin: His speech was in the morning. Then there was a luncheon at the mansion with some industrialists from Europe; he had some phone time and then a function in the back yard later in the afternoon.

Retter: There was a luncheon at the mansion?

Gauldin: Yes. It was with some people from one of the lowland countries—Holland, I think. I was there because they had their own press with them.

Retter: There was a function later at the mansion?

Gauldin: Yes. I remember helping to set up chairs for it on the lawn.

Gauldin's reference to "phone time" is relevant because he revealed that Clinton had just returned from an important speech in Cleveland. "He was walking around with a handful of phone messages from party powerbrokers—for the first time he was being considered as possible presidential timber. It was an exciting time."

A check of newspapers shows no articles mentioning his speech on May 8, 1991, at the Governor's Quality Management Conference at the Excelsior Hotel. However, the day before, an article was published in the *Arkansas Democrat-Gazette* with a dateline from Cleveland:

CLINTON A HIT WITH D.L.C.
DECLARES GOAL TO SAVE U.S.

Gov. Bill Clinton galvanized delegates to the Democratic Leadership Council here Monday, according to the applause meter. The D.L.C. chairman received a standing ovation before and after the 22-minute keynote address. And seven other times during the speech delegates applauded.

For Paula Jones, when she met with Clinton is critical. If it was 2:30 P.M., that would allow time for her to be "visibly shaken" when she returned to the registration desk and coworker Pam Blackard, and then leave work early. If it happened in the morning, however, scores of people could be called to testify as to her demeanor and whether she appeared "visibly shaken" to them. Blackard is an important witness.

Yet, the January 1998 issue of *I.F. Magazine* states:

> ...Blackard has told Clinton's legal team and others that she now recalls Jones mentioning an encounter with Clinton in the morning, not the afternoon. The sources quoted Blackard as saying that in 1994, she initially balked at Jones' request that she sign an affidavit which set the time of their conversation as the afternoon. But Blackard said she relented as a favor to Jones.

The time in question appears to be addressed by Danny Ferguson in his legal response to Paula's complaint, when he states that:

> 7. "...after the speech given by Governor Clinton."

Ferguson is on record as having stated that the speech was given in the morning. Furthermore, a copy of the conference agenda shows that Clinton gave the opening remarks at 8:00 A.M. His name does not reappear on the schedule of speakers for later in the day.

Yet another interesting timing issue: Blackard had told reporters that she had heard the whole story, in X-rated detail, minutes after Paula had returned "shaking" to the hotel lobby from Clinton's room. But Danny Traylor reports that Blackard told him that Jones had added the most dramatic details—about Clinton exposing himself and asking for oral sex—some time later.

OTHER WOMEN

On February 4, 1998, *The New York Times* stated that:

> Despite a relentless three-year investigation of Bill Clinton's personal life in Little Rock and Washington, lawyers for Paula Jones have been unable to find any credible new witnesses who are willing to swear under oath that they had a sexual relationship with him, witnesses and lawyers involved in the Jones case say.

With one exception: The *Times* report noted, in a deposition, a woman named Kathleen Willey said that the president made an unwanted advance to her, calling her, "the single strongest witness to bolster the Jones case and has testified that when she asked Mr. Clinton for a paid position in November 1993, he led her to his private study, groped her and placed her hand on his genitals."

Continuing, the article noted that Mrs. Willey met with *Newsweek* reporter Michael Isikoff and "tearfully described the incident to him. She then sent Mr. Isikoff to a friend, Julie H. Steele, for corroboration."

The article also stated that Ms. Steele "said she backed her friend's story, telling Mr. Isikoff that Mrs. Willey came to her home the evening of the encounter and described it to her. But Ms. Steele later said she told that story to Mr. Isikoff in response to pressure from Mrs. Willey. She said Mrs. Willey telephoned her while the reporter was on his way to her home and told her what to say."

"She did not come to my house that night," Ms. Steele said. "I didn't know a thing about this. I never heard that she had been groped by the president until the guy from *Newsweek* was on his way to my house."

THE MONEY TRAIL

...This is crazy. One London newspaper is offering a half million dollars for a story. There are people out there now who are going to try to cash in.
—Larry Nichols' letter withdrawing his lawsuit against Bill Clinton, January 25, 1992

May 8, 1994: As reported, it started with a question about money. Ambrose Evans-Pritchard wrote in the *London Sunday Telegraph* that Paula's lawyer Daniel Traylor had "...offered to do a deal beneath the table for a suitable sum of money for his client."

Jones issued a statement saying: "My critics have accused me of doing this for financial gain. This is absolutely not true. Had my motivation been financial, I could have already responded to the numerous offers I have had to 'sell' my story. I have not done so because that is not my motivation. In order to remove that issue once and for all, I am announcing today that any proceeds from this litigation, above the costs of the case, will be donated by my husband and me to a Little Rock charity."

March 16, 1997: On *60 Minutes*, Paula Jones was asked, "What is it you want from the president?" Jones replied, "An apology. And it's as simple as that. I want an apology because he did something wrong to me. And I want my reputation back and the lies to stop and an apology."

November 3, 1997: *The New Yorker* magazine writer Jeffrey Toobin reported that Carpenter-McMillan was shopping a book proposal. Called *Still Standing: The Inside Story of Paula Corbin Jones*, it was a "thirteen-chapter outline" that would focus on Jones' case against the President" and promised to be "...an inspiring message which leaves the reader with admiration for the grit, tenacity, courage, and perseverance of a modern-day Joan of Arc."

Toobin confronted her about it: "McMillan told me she had submitted the book proposal without Jones' knowledge," he wrote, "and Jones left a message on my answering machine saying that she had no knowledge of the book project."

ITEM: *Meet the Press*

> Host: Tim Russert
> Guest: Susan Carpenter-McMillan
> Date: January 18, 1998

Russert: But now in the future, will Paula Jones pledge not to receive any money from this lawsuit and refuse to write a book or participate in a movie?

Carpenter-McMillan: Tim, why in the world would any plaintiff make such a stupid pledge?

Russert: *The New Yorker* magazine reported that you pitched a book—*Still Standing: The Inside Story of Paula Jones*. Is there a book proposal? Is a book being written? Will Paula Jones benefit from a book contract?

Carpenter-McMillan: Absolutely no, no, no, and no. I was contacted by a publicist. I had never even seen the proposal. I knew about it when Jeff Toobin of *The New Yorker* wrote his article, and I got the publicist on the phone and I said, "What in the world is this you are floating out there?" And he said, "Well, I thought I faxed you a copy." Of course, Mr. Carville, because of mistakes made in the media, just loves to take that and run with it.

Asked for a comment, Jeffrey Toobin told the author: "Carpenter-McMillan is lying. She worked on the project and knew an agent was trying to set it up."

August 1997: Jones parted with her lawyers Gilbert Davis and Joseph Cammarata after rejecting their suggestion that she settle the case out of court for $700,000, and again stated that the dispute "was not about money." The next month, Dallas attorney Donovan Campbell took over as Jones' lead attorney and promptly announced that the price for settling the case without a trial had tripled to $2 million.

Paula's sister Charlotte was quoted in the *Daily Mirror*, "I can't help feeling that she's in this for the money." "Everyone expected me to be on her side," she told the *Washington Post*, "but I would not lie for financial gain…. I couldn't do that."

The February 27, 1998, *Chicago Tribune* reported that Paula Jones had signed a contract with Bruce W. Eberle and Associates, Inc., a conservative fund-raising business, which guarantees her a minimum net income of $300,000. Jones had been advanced $100,000 and the other $200,000 was to come. The remainder of the donated funds go to Eberle.

The contract has a space for the signature of an officer of the Paula Jones Legal Fund, but the words "Legal Fund" were scratched out and Jones signed it, a copy of the contract obtained by the *Tribune* shows. The paper reported that the first version of the fund-raising letter said, "All I want is my good name back." A later version added "and my expenses covered." In the earlier version, Jones asserted, "I don't want Bill Clinton's money." The new version deletes that line.

In her fund-raising letter sent out by Eberle, Jones says, "Dear Friend: It's an ugly story," and states that any contributions to her legal fund are not for her personal use. "It's not for me. It's all going to help my legal case." Her web site promises donations will be used for "litigation expenses...depositions, investigations, and court appearances."

Then, in a bizarre twist, on March 11, 1998, *Salon* magazine reported that the Rutherford Institute has sent letters to a federal judge accusing the Paula Jones Legal Fund of misleading and possibly defrauding the public in its fund-raising practices.

The problem, *Salon* reports, is that the Rutherford Institute has "not seen a penny of the money raised by the Paula Jones Legal Fund." The "direct mail solicitations of the fund creates a false impression and misleads the public that others besides the Rutherford Institute are paying court costs and legal expenses," said one of the letters obtained by *Salon*. The magazine further reported that Rutherford "threatened to report the alleged fraud by Eberle and the Paula Jones Legal Fund to the Internal Revenue Service, the Better Business Bureau, and attorneys general in all 50 states." The charge was potential mail fraud.

The fund's former attorney, Braden Sparks, was quoted by *Salon* as saying, "Jones needs $300,000 to pay travel expenses and the services of Susan Carpenter-McMillan." Sparks' successor, attorney Brent Perry, was asked how these expenses squared with the fund's appeal for contributions to pay for Jones' legal expenses. He responded, "The money doesn't necessarily go to expenses incurred by lawyers, but it goes to expenses that are related to the lawsuit."

The *Chicago Tribune* reported that the fund is classified as a sole proprietorship and that Jones could treat the donations as personal income. In addition to the direct-mail campaign, donations can be sent via an electronic credit card collection service that takes it to one of two post office boxes in Pasadena, California. "Postal records show one of the boxes is registered to an advocacy group run by Susan Carpenter-McMillan. The other box was opened in November by a Carpenter-McMillan aide."

"We're not getting any of the money," Rutherford president John Whitehead told the *Tribune*. Jones' previous legal team told the newspaper that they had "not received any money since leaving the case in September."

THE QUESTIONS

With Paula Jones prepared to take a sitting president to trial, questions remain. Was the right wing involved from the beginning? And is there more to this moralizing crusade against Bill Clinton than meets the eye?

Two days after Paula Jones filed her lawsuit on May 8, 1994, a British journalist wrote in the *London Sunday Telegraph* that he had "a dozen conversations with Mrs. Jones over the past two months." As to whether the lawsuit was political, he wrote, "of course it is. Put plainly, the political purpose of Jones' lawsuit is to reconstruct the inner history of the Arkansas governors mansion using the legal power of discovery. In effect, two lawyers and their staff could soon be doing the job that the American media failed to do during the election campaign and largely failed to do since." The number of people sub-poenaed, he felt, would be "enormous," and that "it doesn't matter all that much whether Mrs. Jones ultimately wins or loses her case. The ticking time bomb in the lawsuit lies elsewhere, in the testimony of the other witnesses."

The reporter—Ambrose Evans-Pritchard—is not a household name, but to Clinton conspiracy buffs, he is an icon.

The English reporter's involvement in Paula Jones' story is both pivotal and revealing. A week before Jones filed her lawsuit, Evans-Pritchard had written the following in the *Telegraph*: "By pure chance I happened to be present at a strategy meeting last March on a boat in the Arkansas River when her lawyer, Danny Traylor, was weighing up the pros and cons of legal action." He also indicated that Traylor informed Jones that he had "offered to do a deal beneath the table for a suitable sum of money for his client."

How did Evans-Pritchard happen to be in the same boat on the same river with Jones' lawyer? In an interview with the author, Evans-Pritchard maintains that it was "indeed by chance." "Ever since Paula's press conference," he said, "I wanted to meet her, but the [*Washington*] *Post* had an exclusive on her story. When I heard Traylor was on the boat, I asked to meet him."

Traylor expressed his frustration that the *Post* was taking so long to publish Jones' story, and while he wouldn't let Evans-Pritchard contact his client directly, he did consent to let him meet with Paula's mother and sister. Yet when Traylor's patience with the *Washington Post* came to an end, he allowed Evans-Pritchard to talk to Jones directly. Evans-Pritchard's impression was that she was telling the truth, which he expressed in his articles. He also said that he felt the lawsuit was "political" and confided that Paula's husband, Steve, had "an underlying political agenda."

Evans-Pritchard summarized the Jones case by stating that "Paula and Steve Jones were so disgusted by the failure of the [*Washington Post*] to publish their story that they decided to file a sexual harassment suit against the President, forcing the issue into the news pages." With Evans-Pritchard's involvement, Paula Jones suddenly became less about sex and all about the battle for information.

Larry Nichols' comment on January 25, 1992, when he withdrew his lawsuit against Bill Clinton that, "One London newspaper is offering a half million dollars for a story" is curious. If true, why would a "London newspaper" be willing to spend so much money digging for dirt on an American presidential candidate?

Is the crusade against Bill Clinton's presumed sex life driven by moral outrage or politics? Oliver North's March 6, 1998, appearance on *Larry King Live* suggests the former. Asked whether Eisenhower should have been removed from office for having an affair with his female driver, North responded, "Sure." He added that, "I think there ought to be standards. I think the American people have a very firm sense, most of them, to an immutable sense of the Judeo-Christian value system in this country."

The political side, however, was evident on the March 10, 1998, *Rivera Live*. "David Brock," Rivera said, "is the reporter whose 1994 article about Bill Clinton's sex life 'sparked the Paula Jones lawsuit, which led to 'Monica Madness.'" In an open letter to President Clinton in the April 1998, issue of *Esquire* magazine, Rivera quoted Brock as saying, "my ransacking of your personal life had given your political adversaries an opportunity to use the legal process to finish the job that I started." Watching the Monica Lewinsky case unfold left Brock "...chilled. The spectacle seems strangely and depressingly familiar. I had seen it all before: filthy tapes, too many details not to be true, an accuser whose credibility got shakier by the hour, hidden agendas, book deals, friends betraying friends, declarations of war and even talk of 'killing' the president by those who forced the sludge out. Troopergate had come full circle."

Whether driven by piety or politics, Paula Jones and her claim against Bill Clinton revolves around her veracity. Yet, one detail has been overlooked: In her first legal complaint filed by Davis and Cammarata, Jones states that after Clinton exposed himself, she "became horrified, jumped up from the couch, stated that she was 'not that kind of girl' and said, 'Look, I've got to go.'" However, the Rutherford complaint states: "Jones became horrified, jumped up from the couch, absolutely refused to engage in such conduct, and said: 'Look, I've got to go.'" Omitted is the quote, I'm "not that kind of girl."

Alexander Hamilton might have counseled that when it comes to a lady in a hotel room, perhaps it might be prudent to find out what kind of "girl" she really is.

THE PROGRAM

THIRD ANNUAL
Governor's Quality Management Conference
Excelsior Hotel
Little Rock, Arkansas

Wednesday, May 8, 1991

AGENDA

7:30 Registration

8:00 Welcome, Introduction Dave Harrington,
Executive Director, AIDC, Opening Remarks
Bill Clinton, *Governor, State of Arkansas*

8:30 Total Systems Approach to Quality Manufacturing
Lew Springer, *Former Senior Vice President
with Campbell Soup Company*

10:00 *Break*

10:20 Lew Springer—continued

12:15 *Lunch*

1:15 The Improvement Process: How America's
Leading Companies Improve Quality
Jim Harrington, *International Quality Advisor
for Ernst and Young*

2:15 *Break*

2:30 Jim Harrington—continued

3:30 Questions and Answers
Dave Harrington, Moderator

4:00 Adjourn

FROM THE LIBERTY LEAGUE TO THE WEDNESDAY GROUP

The Right Wing

Following the election of Franklin Delano Roosevelt, leading Republicans launched the most intense and concentrated campaign to propagate conservative political and economic thought that the United States had ever witnessed, chiefly in the form of the Liberty League. Dissected, the League's philosophy revolved around Social Darwinism, laissez-faire economics, Old Testament apocalypse, and Constitution and ancestor worship. But above all it was driven by a savage hatred of one man: Franklin Delano Roosevelt.

As early as 1934, the Roosevelt haters were in evidence; by 1936 they were a well-defined cult, often garnishing their sermons with scandalous stories and obscene parody. "Regardless of party and regardless of region, today, with few exceptions," said *Time* in April 1936, "members of the so-called Upper Class frankly hate Franklin Roosevelt." In a piece for *Harper's* in May of the same year, Marquis Childs wrote that most of the upper economic echelon was beginning to share a "consuming personal hatred" for the president.

In the Liberty League thesaurus of hate, Roosevelt was a "renegade Democrat," an immoral liar and tool of blacks and Jews, who was surrounded by radicals who were selling America down the river. The boat for the trip down the river was the New Deal.

There was no doubt that they believed FDR was a dictator, but Liberty Leaguers were not quite sure what kind. Some thought he was a fascist, others believed him to be a Socialist or Communist, while others were convinced he was both. The claim that Roosevelt was a Socialist or a Communist and the New Deal was a Marxist conspiracy was trumpeted more frequently and persistently than the fascist charge.

Yet, if the Liberty League was not always certain what Roosevelt and the New Deal were ideologically, the group was certain that the New Deal meant the destruction of the Constitution. Protection of the Constitution was its moral issue: "If the League has taken issue with the New Deal, it is only because the New Deal has taken issue with the Constitution."

The secretary of the Liberty League, Captain Stayton, wrote: "The public ignorance concerning [the Constitution] is mighty, though there is an affection for it. The people, I believe, need merely to be led and instructed, and this affection will become almost worship and can be converted into an irresistible movement. I think our first appeal should be to the effect that the Constitution is perfect; we seek to rescue it from those who misunderstand it, misuse, and mistreat it."

Accordingly, for the League to appear as the knight errant of the Constitution was to imply that the president and his administration were its enemies, seeking to pervert and destroy it. Defending the Constitution served another practical purpose: It gave the League a measure of righteous immunity. The pose of the Liberty League as the handmaiden of the Constitution was conscious, deliberate, and calculated. For no matter how strong and efficient the group might be, without a moral or emotional purpose the League was doomed. With such a purpose, it could with abandon demonize FDR. The Constitution was chosen because it was noble, patriotic, and sacrosanct. Few issues could command more support or evoke more enthusiasm among people.

To hear the League tell it, there were no other enemies abroad in the land seeking to undermine the Constitution save Roosevelt. More serious was the implication that all of this was cunningly deliberate and calculated, that the president was purposely intent on wrecking the republic and superimposing upon its ruins a totalitarian state, with himself as dictator.

Here was a new dimension in the League's criticism. It was more than a matter of castigating the administration in terms of its wisdom and efficacy, as well as the short- and long-range results of its policies. The new dimension was morality. The League stood for that which was traditional, that which was "natural," that which was virtuous and morally good. The New Deal was not bad in the sense it was imprudent and unwise; it was morally bad.

The Liberty League was really interested in cutting taxes. The problem was that many of its members were men of wealth who believed as they did because it reflected what the philosophy of 19th-century conservatism called Social Darwinism, and who came unglued when Roosevelt said things like "Our enemies are the forces of privilege and greed within our borders," and referred to the wealthy as "privileged princes."

Social Darwinism maintained that life was a race in which the runners all start equal, but the prize went to the swift and able, and was measured in financial terms. "Millionaires are the finest blooms in the garden of America's competitive civilization" and "The business of America is business" were the philosophy's common maxims.

Conversely, according to the League, poverty resulted from the innate inferiority of the poor, the slow of foot; in short, most economic and social problems were the result of individual incompetence. The difference between rich and poor was the result of natural, inherent, innate qualities, not the result of economic conditions or degree of opportunity. With the Depression, the League's philosophy was put to an acid test.

Depression was natural; it was, as one League spokesman put it, sort of cathartic, a physic to purge the economic system of harmful poisons. If depressions were natural, even desirable in a sense, then recovery from depression would inevitably follow if nature was allowed to run its course. The idea of a natural recovery was not a hypothesis or a matter of wishful thinking with the Liberty League: It was a tenet of the faith.

Roosevelt made it clear that he rejected the natural-recovery thesis. "We must lay hold of the fact that economic laws are not made by nature. They are made by human beings," he said. Eventually, suspicions were aroused that the administration was deliberately retarding recovery from the Depression in order to perpetuate FDR's power. Roosevelt's goal, the League maintained, was a planned economy, which could only mean one thing: dictatorship. For Liberty Leaguers, who fervently believed that economic matters were outside the competence of government, economic planning was akin to treason. Such planning is in "conflict with the system of free enterprise," said a League pamphlet. "Democracy cannot live side by side with [planning]." The rhetoric reached a fever pitch. The New Deal must "stop itself or it must be stopped. In short, unless annihilated, it will annihilate the republic."

The public wasn't buying these notions, however. To counteract the perception of a bunch of rich guys with last names like DuPont complaining about higher taxes, the League used this approach: *You* are paying too much in taxes; *your* government has got to reduce its expenditures; what are *you* going to do about it? The League's theme was that the New Deal policies would hurt the "little" fellow. Not coincidentally, every administration proposal was opposed by League members.

The Liberty League learned the hard way that in the battle for America's hearts and minds, he who hesitates is toast. By the time the League got organized, FDR's bold initiative and masterful command of slogans and public relations had already found favor with the public. The basic problem was that the League had to make a popular president the "bad guy," and its results were a disaster. It was an error that conservatives were determined not to repeat. For them FDR was more than a nemesis: He was a success story to be copied.

As they evolved, modern conservatives found a natural enemy in communism. When it collapsed, without missing a beat they switched their invective to government. Still with government as the "enemy," conservatives faced the same problems as had the League: how to convince the public that cutting taxes for the wealthy is a good idea[1].

In 1980, something went virtually unnoticed by the press and public: a 3,000-page, 20-volume report titled "Mandate for Change." Prepared by the conservative

Heritage Foundation, it contained more than 2,000 specific policy recommendations and was delivered to the incoming Reagan administration only weeks after the 1980 elections.

No private group not officially associated with an incoming president had ever presented such a detailed plan for taking over the reins of government. The Heritage plan included the blueprint for Reagan administration policies such as "trickle-down" economics, which featured tax cuts for the wealthy, and "Star Wars," a proposed defense system of space-based weapons for destroying missiles. Heritage director Ed Feulner, in the foreword to the 1984 "Mandate for Leadership," wrote: "The Mandate was designed to be a detailed road map to help the fledgling Reagan administration steer the nation into a sound future, guided by conservative principles. By the end of the president's first year in office, nearly two-thirds of the Mandate's more than 2,000 specific recommendations had been or were being transformed into policy."

In his book *The Transformation of American Politics: The New Washington and the Rise of the Think Tanks*, David Ricci states: "There came into being a network of conservative foundations that had no parallel in the liberal camp." What unified this "network," according to Ricci, was a common vision of "promoting laissez-faire" economics—policies which, not incidentally, would increase the already substantial holdings of the conservative activists.

While the Heritage Foundation is the largest, there are approximately 37 conservative think tanks nationwide, all closely tied to one another. In 1995 major conservative think tanks had a combined budget of $46 million, while the major progressive think tanks had a combined budget of $10.2 million—a 4:1 advantage.

Representing a dramatic escalation in the battle for information to shape public debate, the ramifications of this change have been essentially ignored.

The liberal organization People for the American Way notes: "Because the print and broadcast media are essential in shaping public debate, right-wing foundations actively support conservative newspapers, journals, student papers, television networks, and radio programs that disseminate their message. For example, the *American Spectator* is heavily supported by Bradley, Olin, and Scaife foundations. National Empowerment Television, the ultraconservative cable network sponsored by Paul Weyrich's Free Congress Foundation; William F. Buckley's 'Firing Line'; and a variety of conservative public television programs all receive substantial conservative foundation support. By multiplying the authorities to whom the media are prepared to give friendly hearing, the illusion of diversity is created where none exists. The result could be an increasing number of one-sided debates in which the challengers are far outnumbered, if indeed they are heard from at all."

The bottom line is that conservatives were able to sell to the Reagan administration and to the public the notion that tax cuts for the wealthy were a good idea. With the tax cuts in place, woe to anyone who would threaten to roll them back or take them away.

The Liberty League's tactics of couching political and policy objections in moral and patriotic terms is a lesson that present-day conservatives have taken to heart. It would remain, however, for someone to take the League's legacy and bring it into modern conservative lexicon—someone who could take negative campaigning and personal attack to heretofore-unknown heights. That someone was Lee Atwater.

LEE ATWATER
The Dark Prince of Politics

The time: June 1989, when Lee Atwater was Republican National Committee chairman. **The players:** Atwater, his communications director, Mark Goodin, and then-Representative Newt Gingrich. **The stunt:** Just as Tom Foley was poised to take the gavel from departing Speaker of the House Jim Wright, Goodin circulated a memo from the Republican National Committee to state party chairmen and GOP congressmen. Titled "Tom Foley: Out of the Liberal Closet," the memo compared his voting record with that of Representative Barney Frank (D-Mass.), an acknowledged homosexual. *Time* magazine reported that, for days, an aide to Gingrich had been calling more than a dozen reporters trying to get them to print the homosexuality rumor.

Before Atwater saw that he had gone too far, he stood by Goodin's memo. The next day Atwater called it "no big deal" and "factually accurate"; he professed astonishment that anyone could interpret the memo as a slur on Foley. Publicly, George Bush and other Republicans disassociated themselves from the memo.

By the following day, Atwater was backpedaling, saying he had not approved the memo. "I felt confident that if I had seen this, it would not have gone out." Atwater apologized to Foley; Gingrich also apologized and disavowed Goodin's actions. The next day Goodin cleaned out his desk.

Proving the adage that one cannot unring a bell, by the time Atwater and Gingrich apologized, the rumor had achieved its purpose. Foley was forced to deny it both on national television and before a party caucus. Married 20 years, he had to assure his colleagues he was not a homosexual. (John Brady wrote about the incident in his book *Bad Boy: The Life and Politics of Lee Atwater.*)

It was the standard "bad employee–good superior" game; while the top of the ticket took the "high" road, Atwater threw mud from the low. He not only kept his job, but behind closed doors Republicans celebrated the "smear" as another victory from the undisputed master of character assassination.

Atwater is credited with making modern politics personal and mean. Of former Massachusetts governor and 1988 presidential candidate Michael Dukakis, he boasted that he "would strip the bark off the little bastard," and "make Willie Horton [an escaped murderer] his running mate."

Atwater began his career in politics working for Senator Strom Thurmond, and rose to Republican National Committee chairman by using "wedge" or "values" issues such as crime, gun control, taxes, national defense, abortion, school prayer—whatever it took to win. His tactics were pivotal in repositioning the Republican party in the South, the first step in the process of building a national Republican majority.

Why was Atwater so determined to poke around in other people's private lives? Was he simply anticipating a tabloidization of our times or was he creating it? Was he personally offended by real or imagined marital infidelity, or was it just another ready arrow to be routinely shot from a quiver marked "campaign smears"? In answer to the last question, Brady writes in *Bad Boy*: "At the '84 Republican National Convention in Dallas, Lee had arranged to have a 'workroom' adjoining his two-bedroom suite with [his wife] Sally. Lee escorted women in and out of his 'workroom' like clockwork. Finally, a White House staffer sat down with Lee and told him he was afraid Nancy Reagan would find out about the bimbos on parade. Then Lee would be in trouble with the president. Lee assured his worried colleague that he was being very careful, and Nancy Reagan would be none the wiser. As to how he got 'rid' of the ladies? Lee told them that the Secret Service had to sweep his room for security every three hours, so they would have to be quick."

Whatever the real answers, Atwater took them with him. On March 29, 1991, he died from brain cancer. "My campaign-honed strategies of political warfare were simply no match for this dogged opponent," he had reflected in *Life* magazine. "Cancer is no Democrat."

In what some have called a deathbed confession, Atwater said, "Long before I was struck with cancer, I felt something stirring in American society. It was a sense among the people of the country—Republican and Democrat alike—that something was missing from their lives." His illness showed him what it was—"a little heart, a lot of brotherhood."

In commenting on his death, ABC and NBC included images of Willie Horton as a backdrop for their remarks. At the Democratic National Committee, chairman Ron Brown ordered that the flag be flown at half-staff.

While Atwater used "wedge" politics to win, he promoted "big tent" Republicanism and liked to have a little fun. Many feel that this is what separates him from his legion of would-be Republican imitators—imitators who are too often wrapped in ideology that is both dour and exclusive—two things that Atwater, for all his faults, would never have condoned, and which make the Atwater wanna-bes far more dangerous than the original.

THE WEDNESDAY GROUP

As the 1992 presidential primary drew near and the field of candidates narrowed, in conservative bastions something akin to panic set in. The think tanks, with their bought-and-paid-for writers, were in place, as was the bare-knuckles Lee Atwater–style campaigning apparatus. All they hoped for was that another Democrat—a big-spending, soft-on-crime, union-loving liberal—would enter the ring. It was a Republican knockout formula that had become almost too easy.

Enter Bill Clinton. He wanted free trade, and supported welfare reform and the death penalty. Suddenly, the label game was going to be harder. With the combination of Yale and Oxford with Hope, Arkansas, Republicans faced a cross between JFK and Gomer Pyle. Combine that with an attractive, educated wife, and the result could be a deadly possibility: popularity.

Polling showed that Clinton's policies tested high and that if left unchecked, he could capture the "center." The one area of vulnerability was Clinton himself; he was virtually unknown. As Gingrich's pollster, Frank Luntz, told the author, "It was decided to turn Clinton's '60s generation background against him. The question became: Do you want a guy who smoked pot and protested against his country to be president?" Issues were out; personal attack was in.

But more than anything, what galvanized conservatives was Clinton's stand on raising taxes on the rich and his promise of universal health care. The former was untenable; the latter was a sacrilege. He had to be "defined" before the public got to know and like him; he had to be stopped because a popular president equals a trusted president, a combination that could get something like health care passed and the tax code changed. Dwarfing what was done to FDR, a modern-day Liberty League was formed to coordinate what would become the greatest assault ever launched on a president.

Every Wednesday since Bill Clinton's election, 20 to

30 leaders of national right-wing organizations—from taxpayer and term-limits organizations to the National Rifle Association and the Christian Coalition—have gathered for an hour and a half, over coffee and bagels, in the second-floor Washington, D.C., office of Americans for Tax Reform (ATR). It's a tight group that unites editors, writers, and talk-show hosts with conservative activists. The convener is Grover Norquist, a Harvard graduate and protégé of Lee Atwater's. Norquist was inspired to form the Wednesday Group for one reason: To Stop Bill Clinton.

The group's goal was not to draft and pass legislation but to make it impossible for the Clinton administration to pass its programs. It became one of the principal players in weakening public support for the administration's crime bill; it organized opposition to a Democratic measure requiring lobbyists to disclose their sources of income; and it is credited with defeating national health care.

In the early 1980s, one of Norquist's papers for his MBA studies at Harvard Business School outlined a plan for the national college Republicans to switch from a social club to an ideological, grassroots organization. A young conservative named Ralph Reed helped him to implement it. After a stint as chief economist for the U.S. Chamber of Commerce and as a Reagan staffer, Norquist founded ATR in 1985. The organization has 60,000 members and specializes in putting antispending referenda on state ballots. Pundit and columnist Robert Novak commented that Norquist "thinks God put Republicans on earth to cut taxes."

Norquist has figured out how to keep score. He's developed what he calls the "Taxpayer Protection Pledge," a one-page statement in which signers promise never to vote to increase tax rates and never to eliminate tax loopholes without simultaneously reducing tax rates. Every signature is witnessed, and once a politician takes a pledge, that person is bound for life. ATR promises to do everything possible to make life difficult for candidates who refuse to sign or who, having signed, break their word.

The 105th Congress featured 200 pledge-takers in the House (including four Democrats) and 40 in the Senate (all Republicans). Every Republican presidential candidate in the 1996 race took the pledge (Richard Luger's signature was thrown out because he demanded an exception during wars and depressions), including Bob Dole, who had refused to sign in 1988.

So similar are the anti–federal government views of Norquist and the Liberty League that he and ATR could be called "Sons of the Liberty League." In the May 1995 issue of *GQ* magazine, Norquist told writer John B. Judis that his job was to "hunt down" all federal programs and kill them because they "breed Democrats like cockroaches...you've got to throw the cake in the trash so that the cockroaches don't have something to come for."

As a firm believer that the political longevity of key Democrats has been the party's social programs, Norquist created the Wednesday Group as the New Right's command center. The Republican elite meet once a week, enabling brainy think tank scholars and writers to rub elbows with the slightly less-degreed radio talk-show hosts and grassroots activists types. From the *Wall Street Journal* and the *Washington Times* to the *American Spectator*, any conservative who is anyone is represented.

In the fall of 1993, the *Washington Times* began hammering away at the Clintons' role in the Whitewater affair, as well as the president's widely assumed sexual improprieties. The *American Spectator* ran lurid allegations from Arkansas state troopers of Clinton's sexual adventures while governor, and even included charges that the late Vince Foster had made a sexual play for his new partner, Hillary Rodham Clinton. Rush Limbaugh and other conservative talk-show hosts broadcast these accounts to a growing audience, while the *Wall Street Journal*'s editorial page carried and thus legitimized them among its more elite audience.

But according to Norquist, the real situation that brought them all together was "sheer terror of Clinton's health-care plan."

Not everyone, however, agreed. National health care was overwhelmingly popular with Americans. Polls showed that to be on the wrong side of the issue was political suicide. (Bob Dole was quoted as saying, "It may be good for the country, but I'm not sure it's good for the party.") Its passage in some form was deemed inevitable, a reality that was not lost on Heritage Foundation cofounder Ed Feulner. As the largest and most influential of the conservative think tanks, he wanted to make Heritage a respectable opposition to the Clinton plan. As such, Heritage did something bold: It fashioned its own health-care bill, providing for universal coverage. In doing so, they outraged the right.

"Our friends at the Heritage Foundation," began a letter from Cato Institute founder Ed Crane to its contributors, "have endorsed a mandated, compulsory, universal national health-care plan, which flies in the face of the American heritage of individual liberty and individual responsibility." (The Cato Institute wants to phase out Social Security, replace the income tax with an 18 percent national sales tax, and eliminate the minimum wage, food stamps, Head Start, aid to elementary and secondary schools, and most antitrust enforcement.) Senator Don Nickels, who was sponsoring the Heritage-alternative bill, found himself the object of a letter-writing campaign from other right-wing think tanks protesting his stand.

There were other defectors. When the U.S. Chamber of Commerce endorsed the Clinton plan, the Wednesday Group orchestrated radio talk-show appearances and produced attack videos. Other hard-line think tanks like the Competitive Enterprise Institute and the Citizens for a Sound Economy joined in sounding the alarm, and a door was opened to newer hard-line think tanks.

That was defense. As offense, Norquist provided the critical connection between the Wednesday Group members and the conservative media. When activist Bill Kristol sent a fax to Republicans that said simply, "There is no health-care crisis," it was seized upon by the right-wing media and seemed to turn the tide from the inevitability of universal health care to "maybe not."

Republicans were emboldened. After a year of protest by conservatives, the U.S. Chamber of Commerce reversed its support and declared itself opposed to comprehensive health care. Dole no longer felt compelled to offer a universal health-care package of his own. The tide was shifting, but the battle was far from over. Secure Horizons' "Harry and Louise" television ads—featuring an amiable fellow describing how his insurance plan helped save his off-camera wife—were raising doubts with the public, but something more decisive was needed, something that not only raised questions but gave answers, and offered a reason for the American public to "just say no" to the Clinton health-care plan. The answer would come from money supplied by the New Right's founding father and it would be broadcast from the "mouth" of their jewel in the crown: Rush Limbaugh.

*　　*　　*　　*　　*

Elizabeth McCaughey was a senior fellow at the Manhattan Institute—recipient of $1.17 million from Richard Mellon

Scaife from 1988 to 1994—when she wrote "No Exit." It was published in the February 7, 1994, issue of the *New Republic*. The article's premise was that an outside observer such as herself had read through the health proposal. What she saw was terrifying, and McCaughey wanted to share it before it was too late. She wrote:

> The law will prevent you from going outside the system to buy basic health coverage you think is better, even if you pay the mandatory premium. (See the bill, page 244.) The bill guarantees you a package of medical services, but you can't have them unless they are deemed "necessary" and "appropriate" (pages 90–91). That decision will be made by the government, not by you and your doctor. Escaping the system and paying out-of-pocket to see a specialist for the tests and treatment you think you need will almost be impossible.

It was exactly what Limbaugh needed: something from a respectable publication that would support his all-out assault on the Clintons and their health-care plan. On *This Week With David Brinkley*, Newt Gingrich said that having universal coverage would mean the creation of a "police state." That was effective, but McCaughey's article provided dynamite. What she wrote—and what Limbaugh was able to do with it—may well have been the turning point in the health-care debate.

Limbaugh had a field day. He broadcast McCaughey's breathless conclusions to his audience with numbing regularity. Journalist George Will embellished the claim with a "patients in jail" scenario. He wrote: "It would be illegal for doctors to accept money directly from patients, and there would be 15-year jail terms for people driven to bribery for care they feel they need but the government does not deem 'necessary.'"

In his book *Breaking the News: How the Media Undermine Democracy*, author James Fallows stated, "McCaughey's claims took on momentum and a life of their own, as politicians cited them in speeches and they became taken for granted on talk shows." Writer Mickey Kaus offered in the May 8, 1995, issue of the *New Republic*, "More than any other single event in the debate, what she wrote stopped the bill in its intellectual tracks." (See Appendix B.)

The National Association of Magazine Editors awarded McCaughey the prize for "Excellence in Public Interest." There was, however, one problem. As Fallows noted: "Overlooked was one fundamental point. Nothing in the bill prohibits patients from paying their doctors directly." What was prohibited was patients paying doctors extra for services that the health plan was already paying for. No one was ever prohibited from seeing any specialist they wished to see. The fee-for-service was never in jeopardy. McCaughey's conclusion that health reform would lock everyone into an inflexible, centrally planned, no-options medical system was false. But it was a falsehood that the press did nothing to set straight. On the contrary, it passed along McCaughey's conclusions as true. As Fallows observed, the press did something even more damaging: It viewed the conclusions as "interesting" and "in play."

Two months after the administration conceded defeat in its attempts to change the health-care system, the Republicans unveiled the "Contract with America." It did not include a single word about controlling the cost of medical care.

The mainstream media failed to notice that McCaughey's conclusions about Clinton's health-care plan—and therefore the ensuing debate it engendered—were based on a lie. So complete is the scramble for information, the purview of the New Right is that virtually no one was held accountable. To the contrary, Elizabeth McCaughey—in addition to receiving a national magazine award—is now lieutenant governor of New York; the Wednesday Group cites defeating health care as its major victory; and Limbaugh continues to call the conclusions true. For conservative activists like Norquist, it was just as well the plan was defeated by means fair or foul. A recent poll showed that by 70 percent, Americans chose the Clinton health-care plan over alternative ones when Clinton's name was removed.

According to a *GQ* article: "When asked whether the Wednesday Group's organizing and the *American Spectator*'s and the *Washington Times*' attacks on Clinton's character were part of a common strategy, Norquist said, 'It was all on purpose.'"

Norquist elaborated in an interview with the author:

> **Retter:** Were the attacks on Clinton's character part of a common strategy?
>
> **Norquist:** I'm not quite sure. Obviously, in '93 everybody was going about it in their own way. What you would see with the Wednesday Group was people being made aware of things. I think it's important that if you're going to be fighting Clinton on health care to also be aware of what's going on with Whitewater and this other stuff.
>
> In 1992, Clinton made a list of things he was going to do: He was going to socialize medicine, he was going to socialize pensions, he was going

to send our troops all over the world to play U.N. peacekeepers. We basically stopped most of that nonsense.

Retter: By making the issue of infidelity a litmus test for character, aren't the Republicans concerned that it will come back to haunt them?

Norquist: I understand there was this rumor that Dole had an affair. If it would serve the purpose of the left, that story would have broken, and it would have broken whether Bill Clinton was a Boy Scout or not.

Retter: In a *Vanity Fair* story about Newt Gingrich, writer Gail Sheehy gave names of women who said they'd had sexual relations with the congressman while he was married. If marital fidelity is the test, what does it say about his character?

Norquist: I haven't seen that story. I'm not familiar with it.

Retter: The Sheehy article cites not only the stories from the women but says that he served his first wife with divorce papers while she was recovering from cancer surgery, and basically abandoned his two children.

Norquist: Gingrich is an honorable guy. I mean, there's a whole series of problems you have with Clinton, starting with the small business association loan, Whitewater, and everything—it comes as a package. Gingrich is as honest as the day is long and as poor as a church mouse. With Clinton, it all hangs together.

Retter: But doesn't it hang together because the right wing has a platform with people like Rush Limbaugh, who constantly bash Clinton?

Norquist: Whether it's true or not about Gingrich, it doesn't define him. The reason Clinton is having trouble is that everybody believes this stuff on him. It sticks. It sticks. Everything in his life says, "Yeah, that's the way he treats people; that's the way he treats women."

Retter: How do you legitimately determine a person's character?

Norquist: The things that are legitimate are all financial questions raised, the corruption questions. Public corruption, small business loans. When you take away all the sex stuff, it's how poorly he treats the help. That's what shouts out at me more than the sex stuff. People of a lower social station are treated like shit by both him and his wife. That says an awful lot about a person. Also, if the Clintons are not happily married, they're living a lie. Then, how could you believe anything the guy says is true? The Paula Jones case, that's pathological. It's not bad taste—it's sick.

Retter: Where had you heard the Clintons abused the "help"?

Norquist: [Right-wing author] David Brock. Reporters who travel with them swear it's true.

Retter: But what if it's not true? What if neither what Paula Jones nor Gennifer Flowers claims is true?

Norquist: I don't know anybody who doesn't believe that Clinton isn't a philanderer and treats his wife and other women like dirt. Not anyone. I don't know anybody in this whole world I ever had a conversation with who does not believe in their heart of hearts that Bill Clinton is a philanderer who treats women like spittoons. Everybody has internalized that about Bill Clinton. Did you see (Phil Hartman) last night on Jay Leno playing Clinton? That's what people think of Clinton.

Retter: Yet, Paula Jones' case is having problems, and Gennifer Flowers says she had a 12-year affair that started in a hotel that wasn't yet built. How do you know these stories are true?

Norquist: Everybody has their own sources. I know several Democratic women who say Clinton's pinched them. He got right up after Gennifer Flowers came out and lied about the adultery. "I've caused pain in my marriage." That doesn't count as leveling with the American people. The Clintons *want* to focus on this sex stuff because it's the least of the offenses.

Retter: And yet you aren't demanding an accounting from Newt Gingrich. Isn't that a double standard?

Norquist: Newt Gingrich never tried to set us up with government-run health care—that's why Clinton's team got shellacked in '94.

Retter: What did you and the Wednesday Group think of Elizabeth McCaughey's article about the Clinton health-care plan in the *New Republic*?

Norquist: We were delighted with it. Certainly, we sent it to all of our state activists and radio talk-show hosts.

Retter: Are you aware that in the book *Breaking*

the News, James Fallows demonstrates that McCaughey's thesis about not being able to choose your own doctor or having fee-for-service under the Clinton plan was completely false?

Norquist: I'm not familiar with the book. The bottom line is that we don't like Clinton. He steals our money, he steals our guns, and sends Americans overseas to die.

Retter: Who is the Democrat's Rush Limbaugh?

Norquist: Fascinating question. I don't think there is one. The Democrats haven't had much luck with interactive media.

Retter: Just so it's clear, you're saying the attacks on Clinton were not "all done on purpose"?

Norquist: The implication that it was coordinated is not accurate. It is on purpose that he took each one of those hits.

Like the Liberty League before it, the New Right's penchant for regarding the Constitution as an inviolate document never to be tampered with and reveling in ancestor worship as a panacea for problems in today's America is a volatile mix that, once examined, can be specious.

For example, in 1787, while the Founding Fathers were in Constitution Hall debating the rights of man, liberty, and freedom, outside in the streets a mob was chasing a woman accused of being a sorcerer. When caught, her forehead was cut open to counteract evil spells she'd allegedly cast. While it was an era of high ideals, it was also a time when the average folk were illiterate and many believed in medieval magic. Moreover, the Founding Fathers themselves did not believe in democracy as we know it, and often—as the Maria Reynolds scandal demonstrated—were capable of dirty politics.

Historian Jon Butler points out that America in the 1990s is a far more religious society than it was in 1776. In fact, Butler maintains, the premise that America was founded on religion is not true. "Religion," he states, "played very little role in the American Revolution and very little role in the making of the Constitution." Christianity is not even mentioned in either the Constitution or the Declaration of Independence, although the declaration does ambiguously refer to "nature's god."

The reason for this, Butler maintains, "is that most of the wars from 1300 to 1800 had been religious wars in which Catholics and Protestants slaughtered each other, stuffed Bibles into the slit stomachs of dead soldiers so that they would literally eat the words of an alien Bible, and die with those word in their stomachs." This was the world of government involvement with religion that the Founding Fathers knew, and it was a world they wanted to reject, he maintained.

As for democracy, there was not a single Founding Father who was in favor of women, blacks, or Indians having the right to vote. The notion of minorities holding the same jobs as whites and sending their kids to the same schools was anathema. As for deification, Thomas Jefferson was neglected by Americans for nearly 100 years. In the 1920s Monticello stood in ruins. The chief fund-raiser complained that he couldn't even garner enough money to make the down payment. Jefferson's face didn't find its place on the nickel until the 1930s, and his memorial in D.C. wasn't built until the 1940s—long after Lincoln's and Washington's. He became a hero in the 1930s because the Democrats needed a New Deal hero and, as a spokesman for the common man, Jefferson fit.

Conversely, Hamilton was virtually forgotten until the late 19th century. Then, he was discovered because businessmen needed a hero, and Hamilton—the "patron saint of bankers"—fit. (See Rick Schenkman's book *Myths and Legends of the Founding Fathers* for more details.)

It should not be a sacrilege to know that while the Founding Fathers were giants who created history's most enduring document, they weren't saints. And since, like the Liberty League before it, the New Right is full of reverence and myths when it comes to the constitution and the Founding Fathers, the question is: Is the New Right wrapping itself in sanctimoniousness while employing scandal to destroy opponents in the hope of obscuring the fact that they are about little more than rolling back social programs and supporting tax cuts for the rich?

---

1. This account is given in *The Revolt of the Conservatives* by George Wolfskill.

RUMORS RUN AMOK

Ambrose Evans-Pritchard, Richard Mellon Scaife, and Chris Ruddy, Vincent Foster, and the *Clinton Chronicles*

S ex and the sleaze artist *then*:

Thomas Jefferson had a problem. In Alexander Hamilton he faced a formidable rival; they locked swords on virtually everything. Both were part of President Washington's cabinet: The aristocratic Jefferson was secretary of state, and Hamilton, the "bastard brat of a Scot peddler," was secretary of the treasury. Jefferson's vision for America was an agrarian utopia of small farmers taking care of themselves, selling raw material to Europe. States had the right to their own armies and currency.

Hamilton, however, wanted a central currency, a strong federal government, and a national army that could hold a European invader at bay. Fifteen years older than Hamilton, Jefferson had a high-pitched, tinny voice and was a reluctant orator. Hamilton had a spellbinding presence. He was also a war hero and a favorite of George Washington. Jefferson was neither.

Sex became an issue when Jefferson learned of Hamilton's affair with Maria Reynolds. What to do with the information? Jefferson could spread it around at dinner parties; adultery was always good for getting jaws to drop and tongues to wag. But so what? The same thing was being said about Jefferson at the same dinner parties; besides, Hamilton could deny it.

It was a defining moment when Jefferson decided to subsidize writer James Callender, whose genius was that he could make a cookie recipe seem sinister. Little is known of Callender other than that he was a poison pen for hire and bounced from one cheap flophouse to another—always broke. He solved Jefferson's problem of how to put the smear on the information highway of 1796 with his book, *The History of the United States for 1796*, in which he accused Hamilton of adultery (true) and with using taxpayers' money to pay for his mistress (untrue). Suddenly, editors editorialized, partisans demanded investigations, and Hamilton was put in the impossible position of trying to defend a negative.

Jefferson's relationship with Callender came close to exposure in 1803. A small-town newspaper editor named Harry Croswell had written that Jefferson paid Callender to call George Washington "a traitor, a robber, and a perjurer." Croswell excoriated Jefferson for "slandering the private characters of men, who, he well knew, were virtuous."

Jefferson sued him. The editor was indicted for seditious libel. He was charged with "deceitfully, wickedly, maliciously, and willfully traducing, scandalizing, and vilifying President Thomas Jefferson," and "representing him to be unworthy of the confidence, respect, and attachment of the people of the United States." Under existing New York law, proof of the truth of the story was irrelevant. Such evidence could not even be submitted to the jury for its consideration. The only question left for the jury to decide was whether the editor had in fact printed the story.

Hamilton represented the editor and knew that the one person who knew whether the editor's article was true was Callender. He was Hamilton's star witness against Jefferson. Callender, however, was found dead in an alley before he could testify. Without him, Hamilton continued the case, arguing that "it ought to be distinctly known whether Mr. Jefferson paid someone to call George Washington a traitor."

Croswell lost, but public sympathy for him helped push a bill through the legislature to correct the dictum that the truth could not be introduced as a defense to the charge of libel. It became law in 1805. On appeal, the court ordered a new trial. Fearing that this one would elicit testimony about the money he had paid Callender, Jefferson dropped the suit. The editor was troubled no more. Jefferson never instigated another such prosecution.

But the incident forever changed the American political landscape. A lesson was learned: While a politician can talk issues until the cows come home, when it comes to winning an election, nothing works better than a little well-placed sleaze.

Sex and the sleaze artist *now*:

Unlike James Callender, who never saw the front door at Monticello, smear artists are not always down-on-their-luck hacks. Sometimes they hail from Oxford, take high tea, and have hyphenated last names, like Ambrose Evans-Pritchard, Washington correspondent for the *London Sunday Telegraph*. He is one of the foot soldiers in a network that seeks to influence American opinion through the Internet, print and television media, and talk radio. Supported by members of the right wing, this network exists to remove Bill Clinton from the political scene.

On January 9, 1997, at the White House, Press Secretary Mike McCurry was conducting a press briefing on an upcoming NATO summit and Russian President Boris Yeltsin's illness. A reporter's first question was about a "300-page report" put together by the White House and the Democratic National Committee. "Why," the reporter asked, "would the White House waste its time putting together this 'media food chain' theory?" McCurry explained that the document was a two-and-a-half-page cover sheet attached to more than 300 pages of news clippings. He went on to say that "wealthy philanthropists" subsidize "organizations that present themselves as news organizations." They "plant their stories" on places like the Internet, and then these stories are picked up, "typically in London, typically by one reporter," and the "stuff gets fed back into news organizations here," he maintained.

The "one reporter" McCurry was referring to was Evans-Pritchard. The "wealthy philanthropist" McCurry alluded to is Richard Mellon Scaife, heir to the Mellon fortune, with an estimated net worth of more than $800 million.

THE WEALTHY PHILANTHROPIST— RICHARD MELLON SCAIFE

Karen Rothmyer, an editor for the *Columbia Journalism Review*, was writing a story in 1981 about Richard Mellon Scaife. After several unsuccessful efforts to obtain an interview, she decided to make one last attempt in Boston, where Scaife was scheduled to attend the annual meeting of the First Boston Corporation.

Scaife, a company director, did not show up while the meeting was in progress. Reached eventually by telephone as he dined with the other directors at the exclusive Union Club, he hung up the moment he heard the caller's name. A few minutes later, he appeared at the top of the Club steps. At the bottom of the stairs waited Karen Rothmyer. According to Rothmyer, the following exchange occurred.

> **Rothmyer:** Mr. Scaife, could you explain why you give so much money to the New Right?
>
> **Scaife:** You fucking Communist cunt, get out of here.

The rest of the five-minute interview was conducted at a rapid trot down Park Street, during which Scaife tried to hail a taxi. Scaife volunteered two statements of opinion regarding Rothmyer's personal appearance—he said that she was ugly and that her teeth were terrible—and also that she was engaged in "hatchet journalism." Rothmyer thanked Scaife for his time.

"Don't look behind you," Scaife offered by way of a good-bye. Not quite sure what this remark meant, Rothmyer suggested that if someone were approaching, it was probably her mother, whom she had arranged to meet nearby. "She's ugly, too," Scaife said, and strode off.[1]

With the exception of an interview he gave on August 13, 1995, to the *New York Times*, Scaife has been unapproachable. The *Times* noted that he "holds few political views that could not be expressed on the editorial page of the *Wall Street Journal*...and bears no apparent animus toward President Clinton, whom he calls a likable fellow." During the two-hour interview, Scaife "often turned to the president of the Scaife foundations, Richard M. Larry," to answer questions. Scaife impressed the interviewer as soft-spoken. Only when the "larger political landscape" was discussed did he raise his voice, stating that the Democratic Party is based on "class warfare" and the "demonization of public figures." It was ever thus, Scaife said, "...from Herbert Hoover in the 1930s to Newt Gingrich today. They have to maintain a symbol of hatred."

It is very difficult to find a photograph of Scaife that is less than 25 years old. Along with revealing that Scaife is a fourth-generation heir to the Mellon Bank fortune and that his personal worth exceeds $800 million, the facts most often mentioned are that he was thrown out of Yale twice and is "insecure" about his intellectual abilities. He has been depicted as someone who cannot look his employees in the eye and fires those who disagree with his conservative political views. Invariably, also mentioned is that he was an alcoholic and that he went through a bitter divorce that lasted eight years. What emerges is an unflattering portrait of a secretive, wealthy right-wing crusader who has a personal obsession to destroy Bill Clinton.

Seldom mentioned is that, after leaving Yale, Scaife got a degree from the University of Pittsburgh, has a good second marriage, and, in the mid-'80s, was successfully treated for alcoholism at the Betty Ford Clinic. Also seldom reported is that in 1992 he gave $1 million each to the Salvation Army and the Pittsburgh Symphony. He is pro-choice, opposes NAFTA, and has little interest in the religious right. But regardless of the depiction, one fact remains: Perhaps as much as anyone else, Scaife deserves credit for creating the New Right and transforming the GOP into the majority party.

In 1970, Richard Scaife was one of 16 guests aboard

the yacht, *Sequoia*, for an evening dinner cruise. The host was Richard Nixon, and the cruise was about money—$100,000 per guest to be exact. But then, money is what his relationship with Nixon was about. In 1968, Scaife was finance chairman for the Committee to Elect Nixon. For Nixon, however, Scaife was a very special "fat cat." In 1972, he gave Nixon's Committee to Re-elect the President more than $1 million—parceled out in 334 checks for about $3,000 each to avoid gift taxes. This made him Nixon's second largest contributor. It was reported that Scaife also gave $47,500 for Nixon's illegal "Townhouse" slush fund in 1974, which was run by Nixon's chief of staff, H.R. Haldeman. But darker plans were considered. As Watergate unfolded, at least one top Nixon aide thought the best way to muzzle the *Washington Post* was to convince Scaife to buy it. The evidence was discovered by reporter Nicholas Lemann in the Nixon Archives, and was in presidential assistant John Erlichman's notes on a December 1, 1972, meeting with Nixon: "*Post*. Scaife will offer to buy it."

However, as the Watergate scandal dragged on, Scaife's disenchantment with Nixon grew. In the waning days of Watergate, even his newspaper was editorializing for Nixon to resign.

It marked a turning point. After Nixon, Scaife began to invest in conservative ideology rather than individual candidates. He had embarked on a bold new course of philanthropy. He provided the money to build nothing less than a parallel network that would outspend and out-maneuver the liberal "Establishment." He put in place a well-financed army of handpicked universities, thinkers, activists, media outlets, and politicians to carry out his agenda. The current GOP proposals to restrict governmental regulations, oppose affirmative action, cut taxes, set term limits, revamp welfare and limit civil liability awards, and balance the budget all have some roots in Scaife-funded groups.

But he's more than just the financial deep pocket who paid for the New Right. Richard Scaife has created an aggressive network of think tanks that recognize that, unlike in Vice President Spiro Agnew's day, the media are no longer simply the enemy; they are just another institution capable of being influenced, as well as intimidated. By spending an amount totaling more than $200 million—roughly $20 million a year, which translates into $400,000 a week—Richard Scaife can do both.

THE DEATH OF VINCENT FOSTER

Ambrose-Evans Pritchard

An example of how the "media food chain" works is the Helen Dickey story, which emerged after the body of White House counsel Vincent Foster was found in a Virginia park on July 20, 1993. Evans-Pritchard reported in the April 9, 1995, *Sunday Telegraph* that Arkansas state trooper Roger Perry had talked to Chelsea Clinton's governess, Helen Dickey, about "Vince Foster's death, hours before his death was supposed to have become known."

The story received major coverage by the Scaife-funded Western Journalism Center and the Scaife-owned Pittsburgh *Tribune-Review*. From these fringe right-wing publications, the story hit the Internet and the London tabloids, where it was reproduced for a far wider audience. Subsequently, right-of-center papers, including the *Washington Times* and the *New York Post*, covered the Dickey story as a legitimate news item. This in turn gave Senator Alfonse D'Amato's staff the needed justification to investigate the issue, which lent the story further credibility and prompted other members of the mainstream media to cover it.

The process by which articles published in London tabloids reappear in American news outlets is called the "blow back." Evans-Pritchard is undisputedly the blowback king, and a review of his articles in the *Sunday Telegraph* from March to November 1994 shows why. (See Appendix C.) From the troopers' tales to Vince Foster, "murdered spy," Evans-Pritchard has been at the epicenter of almost every salacious and criminal story about Bill Clinton to date, including Paula Jones.

In late 1992, Evans-Pritchard moved to D.C. as Washington correspondent for the *Sunday Telegraph*. He claims his first impression of Clinton was positive, and he remembers thinking that the Democrats had a most impressive president-elect. It was an impression that would not last long, however. In Little Rock, he met and courted Clinton's enemies, Cliff Jackson and Larry Nichols, and before long Evans-Pritchard was on his way to being singled out by McCurry as that "one reporter."

He takes umbrage at the assertion that he has done anything more than report things as he sees them, and denies any "cabal" with Scaife. "I had never met the man," he assured the author, "until the White House report came out and linked us as co-conspirators. Scaife called and suggested we have lunch." It was, he said, both innocent and innocuous. He described Scaife as pleasant and a bit "dotty."

Why has the White House singled him out? Evans-Pritchard explains in his January 12, 1997, column, "Why Is Clinton Persecuting Me?"

What seems to cause intense frustration at the White House is the emergence of a new mass media that does not respond to the usual levers of control. A foreign newspaper such as the *Sunday Telegraph* can run stories that are picked up by the Internet and transmitted instantly across America.

The radio talk shows—predominately right-wing—then provide broader amplification, ensuring that the stories reach 10-20-30 million people. The White House is clearly alert to the dangers posed by this samizdat network, but has not figured out a way to jam the transmissions. So it has resorted to shameless propaganda...

On March 27, 1994, Evans-Pritchard wrote:

The radio talk shows have been running at about one a day. I stand by the window of the *Telegraph* offices at 13th and "F" Street, telephone in hand, and broadcast out into the hinterland. Texas, Colorado, New England, California: huge audiences of people I know nothing about, all eager for the latest details about Whitewater. It is an eye-opener. The callers talk about the president of the United States in a tone of undisguised contempt, and they want to know the answer to everything...

Why does Evans-Pritchard seem so determined to destroy Clinton, and why is it so personal? One explanation would be that papers like the *Sunday Telegraph* are only following their brand of British conservatism, which treats political opponents like roadkill. In Evans-Pritchard, the paper has not only a reporter who fits comfortably into that tradition but also one who professes to believe what he writes.

Scandal sells papers and builds viewership. And if in

the process it destroys political opponents, so be it. Witness the controversy that was whipped up around the Clintons about the death of Foster. In a transcript of his appearance on George Putnam's talk show, broadcast on KIEV in Los Angeles, March 3, 1997, Evans-Pritchard stated that he was in possession of an "absolutely authentic" photograph that proved Vince Foster died from a gunshot wound to the neck, and that he'd passed it on to a "prosecutor who is currently serving on the staff of Kenneth Starr."

The photograph showed the wound, "from the right-hand side about halfway along the jaw and about an inch below the jaw." There was, according to Evans-Pritchard, no exit wound from the back of the head, and a photograph purporting to show such a wound was "dummied-up to mislead investigators and the Congress." In the "dummied-up" photo there was a smear of blood that investigators claimed was a "contact stain from the head bouncing against the shoulder, but, in fact, that wound on the neck is the origin and source of the blood that comes down the neck and trickles down the collar."

Why does a reporter from an English newspaper have this information? "It's logical," Evans-Pritchard told Putnam, "that a foreign or an alternative kind of newspaper would be the ones investigating this. It'd be too hazardous for somebody from a major paper to commit themselves to a position that's inconsistent with the consensus." He concluded that the Clinton administration is "a very corrupt group of people."

On the same program, he referred to Foster's death as the "Rosetta stone" on Clinton and his administration.[2] Yet Evans-Pritchard bristled when the author asked about his comments that Foster had been murdered. "I never said he was murdered," Evans-Pritchard snapped. As for what he thinks of the independent counsel's conclusion that Foster committed suicide, thereby rejecting Evans-Pritchard's photograph and theory, he fumed: "Kenneth Starr is a moral coward."

His frequent radio talk-show appearances and articles demonstrate that, wittingly or not, Evans-Pritchard's role is to sound the alarm against the "corrupt Clinton and the people who surround him." While Evans-Pritchard may not be a personal friend of Richard Scaife's, he knows the right wing's information highway and is all too pleased to be its Paul Revere. But Richard Scaife has a reporter even closer to home: Chris Ruddy.

Chris Ruddy

Ruddy is the son of a Nassau County, New York, policeman, and is a graduate of St. John's University and the London School of Economics. While an editor of the now-defunct conservative monthly the *New York Guardian*, he attacked the accuracy of a Public Broadcasting Service documentary called *Liberators: Fighting World War II on Two Fronts*. It purported to tell the heartwarming story of a black infantry company liberating the Nazi concentration camp at Buchenwald. The problem was, it wasn't true.

The black infantry company, Ruddy reported, was 60 miles away when Buchenwald was liberated. The documentary, he concluded, "offered a prime example of how the media can manipulate facts and narratives to create a revised history both believable and untrue."

Ruddy began work on the Vince Foster story in late 1993, just a few months after the story broke. In January 1994, the *New York Post* ran his first story, which quoted two of the first emergency personnel on the scene as saying Foster's body did not look like other suicides. Ruddy says he was dismissed from the *New York Post* because the paper did not want to support his continued investigation of Foster's death. The *Post* has said that he left on his own to pursue other opportunities.

Before he hooked up with Scaife's Pittsburgh *Tribune-Review*, Ruddy was sponsored by the Western Journalism Center (to which Scaife was a major contributor). Once he was hired by the *Tribune-Review*, he became the only reporter working full-time on Foster's death. The significance of Ruddy being hired by a newspaper owned by Richard Scaife is that Foster's death became a driving force in the attempt to discredit Bill Clinton.

It seemed to be working. A *Time*-CNN poll in August 1995 showed that only 35 percent of Americans surveyed were convinced that Foster had committed suicide. Twenty percent said they thought he had been murdered. Yet, besides what the conspiracy-theorists were telling them, what did Americans know about Vince Foster or the case?

*   *   *   *   *

Bill Clinton and Vince Foster were childhood friends from Hope, Arkansas. When Clinton became president, he brought Foster, who was Hillary's law partner, to Washington to work in the White House counsel's office. Foster's family stayed in Little Rock to finish the school year and he moved in with his sister, Assistant Attorney General Sheila Anthony, and her husband, former Representative Beryl Anthony.

Appointments that Foster helped organize, including the attorney general bids of Zoe Baird and Kimba Wood, as well as the firing of seven White House travel office workers and its aftermath, had turned out badly. An editorial in the *Wall Street Journal*, headlined "Who Is

Vincent Foster?" complained the White House wouldn't provide the paper with a photo of Foster when it asked for one and stated that it was filing a Freedom of Information Act request for the photo.

Foster, for the first time in his life, encountered failure. He had trouble sleeping. He looked gray. He seemed unable to concentrate and talked of quitting his job. His sister worried about him and on July 15, 1993, gave him the names of three psychiatrists. The list was in his pocket when he died.

He phoned his family physician in Little Rock on July 19, the day before he died, and said he felt depressed. The doctor, who had in December prescribed a sleeping medicine called Besoril, prescribed a mild antidepressant called Desyrel to help him sleep. Foster took one tablet that night.

At lunch on July 20, he ate a hamburger and fries in his White House office and went out after 1:00 P.M., telling his secretaries they could finish the M&Ms on his plate. He said he'd be back. The last person reputed to see him alive was one of his aides, Linda Tripp.

Between then and mid- or late-afternoon, Foster turned off the George Washington Parkway at Ft. Marcy Park in McLean, Virginia. The temperature was about 100 degrees. He left his coat in his car, walked some 200 yards into the park, sat down on the side of the battlement, not far from a cannon, put a gun's pistol barrel in his mouth, and pulled the trigger with his thumb.

He fell straight back. His hands fell to his side, his thumb caught between the trigger and the trigger guide. There his body lay until it was found at about 5:00 P.M.

That's the official version. It's not the one Chris Ruddy accepts. The Western Journalism Center's winter 1995 newsletter features Ruddy on the cover and covers his disagreement with the conclusions that Foster committed suicide. His list includes unanswerable questions as to why "a devoted family man with three children" would leave no suicide note or not make final arrangements. He fretted about the lack of blood at the scene and fingerprints on the gun, and about carpet fibers found on Foster's clothing. But his most startling charge was that "Foster fired the gun using his right hand, even though he was left-handed."

For such "scoops," the WJC honored Ruddy with a Courage in Journalism award. CNN pundit Robert Novak was the awards presentation host. "Why," WJC founder Joseph Farah wondered, "should the elitist Pulitzer board have a monopoly on setting the editorial agenda of American journalism? We think it's time someone honored those courageous souls who step forward and challenge the conventional wisdom of the day and do battle in the marketplace of ideas." People like Reed Irvine praised the *Tribune-Review* for its boldness.

60 Minutes, however, was not happy. Ruddy edited the script and appeared in *Unanswered: The Death of Vince Foster*, the video produced by the National Taxpayers Union's newsletter, "Strategic Investments." The video begins with a narrator declaring that it had "gone forward and done what *60 Minutes* didn't do," which was to investigate Vince Foster's death. "That got our attention," responded *60 Minutes* correspondent Mike Wallace. He addressed Chris Ruddy's most significant assertions point by point.

1. Ruddy was asked about his assertion that there was a suspicious lack of blood at the scene.

Ruddy: [Fairfax County Medical Examiner] Dr. Haught, in his FBI report and interviews with me, said there was not a lot of blood behind the body."

Haught, asked by Wallace if he told Ruddy there was a "suspicious lack of blood" at the scene, said, "absolutely not."

Ruddy responded, "I don't know why he's suddenly changed his story."

2. Was the body moved to Ft. Marcy Park, as Ruddy has alleged, because of the numerous and varied carpet fibers found on Foster's body?

> **Wallace to Ruddy:** Do you genuinely believe that he was rolled up in a carpet and brought there?
>
> **Wallace:** Foster's wife, Lisa, had just put new carpets in their home."
>
> Wallace went on to point out that she had them put in several places and they had different colors, and carpet fibers of these colors were found on Foster's clothing.
>
> **Ruddy:** I don't have any evidence that he was rolled up in a carpet.
>
> (The fact is that had the 6'4", 200-pound Foster been rolled up in a carpet, there would have been more, not less, blood and fibers on him and his clothing.)

3. Why did the left-handed Foster use his right hand to kill himself?

> **Wallace:** The fact is that Foster was right-handed, not left-handed.

"Wallace," the *New York Times*' Frank Rich noted, "dutifully deflated the more widely circulated conspiracy theories" about Foster's death. Perhaps. But the fact is that by the time *60 Minutes* got around to its report on Foster, Ruddy had been pursuing it for a year and a half in print and on the Internet. There had been time to produce and distribute two videos that featured Ruddy and his theories, to reprint Ruddy's articles in the mainstream press, to raise $500,000 in donations, to make countless radio talk-show appearances—all of which happened without the mainstream media taking notice. By the time they did, it was too late—too late for something as simple as whether Vince Foster was right- or left-handed to matter. By then millions of Americans were already convinced that something dark and sinister involving the Clintons happened the day Vince Foster died.

Through it all, the role of the man most responsible for creating this alternative-news network was virtually ignored. But then, that was exactly the way Richard Mellon Scaife wanted it. The *60 Minutes* report denied him the Rosetta stone that he intended Vince Foster's death to be. But, with polls continuing to show that a majority of Americans still questioned whether Foster's death was a suicide, Scaife had won a big battle. And since it was a battle for control of information, it was an important one.

*　*　*　*　*

It would be a mistake to conclude that anything but a small portion of Scaife's philanthropy supports the Foster suicide skeptics. In 1993, he gave $17.6 million to 150 nonprofit groups. As mentioned, included in his largess was more than $1 million each to the Salvation Army, Goodwill, and the Pittsburgh Symphony. The bulk, however, went to the New Right, with the Heritage Foundation receiving the largest single amount. From 1988 to 1994, it has received more than $7 million. Still, in terms of dollar amounts, Scaife's support for the Foster conspiracy is small but significant, as the following breakdown demonstrates:

$230,000 to the Western Journalism Center (WJC) 1995

The WJC was founded in 1991 by Joseph Farah as a nonprofit organization. Until reprinting criticisms of independent council Robert Fiske's investigation into Foster's death, it was moribund. The WJC first printed the article, "Vince Foster's Death: Was it a Suicide?" and then paid to have it reprinted as a full-page ad in the *New York Times, Chicago Tribune, Los Angeles Times, Washington Post,* and other large newspapers. Included in the reprint was an ad soliciting funds, which raised a reported $500,000. As Farah acknowledged, "...it was our sponsorship of investigative investigation into the death of Vincent Foster that really put Western Journalism Center on the map."

$355,000 to Accuracy in Media (AIM) 1995

Reed Irvine is chairman of AIM. He has written numerous articles questioning Foster's death. AIM released a report, "The Trial of Vince Foster," and produced a television show, *The Other Side of the Story.* Among his theories: Vince Foster was lured into a "sex trap" from which he fled to the park, where his body was found. "It's the biggest scandal in postwar history," Irvine says.

$175,000 to National Taxpayers Union (NTU) 1995

Chairman James Dale Davidson also publishes a newsletter, "Strategic Investments," which produced the video, *Unanswered: The Death of Vincent Foster*. On Pat Robertson's *700 Club*, Davidson said that Foster's death was clearly a murder and that top people in the news media knew that a cover-up was taking place. "Mr. Clinton," Davidson predicted, "will be eliminated from the political scene, hopelessly and totally discredited."

$5.5 Million to The Free Congress Foundation and National Empowerment Television (NET) 1988 to 1994

This group is headed by Paul Weyrich, who said, "In any kind of battle, communication is number one." NET broadcasts Reed Irvine's show, *The Other Side of the Story*, and offers videos produced by Foster-conspiracy organizations.

Aside from funding from Scaife, these organizations primarily rely upon Evans-Pritchard and Ruddy for stories about Vince Foster.

* * * * *

On March 9, 1994, the Washington consulting firm of Johnson Smick International published a newsletter that stated that "investigators" believed White House deputy counsel Vince Foster had died in a "safe house" in suburban Virginia. The house had been rented as a retreat for Clinton administration officials from Little Rock. It was from this house, according to the "investigators" cited by Johnson Smick, that Foster's body had been transported to Ft. Marcy Park, where it was found.

The next day, radio talk-show personality Rush Limbaugh read the account to his radio audience, adding that the "secret hideaway" where Foster was killed was an apartment belonging to Hillary Clinton. From newsrooms to government offices and back again, phone lines sizzled with the "news." A kind of delirium set in. Rumors piled upon rumors. The financial markets trembled. Limbaugh was blamed by many analysts for a 23-point drop in the Dow Jones Industrial Average.

By the following day it was over. With the dawn came the fact that the rumor was baseless. There was some hand-wringing and concern about ethics in the press, but the question of how a scurrilous rumor made its way from a small financial newsletter to Rush Limbaugh's nationally syndicated show obscures the point. A direct link between Foster's death and the Clintons had successfully been made on national radio. It had already been on the Internet for more than a year.

When confronted by James Carville on *Nightline*, Limbaugh stated that he told his audience it was a rumor and repeated it as an "example of what's flying around out there." Not true. He cited it as a news item. The part about "Hillary's apartment" was not in the newsletter, which made reference to a "safe house" and did not mention the first lady. Limbaugh has neither admitted nor apologized for his role in spreading a lie. (See Appendix D.)

THE CLINTON CHRONICLES

Rumors bounced from barroom to Internet to radio talk show, rarely hitting newsprint. Eventually, they ended up in Hemet, California, with a man named Pat Matrisciana. Matrisciana is the producer of the wildly successful *Clinton Chronicles*, which is distributed by the Reverend Jerry Falwell, broadcast on National

Empowerment Television, promoted by the Rutherford Institute, and praised by Pat Robertson on the *700 Club*. The tape sells for $19.95, and it has been estimated that anywhere from 100,000 to 300,000 copies have been sold. Copies have been hand-delivered to every congressman.

Matrisciana is founder of Citizens for Honest Government. His company, Jeremiah Films, offers—in addition to a book version, an updated *The New Clinton Chronicles—The Death of Vince Foster: What Really Happened?; The Mena Cover-up: Drugs, Deception, and the Making of a President; Vince Foster: The Ruddy Investigation;* and *Intelligence Files: A Collection of Official Documents Pertaining to the Criminal Activities of Bill Clinton.*

The company also has made antihomosexual videos that have been used in campaigns against gay civil-rights measures, and warn that civil-rights protection of gays will lead to taxpayer funding of sex-change operations. "We try to hit issues that are not basically touched by the mainstream media," Matrisciana has said. "We basically espouse what could be considered old-time values I think the average American needs to know."

After Matrisciana finished an antigay videotape called *Gay Rights, Special Rights*, a friend urged him to go to Arkansas and meet with Larry Nichols. He did so and told the author that "when I first met [Nichols] he was in very, very bad shape. He'd lost his house, he was on unemployment. He was beaten down, broke, and in debt."

Matrisciana learned that Nichols had worked for the Arkansas Development Finance Agency (ADFA). He already knew that Nichols was indirectly responsible for Gennifer Flowers. "I would say that Nichols is an Arkansas 'character,' but by and large, his information is true. He has an uncanny insight as to how things function in Arkansas."

The *Clinton Chronicles* begins with a statement: "All information presented in this program is documented and true," and ends with a warning: "If any additional harm comes to anyone connected with this film or their families, the people of America will hold Bill Clinton personally responsible." In between, Clinton is depicted as a drug-running, cocaine-addicted murderer.

Many of the charges hinge on the reason Clinton created the ADFA. Clinton's story is that in 1985, it was part of a package of economic-development legislation he endorsed, which allowed the issuing of tax-exempt bonds for industry, government, and housing projects. However, the *Clinton Chronicles* charges that the ADFA was created to launder $100 million in drug money being funneled monthly into the small Polk County town of Mena in the 1980s. Larry Nichols, who was the ADFA's former research and marketing director, is Clinton's chief accuser in the video. Some of the charges—and their refutations:

CHARGE: Clinton had to sign off on every loan ADFA made.

FACT: Clinton did not have to sign off on every loan the ADFA made. However, state and federal regulations require the governor to authorize the issuance of most ADFA bond issues after a public notice and hearing. Bond issues are also reviewed by a loan officer, loan-review committee, and the ADFA Board of Realtors.

CHARGE: There were no payments made on the loans.

FACT: The ADFA has documentation on the repayment of loans since 1977. Housing loans had an annual loss rate of less than half of one percent. ADFA loans to industry had a loss rate of 1.3 percent. That compares favorably with loss rates nationally.

CHARGE: The ADFA was created to launder $100 million a month in drug money coming into Mena.

FACT: As of 1994, in the ADFA's nine-year existence, it had $1.7 billion in loans. If ADFA laundered $100 million a month for even one year, that equals $1.2 billion.

CHARGE: Tyson Foods received $10 million from the ADFA and never paid it back.

FACT: According to the authority records, the ADFA never made a loan to Tyson Foods.

CHARGE: The ADFA routinely transferred $5,000 to $10,000 to Clinton to fund his travel to see women.

FACT: The ADFA has been independently audited since its inception. Audits show the ADFA has never transferred money to Clinton.

CHARGE: Former Associate U.S. Attorney General Webb Hubbell shared the first loan with POM Inc., which his father-in-law, Seth Ward, owned. The $2.85 million loan was never repaid.

FACT: Planters Lumber Co. of North Little Rock received the first ADFA loan. POM Inc. received the ADFA's third loan, for $2.75 million and, according to ADFA records, repaid the loan in full in 1989.

The loan to POM Inc. is important because of the connection to Webb Hubbell and, therefore, to Clinton. POM makes parking meters, selling 50,000 to 70,000 annually in 72 countries, and is the largest of three parking-meter manufacturers in the world. The *Clinton Chronicles*, however, charged that it used the loan to make compartments for nose cones on airplanes where drugs could be stashed. Skeeter Ward, POM's president and chief executive officer, called the nose-cone charge "ludicrous."

As if allegations of drug-running and being a coke-head weren't bad enough, *Chronicles* purports to expose a mysterious beating and murder. *New Republic* writer L.J. Davis came to Little Rock in early 1994 to look into alleged conflicts of interest involving the Clintons. The result of Davis' investigation became the magazine's April 4, 1994, story, titled "The Name of the Rose." It was an unflattering portrait of Clinton's governorship and the Arkansas legal and financial community. He likened them to a cozy conspiracy in a Third World country. Little Rock reporter Gene Lyons says that Davis' main focus of conspiracy was the Stephens, Inc. investment banking empire and Clinton's alleged role in "stuffing their coffers with illicit bond money through ADFA." To the contrary, Lyons told the author that family patriarch Jack Stephens is a Republican and a Bush supporter who has bankrolled every Clinton challenger except Sheffield Nelson. In the last decade, Stephens' fees from bonds actually declined after Clinton established the state bonding authority in 1985. Wall Street firms such as Paine Webber and Merrill Lynch became bigger players in Arkansas bond underwriting. Clinton had cost Stephens millions of dollars. "Davis," concludes Lyons, "could not have gotten the story more incorrect."

While Davis got a number of things wrong, within days of his article's appearance, a March 23, 1994, editorial titled "Censored in Arkansas" ran in the *Wall Street Journal*. It was reported that while researching his article, Davis had been coldcocked by an unknown assailant in his Little Rock hotel room. He'd awakened several hours later with a lump on his head. "The room door," the editorial stated, "was shut and locked. Nothing was missing except four 'significant' pages of his notebook that included a list of his sources in Little Rock."

Warned by a mystery phone call that his life would be in danger the closer he approached "the red zone,"

Davis beat it back to the safety of New York, where he told reporters that his doctor thought the lump on his head had been caused by a small, blunt object. Feeling that Clinton and his thugs were getting off too easily, the *Wall Street Journal* minced no words: "The respectable press is spending too much time adjudicating what the reader has a right to know, and too little time with the old spirit of 'stop the presses.'"

Reading the account on his radio show, Rush Limbaugh intoned that in Arkansas, "They're dropping like flies." The *Arkansas Democrat-Gazette*, however, was puzzled. In short order, reporters tracked down Davis' assailant. It seemed that, on February 14, during the same four hours Davis claimed he spent facedown on the carpet in his Little Rock hotel room, he'd actually been seated upright on a stool in a bar called Filibuster's. Davis' assailant was a half dozen or so straight gin martinis. His bar tab supported the account.

Then there's the "strange" death of 38-year-old Kathy Ferguson, the former wife of Danny Ferguson, the Arkansas state trooper associated with Paula Jones. *Chronicles* reports that Kathy Ferguson was told by her ex-husband that Paula Jones' allegations were true. Then in May 1994, Jones filed suit against the president and Danny Ferguson. Five days later, Kathy Ferguson was found dead in a boyfriend's apartment. She'd been shot in the head. "Typically," the *Chronicles* narrator said, "the police ruled suicide." Limbaugh informed his listeners of Ferguson's "mysterious" death, and once again commented that in Arkansas, "They're dropping like flies."

Yet, neither the video nor Limbaugh informed the audience that Ferguson had quarreled with her boyfriend. A friend told police of pleading with Kathy not to take her life, and Kathy left a note to her boyfriend that said, "I can't stay here any longer. Things will never be the same for us.

I can't handle that." Fifty-one police department photographs documented that the wound was self-inflicted.

Also appearing in the *Chronicles* is a man named Jerry L. Parks. Parks is prominently cited as one of the countless who have been murdered, and is described as a "member of then-Governor Clinton's security detail." Parks' son says that his late father had kept a file on Clinton's sexual indiscretions and that his father's home was burglarized shortly before his murder. The *Arkansas Democrat-Gazette* checked police records but found no report of a burglary. It also found that Parks' security company merely secured entrances and that Parks had no personal access to Clinton.

Matrisciana admitted to *Arkansas Democrat-Gazette* reporter Carrie Rengers on October 30, 1994, that much of the *Clinton Chronicles* video is based on Larry Nichols' files. Although Matrisciana won't share that documentation, he said he feels confident it's accurate. When told about some inaccuracies, Matrisciana said that he only produced the video and didn't research it personally. He won't say who did.

"Our objective was to get the word out. So much of this stuff was not carried by the national media, and we felt that the American people deserved the right to know about their president. Frankly, we were very upset that this wasn't done by *60 Minutes*. I don't particularly like doing this—it's like shoveling manure—I'd rather be riding the horse," said Matrisciana.

Retter: How was the *Clinton Chronicles* scripted?

Matrisciana: We did it totally in-house. Larry Nichols was simply a guy that we interviewed. He has absolutely zero ownership. We dug everything up ourselves. We spent hundreds of thousands of dollars over the last few years in digging up evidence.

Alexander Hamilton and Aaron Burr dueled to the death (Hamilton's) in 1804.
This was the culmination of a years-long rivalry, part of which included Burr
representing Maria Reynolds—a woman who claimed to have had an affair
with presidential hopeful Hamilton. These revelations derailed Hamilton's
presidential ambitions, and, for the first time, introduced to America the
combustible mix of Sex and Politics.

AP/Wide World Photos

AP/Wide World Photos

Gennifer Flowers claimed that Bill Clinton had been her lover for 12 years—while he was governor of Arkansas. The accusation was accompanied by tapes and received tremendous media coverage, almost derailing Clinton's presidential campaign just as it was getting started. Larry Nichols (below, left), an Arkansas native angry at Governor Clinton for unrelated issues, helped fan the flames of Gennifer's accusations.

AP/Wide World Photos

Corbis-Bettmann

Corbis-Bettmann

In 1991, Paula Corbin Jones alleged that Bill Clinton had made an unsolicited advance toward her. Her decision to sue for damages set off a chain reaction that almost forced the first sitting president in United States history to appear as a defendant in court. Cliff Jackson (right), an Arkansas political operative and former Clinton friend, helped propel Paula onto the national stage and into the arms of conservative groups willing to underwrite her lawsuit against the president.

Corbis-Bettmann

Franklin Delano Roosevelt was the target of vicious personal attacks by the Liberty League, a group of conservatives who tried to undo the New Deal and bring down his presidency. The modern-day version of personal attack politics included the insinuation by many conservatives that, among other things, first lady Hillary Rodham Clinton was a lesbian.

Corbis-Bettmann

Rush Limbaugh (above, right, with President Bush) became the mouthpiece of the Republican party with his nationally broadcast radio show. Grover Norquist (bottom, left) takes credit for forming the Wednesday Group, which has met almost every Wednesday since Clinton's inauguration. Its stated mission: to disable Bill Clinton. Richard Mellon Scaife (bottom, right), a billionaire heir to the Mellon fortune, has generously funded numerous right-wing think tanks and nonprofit organizations, as well as conservative media that have been the sources for some of the more sensational charges spread about the Clinton administration.

AP/Wide World Photos

AP/Wide World Photos

Corbis-Bettmann

AP/Wide World Photos

AP/Wide World Photos

Speaker of the House Newt Gingrich (above, left) and the Reverend Jerry Falwell (above, right) were two high-profile promoters who questioned whether Vincent Foster's (left) death involved foul play. Falwell also hawked the notorious *Clinton Chronicles* video, which charged that Bill Clinton was a cocaine smuggler who was directly responsible for the deaths of dozens of people. Even after independent counsel Kenneth Starr's investigation ruled Foster's death a suicide, many, including Richard Mellon Scaife, insisted that this incident was the "Rosetta Stone" of the Clinton Administration.

Michael Isikoff (right), originally reporting for the *Washington Post,* and later for *Newsweek,* became an early Paula Jones advocate after he was introduced to her by Cliff Jackson. Along with Pat Robertson's (middle) *700 Club,* he was most responsible for bringing the story to the attention of the American public. Joe Klein (bottom), then reporting for *Newsweek,* wrote a thinly disguised fictionalized account of the Clinton campaign in his steamy bestseller, *Primary Colors.* In a brilliant marketing ploy, Klein used the pen name Anonymous to make the book appear like it was written by a Clinton campaign insider. The book promoted the concept of Clinton as an out-of-control womanizer.

AP/Wide World Photos

AP/Wide World Photos

AP/Wide World Photos

AP/Wide World Photos

AP/Wide World Photos

Bill Clinton had to stand before the American public and deny yet another accusation of sexual impropriety in January of 1998, this time involving a White House intern named Monica Lewinsky. The first lady then appeared on national television and suggested that a "vast right-wing conspiracy" was behind the efforts to unseat her husband.

Sporting a recent makeover by her new handlers, Paula Jones nearly became the first United States citizen to get her day in court with a sitting president. Although her suit asked for $2,000,000 in damages, she claimed that her only motivation was to get her reputation back. Her legal fees are being underwritten by the conservative Rutherford Institute.

Independent council Kenneth Starr, originally charged with looking into a $45,000 real estate investment by the Clintons in an Arkansas land development called Whitewater, has been allowed to extend his investigation to include Foster's suicide, Travelgate, and Troopergate, at a cost to taxpayers of over $40,000,000. With the introduction of Monica Lewinsky, Jones' case eventually provided the vehicle for Starr to look into every facet of Clinton's personal and professional life and haul many members of the White House staff before a grand jury.

AP/Wide World Photos

AP/Wide World Photos

Retter: Regarding fact-checking?

Matrisciana: We're certainly responsible for what goes in the film.

Retter: What about the statement that Clinton was "hooked" on cocaine? Where did you get that?

Matrisciana: Medical doctors.

Retter: Are you connected with Richard Mellon Scaife?

Matrisciana: Well, of course, Christopher Ruddy is employed by Richard Scaife and he's done things for us. We feel that Chris Ruddy's stuff should go out, so indirectly we've had some contact, but I don't know Richard Scaife and have never gotten any money from him.

Retter: What if someone from the media wanted to check your facts?

Matrisciana: If somebody were very serious and wanted to know my sources, I would certainly cooperate.

Retter: Describe your connection to Paula Jones.

Matrisciana: I gave her a thousand bucks. I'm totally convinced that her story is true.

Besides the *Chronicles* video, there is an active cottage industry of people convinced that dark, foul deeds and Clinton are one and the same. Referring to the numbers of people who have supposedly met an untimely end because of Clinton, an Indianapolis lawyer named Linda Thompson has coined the phrase "body count." The 'count' is as high as 56, 35 of which resulted from the crash of Department of Commerce Secretary Ron Brown's plane in Croatia on April 3, 1996.

In *Chronicles*, the narrator intones: "At the time of his election in 1992, most Americans were not aware of the extent of Clinton's criminal background." With 52 "murders" to his credit, drug-running netting $100 million a month, the whole state of Arkansas being his personal criminal empire, a state trooper claiming to have arranged more than a hundred sexual assignations, and hapless reporters he ordered beaten up and intimidated, it's no wonder that *Chronicles* ends with a call for Clinton's impeachment.

Conservative William Bennett has denounced the *Chronicles* video as "counterproductive" and harmful to the conservative cause. He is the only major Republican to publicly repudiate the video. Bennett, however, sits on Richard Mellon Scaife's board and has been a repeat guest on Rush Limbaugh's radio talk show.

1. This account was given in the July/August 1981 issue of the *Columbia Journalism Review* in an article by Karen Rothmyer titled "Citizen Scaife."

2. Rosetta stone: A basalt tablet, inscribed with a decree of Ptolemy V of 196 B.C. in Greek, Egyptian hieroglyphic, and Demotic, that was discovered in 1799 near the town of Rosetta, Egypt, and provided the key of decipherment of hieroglyphics.

THE RELIGIOUS RIGHT

Falwell and Robertson

Bill Clinton has turned the White House into a whorehouse.
> —Reverend Jerry Falwell, on
> *Politically Incorrect*, June 10, 1997

In the 1930s, a priest was second in popularity only to Franklin Roosevelt. Broadcasting every Sunday from the Shrine of the Little Flower in Royal Oak, Michigan, Father Charles E. Coughlin was a force to be reckoned with. In 1934, when he launched his own party, the National Union for Social Justice, more than five million listeners signed up within two months.

At first, he was a supporter of FDR, but as the economic advice Coughlin offered the president was ignored, Coughlin turned against him. The New Deal, he fulminated, had communistic tendencies, and Coughlin was nothing if not anticommunist. He was also anti-Semitic and attacked both the labor unions and the captains of industry. He took to calling FDR "the great betrayer" and "double-crosser." In 1936, Coughlin said, "When any upstart dictator in the U.S. succeeds in making this a one-party form of government, when the ballot is useless, I shall have the courage to stand up and advocate the use of bullets. Mr. Roosevelt is a radical. The Bible commands 'increase and multiply,' but Mr. Roosevelt says to destroy and devastate. Therefore, I call him anti-God." (*This Fabulous Century, 1930–1940*, published by Time-Life Books)

By the mid-'40s he was off the air, but not before he had done something that had never been done before: Coughlin used a brand-new medium to carry his invective directly into America's living rooms.

*   *   *   *   *

I believe there'll be a constitutional crisis as impeachment proceedings begin.
      —Jerry Falwell, on *Politically Incorrect*

Jerry Falwell was born August 11, 1933, in Lynchburg, Virginia. In 1956, he graduated from Baptist Bible College in Springfield, Missouri, and returned to his hometown, burning to assemble a large flock for his newly founded Thomas Road Baptist Church. Radio and television seemed like good, if unconventional, ideas. Paying a radio station $7 a day to broadcast his sermons and $90 to a local TV station to air his Sunday sermons, his show, *The Old Time Gospel Hour*, was soon picked up by stations around the country.

At the height of his success in 1980, Falwell was heard on 280 radio stations and seen on more than 300 television stations. His church had grown from 35 members to 22,000, one of the largest Protestant congregations in America. Founder and chancellor of Liberty University and founder of the Moral Majority, he was credited with delivering the evangelical vote to Ronald Reagan. *U.S. News & World Report* said he was one of the 20 most influential people in America.

The Moral Majority reflected Falwell's views by opposing abortion, gay rights, the Equal Rights Amendment, and pornography. It supported prayer in schools. Falwell said that he spoke for millions, and the money rolled in. From its founding in 1979 until its demise a decade later, it took in $69 million in donations.

Foreign affairs interested Falwell as well. The Associated Press reported on May 20, 1992, that he traveled to South Africa and pronounced Prime Minister Desmond Tutu a "phony" and announced a campaign "for millions of Christians to buy Krugerrands" as a "reverse campaign" against the Pretoria regime. Likewise, he went to the Philippines and said that the United States should stop "bellyaching" and give "unswerving support" to President Marcos.

But then came the 1987 sex-and-money scandal of Jim Bakker. Jimmy Swaggart got caught with a prostitute—twice. Donations slumped. Contributions slipped from $135 million in 1986 to less than $100 million the following year—and never rebounded.

In 1988, Falwell disbanded the Moral Majority and left television except for local stations and religious outlets. Five hundred people were laid off at his ministries. He hired AMI Securities to sell three bond issues on behalf of *The Old Time Gospel Hour*. Falwell pitched the bonds as a way to earn high interest—9 to 12 percent. "Your monies then go to work building churches and Christian ministries," he wrote in a letter to supporters.

More than $32 million worth of bonds were sold. Shortly thereafter, AMI was indicted by the SEC for fraud. On May 20, 1992, the Associated Press reported that "AMI was backed by Charles Keating and his Lincoln Savings and Loan. When the Resolution Trust Corporation took over Lincoln Savings, it also received the deed of trust of Thomas Road Baptist Church. The Associated Press later revealed that Falwell used his church as collateral 11 times."

* * * * *

Evangelist Jerry Falwell is selling a videotape that contains scathing attacks on President Clinton, charging, among other things, that the president ordered the murders of "countless people."
—*Washington Post*, May 21, 1994

It is not without a certain irony that when the Wednesday Group convenes, myriad representatives of the Christian Coalition are in attendance, but not the man who first merged television with the religious right. The Reverend Jerry Falwell is somewhere outside the insiders. The reasons, however, are not clear. Certainly, his diminished flock and financial problems tag him as yesterday's news. But the main reason for his disgrace is his association with the *Clinton Chronicles* videotape.

In May 1994, CNN's *Crossfire* began with a clip from the video showing an unidentified man standing by railroad tracks in Arkansas, and saying: "People are dead in Arkansas. There are people that are dead, yeah. When I started this, I knew that I might be one of the unsolved mysteries in Arkansas. There were boys on a railroad track. There were countless and countless people that mysteriously died that, as it turned out, had some connection to Bill Clinton. I believe this is going on today."

Liberal cohost Michael Kinsley could hardly contain himself. "Jerry Falwell, where is your evidence? Who has died by opposing Bill Clinton in Arkansas?"

Falwell responded, "I have on hours of videotapes produced the comments, the testimonies, the views of the Arkansas people who are saying these things."

Kinsley: "You've got some jerk in Arkansas. He doesn't have any evidence either."

In an interview for this book, Pat Matrisciana, founder of Citizens for Honest Government and *Clinton Chronicles* creator, was asked about Jerry Falwell: "He did some infomercials—he bought time and would ask for a donation—and sold lots and lots of videos. He became our largest distributor. What happened was he took the flack—I was pretty low-key and was not trying to get a lot of media attention. When the video came out, it was the 'Falwell video.'"

Falwell defends the video by saying, "I felt that there were enough obvious truths to do what I did." And he only did it because the national media were being "hypo-critically quiet."

In an exchange with *Newsweek*'s Jonathan Alter on Charles Grodin's CNBC show on February 19, 1998, Falwell said something startling:

> **Alter:** Jerry Falwell, you have a video out which bears false witness—which is really a sin—against President Clinton. You accuse him of murder...
>
> **Falwell:** That is totally untrue. Citizens for Honest Government in California produced that film. I was given a single copy, and I gave that

particular copy to someone in Washington, who then accused me of circulating it. We did not.

Alter: You give the introduction to the film! And then introduce crazy people who say, "Bill Clinton killed my father! Bill Clinton killed my brother!"

Falwell: I did not introduce the film, and you're wrong.

Alter: Did you not participate in that video?

Falwell: Absolutely not!

Grodin: Are you on the tape, Reverend?

Falwell: I don't know if they put me on the tape or not.

Responding to press inquiries, Falwell's spokesman, Mark Demoss, said, "We had no involvement with the video until long after the fact. The only role of Revered Falwell was to tell the American people about it." However, the March 1998 issue of *Salon* magazine uncovered a fund-raising appeal by Falwell that shows he was indeed involved with the video. In August 1994, in a direct-mail solicitation, he asked supporters to "help me produce a national television documentary which will expose shocking new facts about Bill Clinton." The letter stated that Falwell was ready to make it available "as soon as I can raise approximately $40,000 needed to produce this video."

Pat Matrisciana told *Salon* that "more than 150,000 copies had been sold." The success was due to Falwell's promotion on *The Old Time Gospel Hour*, as well as the infomercial. As reported in the January 27, 1995, *Washington Post*, "Falwell has sold as many as 40,000 copies of the *Clinton Chronicles* by offering them during broadcasts of his weekly *Old Time Gospel Hour*, said his spokesman Mark DeMoss." In the infomercial, Falwell interviews a silhouetted individual whom he identifies only as an "investigative reporter."

"Could you please tell me and the American people why you think that your life and the lives of the others on this video are in danger?" Falwell asks the man.

"Jerry, two weeks ago we had an interview with a man who was an insider," the mystery man replies. "His plane crashed and he was killed an hour before the interview. You may say this is just a coincidence, but there was another fellow that we were also going to interview, and he was killed in a plane crash. Jerry, are these coincidences? I don't think so."

Falwell reassured the man, "Be assured, we will be praying for your safety." When the *Salon* reporter told Matrisciana that he sounded like the man in silhouette, Matrisciana acknowledged that he was the mystery man. "Obviously, I'm not an investigative reporter," Matrisciana admitted, "and I doubt our lives were actually ever in any real danger. That was Jerry's idea to do that.... He thought that would be more dramatic."

Salon also reported that Matrisciana's Citizens for Honest Government funneled money to Larry Nichols, who narrated the *Clinton Chronicles*, despite his frequent denials that he has ever received any money for his appearance in the video or his other anti-Clinton efforts. Nichols "received more than $89,000 in 1994 and 1995 from Citizens and [Matrisciana's film company] Jeremiah Productions." Former employees, however, "say that Nichols boasted of earnings as high as $200,000 from selling copies of the *Clinton Chronicles*" and other anti-Clinton material supplied by Matrisciana.

∗   ∗   ∗   ∗   ∗

PAT ROBERTSON

1960

> *As Election Day approached, Billy Graham wrote an article for* Life *magazine, offering a warm appraisal of Nixon and, without naming Kennedy, observing that it would be inappropriate for a candidate to win because he was "more handsome or charming, or because he happened to be richer, better organized, and more ruthless." Before the article could appear, however, Graham got cold feet and persuaded publisher Henry Luce to pull it and to run instead a nonpartisan article on why Christians should vote. When word of what he had done leaked out, Graham told reporters that "I have come to the conclusion that my main responsibility is in the spiritual realm and that I shouldn't become involved in partisan politics." Given that the election was one of the closest in American history, many observers, including Richard Nixon, believed such an article could have brought victory to the Republican ticket.*
> —William Martin, *With God on Our Side*

The same year as Billy Graham's quandary, a young Pat Robertson walked into a defunct UHF station in Portsmouth, Virginia, and announced to the owner: "God has sent me here to buy your television station." For $37,000, it was his, and the Christian Broadcasting Network was born, chartered as a nonprofit organization "for the purpose of bringing glory to Almighty God." By buying a TV station first, Robertson was practicing sound economics: Control the source. It marked one of many differences between Robertson and Falwell.

Marion G. "Pat" Robertson was born March 20, 1933, in Lexington, Virginia, and grew up in an atmosphere of power and prestige. His father, A. Willis Robertson, was a longtime Democratic U.S. senator from Virginia and chairman of the Banking and Currency Committee. The young Robertson seemed destined for success: military prep school, Phi Beta Kappa at Washington and Lee University, Yale Law School, a wife and baby son, and a promising job in the electronics industry. But at age 26, "suddenly it all seemed empty," Robertson wrote in his autobiography, *Shout It From the Housetops*. He quit his job, entered the New York Theological Seminary, and plunged into the Christian movement.

Robertson's charismatic views had an advantage over Falwell's fundamentalism. Falwell's Baptist position was that there was one correct interpretation of the Bible: Life involved a lot of self-restraint and denial. All the rewards were in heaven, and his sermons were no more than stern lectures. Conversely, Robertson's Pentecostal-like beliefs urged a strong, close relationship with God. There is joy and wealth to be had here on earth. The *700 Club* was run like a snappy talk show, with current events mixed in with attractive guests providing healthy-living advice and recipes. It doesn't preach deferred benefits. Heaven can wait.

Still, when Robertson first went on the air in 1961, he had little money and knew nothing about broadcasting. But he "rigged old tubes and wires and stood before the camera to establish God's beachhead in Tidewater," he explained in his autobiography. As money rolled in, he plowed it back into satellite and cable television, amassing a communications empire. He bought the Family Channel and founded a university. When the Bakker scandal hit and donations plunged, Jerry Falwell was forced to keep spending to buy airtime on other peoples' networks. Thanks to cable Robertson was able to ride it out.

PAT ROBERTSON FOR PRESIDENT

I have never had this kind of precision demanded of me before. I would ask a little mercy.
—Pat Robertson on the campaign trail

When Robertson announced his bid for the 1988 Republican presidential primary, he did more than stun the political world, he met the secular press. Curiously, for someone who had spent years in broadcasting, it was not a happy meeting. In an interview with the *Washington Post*, Robertson said that the scrutiny of running for high office was becoming "embarrassing for my family" and "painful."

One of the reasons for his discomfiture had to do with questions about his 1954 marriage. The *Wall Street Journal* reported that he was married on August 27, 1954, and that his son was born 10 weeks later. Yet, in an October 8, 1987, interview with the *Post*, he had said that he was married on his birthday, March 22, in 1954. "I did give an honest answer," Robertson explained, saying that he and his wife have always considered March 22, 1954, the day they were married because "our son was conceived on that day." The couple's legal marriage on August 27, "to us, wasn't any big deal," he added.

Asked about his autobiography, in which he says he received precise guidance from God on details of his personal life and his business, and that he argued with his wife, Dede, in the early years of their marriage, Robertson said, "The book sets up conflict between Dede and me for dramatic purposes." He did not want readers to draw inaccurate conclusions about his marriage.

Another passage he was asked about concerned a message he'd heard from God in 1966. In the original edition of his book, Robertson wrote that God told him that a minister should not get involved in electoral politics. "The Lord refused to give me the liberty," he wrote. "I have called you to my heart, you cannot tie my eternal purposes to the success of any political candidate." The *Post* noted that after Robertson announced his intention to seek the presidency, the Christian Broadcasting Network reissued the autobiography with the message from God excised.

Similarly, Robertson wrote in 1982 that he had received a message in which, "God told him to stick to his ministry work." Recently, the *Post* wrote, "Robertson has said that the guidance has changed and that he has a 'direct call and leading from God' to run for the presidency." Moreover, he claimed to have done "graduate study" at the University of London, but it was revealed that the work was actually an art class for summer tourists; he also said he was on the board of directors of a Virginia bank, which the bank has denied. And his "war service" in Korea was found to be exaggerated.

The candidate told the *Post* on October 8, 1987, that it would be an error to suggest that "there has been a pattern of deceptions" in his writings and speeches. He said he may have occasionally—and inadvertently—said something "imprecise," and that he may have used a "malapropism" on occasion. But he added emphatically that "I have not lied about my marriage or anything."

Robertson made integrity and moral values the core issues of his presidential campaign. In the speech for his declaration of candidacy, he said, "We must bring back the old-fashioned concept of moral restraint and abstinence before marriage."

But the questions kept coming. An angrier Robertson said, "I think frankly it is outrageous to pry into a man's past and try to do damage to a man's wife and children under the guise of journalism," he told the *New York Times* on October 9, 1987.

In his run for the presidency, Robertson lost badly. In his home state, Virginia, he finished a poor third to Bush and Dole, garnering only 15 percent in the primary. He may have been out of the presidential sweepstakes, but it wasn't all in vain. In the process, Pat Robertson had become a national figure and was able to build a grassroots political organization in 32 states. In fund-raising efforts, he was second only to Bush.

Early in 1989, Jerry Falwell folded the Moral Majority to devote more time to his financially troubled ministry in Lynchburg. Almost simultaneously, Robertson launched the Christian Coalition. The torch had been passed. Instead of proclaiming itself a forum for the majority, the Christian Coalition spoke for a distinct minority. It moved aggressively, and quietly, to identify like-minded voters and get them to the polls. Unlike Falwell, who identified himself with the top, Robertson concentrated on building a grassroots base from the ground up. With the *700 Club*, he had a forum to rail against Medicare, gays, Social Security, public schools, health-care reform, Democrats, and, especially, Bill Clinton. "Many Christians are not planning on celebrating this Inauguration Day...because it represents the repudiation of our forefathers' covenant with God," he said in the January 1993 issue of *Christian American*.

With the Christian Coalition, millions of dollars were being spent to defeat health-care and lobby reform, and promote the Republican Party's Contract with America. In the '94 elections, radio ads in 40 congressional districts ran in 18 states. Thirty-three million voter guides were distributed the Sunday before Election Day. Three million voters were contacted by phone banks, *The Hill* reported on March 13, 1996. For the '96 elections, plans were for 67 million voter guides to be distributed. Pat Robertson had dwarfed anything accomplished by Falwell's Moral Majority. He had succeeded in becoming for the Republicans what the labor unions were for the Democrats. Yet, unlike the unions, he is one person in control of a tax-exempt empire, which poses a question: Is Pat Robertson working for God or man?

THE PREACHER AND THE DICTATOR

The young Virginian who pilots planes for Robertson's organization explained the scenery was new to him because Kikwit wasn't on the plane's normal itinerary. Most of his flights took him deep into Zaire's interior, "where a bunch of former Navy SEALS from Vietnam days are running a diamond mine for Pat Robertson."
　　　　—Laurie Garrett, "The Plague Warriors,"
Vanity Fair, August 1995

1995

Laurie Garrett was confused. She was going to a hamlet called Kikwit, in Zaire, to report on the deadly Ebola virus for *Vanity Fair*. The problem was getting there. Upon arriving in Zaire, she'd discovered that all commercial flights to Kikwit had been canceled, and only humanitarian relief flights were allowed to land. Garrett's problem was solved by Pat Robertson. She had met him the day before by the pool at the Inter-Continental Hotel in the capital, Kinshasa. He had heard of her book, *The Coming Plague*, and offered her a ride on one of his planes taking medical supplies to Kikwit the next day.

Although she'd found a way to get to the plague's center, she was confused. For no sooner had she strapped into her seat (Robertson was not on the flight) than she looked around the plane's interior. Days before, the press corps had been invited by Robertson to witness the plane being filled with what was represented as a great humanitarian effort from the Christian community. "What the press didn't know," Garrett came to realize, "was that most of what they saw was for Robertson's staff and had nothing to do with Kikwit and the Ebola epidemic." With the staff's supplies off-loaded, the "massive" donation "amounted to about 10 boxes strapped together in the middle of this huge cargo plane," she told the author. "My stuff took up almost as much room." Even more disturbingly, Garrett noted, "It was mostly aspirin and medicines that had nothing to do with treating the Ebola epidemic. The kinds of things that really would have helped, like protection from blood, weren't included," she explained.

As it turned out, this was not Garrett's first contact with the Pat Robertson organization.

Before Garrett, the science and medicine editor for *Newsday*, left for Zaire, a television crew requested an interview. Most of the questions were about her book on plagues. However, while in Zaire, Garrett learned that clips of her interview—without her knowledge or permission—were being shown in the middle of a *700 Club* pitch to raise relief money for the troubled country.

Ironically, Garrett's printing of the offhanded comment from Robertson's pilot about the diamond mines may be the first time the outside world learned about the televangelist's mixing of business and evangelism. What follows is the strange story of a man of God and his friendship with a dictator, a story that ultimately pitted Pat Robertson against Bill Clinton.

* * * * *

Robertson's ties to Mobutu—which first developed about two years ago—were highlighted when the Zairian leader appeared in public in the capital city of Kinshasa for the first time in about a year to greet the 64-year-old American televangelist.
—Newsday, May 21, 1995

Until recently he was one of the world's longest-reigning dictators. President Mobutu Sese Seko came to power in 1960 when civil war broke out after the then-Republic of the Congo gained independence from Belgium. In Cold War days it was important turf, and the United States and Russia were locked in a bitter conflict, backing opposite sides. With assistance from the CIA, Mobutu emerged victorious in 1965.

In 1971 he renamed the country Zaire. Mobutu's government was seen as a bastion of anticommunism. During the Reagan years, Mobutu let the CIA use Zaire to launch a secret war against communists in neighboring

Angola. The United States gave him more than $1 billion in aid and helped him get millions in World Bank loans. They ignored Mobutu's corruption because he was furthering U.S. policy.

How corrupt was he? "He set up the country with no checks and balances," said Garrett. "He looted like it was a private store." A 1992 World Bank investigation estimated that up to $400 million—one fourth of Zaire's export revenues, most of it from the state-owned mining conglomerate—inexplicably vanished from the country's foreign exchange accounts in 1988. Mobutu has amassed a personal fortune estimated at $6 billion, most of it tucked away in Swiss and Belgian bank accounts.

However, under Mobutu, Zaire lacked public transportation, telephones, and health care. Entire cities were without electricity. The economy collapsed. The per capita annual income dropped from $500 in the early '70s to an estimated $115 in 1992. Inflation ran as high as 12,000 percent, with unemployment at 80 percent. In 1991, a national conference was called to move the country toward democracy. For more than a year, Mobutu thwarted it. One day in February 1992, hundreds of thousands of Christians poured into the streets of Kinshasa for a pro-democracy rally after church services, demanding resumption of the conference. It was the biggest political demonstration in Zaire since the country gained independence. Mobutu's soldiers opened fire, killing about 200.

Mobutu was in trouble, so among other things, he called Pat Robertson. Less than three weeks later, Robertson was on the state-controlled television station, embracing Mobutu, calling him a fine Christian, reportedly saying, according to the January 26, 1997, *Virginian Pilot*: "You don't have to worry about the political situation...because God loves your country, you only have to

care about the kingdom of God...Mobutu is a good man.
He got his power from God."

* * * * *

*Viewers could see Robertson on a program
called* Sign of the Times, *suggesting that the
Ebola outbreak was sign of a coming plague
and pestilence referred to in the Bible.*
                              —*Newsday*, May 21, 1995

When Robertson visited Zaire in 1995, Mobutu sent one
of his personal Boeing 707s to bring him and his party
of 15. On arrival, Mobutu received his guests on the
presidential yacht. There was a ride up the Congo to
visit a presidential estate. The February 27, 1995, issue
of *Time* reported that the two seemed to get along
extremely well.

But something had happened in the years since the
uprising in 1992 and Robertson's visit in 1995. The dictator's horrific human-rights record and refusal to embrace
democracy had led to the withdrawal in 1993 of economic
aid from Zaire's three main trading partners—the United
States, France, and Belgium. The new Clinton administration was taking a hard line and barred Mobutu from
entering the country. Meanwhile, little was known about
Robertson's private business ventures with Mobutu. His
company, African Development Co., had, in addition to
the diamond mines, branched out and invested in lumber
and gold mines.

After Mobutu's lavish welcome for Robertson, the
two held a press conference. Robertson was "highly critical" of Clinton's sanctions against Mobutu and promised to
enlist the help of Republicans like Jesse Helms to change
the U.S. position. "I think Mobutu cannot understand why

the U.S. has turned against him," Robertson said. "And neither can I."

Claiming that he lost millions of dollars, Robertson would subsequently shut down his for-profit business ventures in Zaire. The coupling of televangelist and dictator was over, ending it as it began, over money. Robertson was comingling business and religion with a brutal dictator who looted and killed his own people. Human-rights organizations charge Mobutu with personally ordering the execution of hundreds of his countrymen. None of this ever seemed to bother Robertson, who ignored warnings from his followers as well as from the State Department that he was helping to prolong a reign of terror.

Laurie Garrett told the author that with the enormous natural resources Zaire possesses, it should not only be the richest country in Africa but one of the richest in world. Since Robertson refuses to open his books, there is no way to know how large his Zaire holdings in diamonds and gold were, the extent of his profits and losses, or whether tax-exempt funds were involved. It is alleged that he also had investments in neighboring Angola.

Garrett added, "The only president who stood up to Mobutu is Bill Clinton." Many find a certain irony that the raging debate over the president's "character" is being led by someone who may have many questions about his own to answer.

THE CAMPAIGN OF DISINFORMATION

Gary Aldrich, Troopergate, and Whitewater

It might have been an electric moment on television. Former FBI agent Gary Aldrich had just been a guest on ABC's *This Week With David Brinkley*. The next guest, George Stephanopoulos, appeared right after Aldrich and charged that a member of the Dole campaign was accompanying Aldrich. In his book *Unlimited Access* Aldrich had portrayed himself as a reluctant author who only told his story because he was interested in the "honor of the presidency and with national security," not for political reasons. He stated that he "had little interest in politics."

Yet, Stephanopoulos was charging that while in the green room waiting to come on, he encountered a man with Aldrich whom he knew to be a Republican operative. "This is a character test for Senator Dole. He should denounce the book, and he should cut all ties to all those connected with this campaign of character assassination," Stephanopoulous insisted.

Aldrich, who was still within earshot, might have

been asked to return to confront his accuser. The moment passed, though, and the confrontation never occurred. What did occur was that Aldrich's first live interview had not gone over as planned.

In the weeks leading up to publication, Aldrich and his book were trumpeted on the coast-to-coast right-wing radio talk-show and print circuit as an electrifying exposé of the Clinton administration. It looked damning. Posted to the White House as one of only two FBI agents, Aldrich's job was to perform background checks on appointees. He viewed it as a "peaceful yet dignified way to close an eventful career spent nabbing mobsters, drug dealers, and white-collar criminals." Yet, as stated in his book's jacket copy, "what he witnessed in the first months of the Clinton administration left him deeply troubled." Then alarmed. Then angered. And finally, halfway through Clinton's (first) term, so thoroughly outraged that he "felt compelled in conscience to leave the FBI."

And write a book. By doing so, Aldrich had violated federal guidelines governing what former officials may divulge from their access to privileged information, and he could potentially be sued by the Department of Justice. In the eyes of people like Rush Limbaugh, taking such a chance only added to Aldrich's credibility.

What he had to say was explosive. Aldrich charged, "The president cannot be located by staff for hours at a time," and that he was a "frequent late-night visitor to the Marriott Hotel in downtown Washington," where he meets for trysts with a "female who may be a celebrity."

Kirby Smith, manager for the Marriott Hotel in Washington, D.C., said: "The garage area that's in question is manned by our security 24 hours a day, so they would have to get past that post, and then the hotel is still somewhat active during the off-hours."

Aldrich also claimed that Vince Foster committed

suicide because he feared his affair with Hillary would be exposed, and that the first lady's Blue Room Christmas tree included drug and sexual ornaments.

In the *This Week* interview, George Will said, "The heart of your book and what makes you think it's important are what you have to say about security provisions at the White House. But before people can get to that, they have to answer a threshold question: Can you be believed? To that end, I want to examine with you the sourcing you have on two matters. One is the alleged Marriott trysts, and the pornographic Christmas tree ornaments."

Will added that before the broadcast he had spoken to the person who was the source for Aldrich's claim about the president and the Marriott. Will identified him as David Brock, and reported that while Brock said Aldrich got the information from him, he was "appalled" that it had been used because the information "was not verified." Aldrich replied that he found Brock's comment "bizarre."

Will then asked about the Christmas tree ornaments that Aldrich claimed were pornographic, and "drug paraphernalia, syringes, heroin spoons, crack pipes, et cetera."

"Ann Stock, the White House secretary," Will continued, "who is responsible for screening [these ornaments], flatly denies this. If she is willing to take a lie-detector test on this, are you?"

Aldrich replied, "I'm willing to swear under oath to anything that I have in this book." Will did not press for a direct answer about taking a lie-detector test. Still, Aldrich did more than just avoid answering the question. He failed to reveal how he could prove the truth about the pornographic ornaments. The proof he managed to offer was right in his book, on page 105. It reads: "'Hey, Gary. Come over here.' I walked over. It was another leaping lord's ornament. Each 'lord' had a wooden body with a photograph of Rush Limbaugh for a head. A dozen ditto-heads, suitable for hanging, but nobody had the guts to hang Rush Limbaugh on Hillary's tree, so back in the box it went. First, though, I held the Limbaugh ornament up, while someone took a picture of me."

On the June 30, 1996, edition of *This Week*, Sam Donaldson noted that the "other salacious story" in the book involved Craig Livingstone's telling Aldrich why Vince Foster committed suicide. Livingstone was the former head of White House security.

> **Donaldson:** You say that Livingstone told you that Foster was worried that rumors that he had had an affair with the first lady were surfacing again. Now, is it your claim that he told you that Foster told him that? Livingstone said: "Foster told me this"?
>
> **Aldrich:** No, he didn't tell me that Foster told him this. The—he told me this in the walk-in safe, as I described in the book—in a matter-of-fact way, as if it was common knowledge. I hadn't—I had no idea what he was talking about. I was absolutely shocked to hear this information in the summer of 1993.
>
> **Donaldson:** So you don't know that the story [about Foster's concern] is true?
>
> **Aldrich:** No, of course not.
>
> **Donaldson:** But you're a trained FBI agent. Didn't you say to him, "Mr. Livingstone, how do you know that Vince Foster was worried about that?"
>
> **Aldrich:** This was not the time or place to cross-examine Livingstone.

As the interview proceeded, it revealed that the only thing in Aldrich's book that was not secondhand—even third- and fourthhand—were the obscene Christmas tree ornaments. According to Aldrich, he had witnessed those himself. Aldrich wrote: "How did [the gingerbread man] fit into the "Twelve Days of Christmas?" Then I got it. There were five small gold rings I hadn't seen at first: one in his ear, one in his nose, one through his nipple, one through his belly button, and, of course, the ever-popular cock ring."

Aldrich continued, "I came back later and took some pictures of the tree and Mr. Gingerbread Man with rings side out. I knew nobody would believe this without photographic proof." However, no pictures were offered by Aldrich to support his claim, nor were any presented in his book.

He did offer a letter sent to hundreds of thousands of people across the country. It read: "The Clintons and the rest of their administration have launched a political vendetta against me because I told the truth about what goes on in their White House." As one man against the government, Gary Aldrich was asking for money.

Ignoring the challenge to his credibility from *This Week*, journalists, and others, Aldrich's book went on to become a best-seller. Six months after his encounters with George Will and Sam Donaldson, *Unlimited Access* had sold a half-million copies and was in its 12th printing. Nevertheless, The Southeastern Legal Foundation sent out 360,000 copies of a letter asking that $29 be sent "right away" for a copy of the book, claiming that the Department of Justice was threatening to withhold Aldrich's book royalties for violating federal disclosure laws.

The lawsuit was never filed, and Aldrich received his royalties. For a brief time, he usurped David Brock as the right wing's favorite author. Aldrich found favor because he showed the Clintons to be immoral and unprincipled. Brock, however, would lose favor for the opposite reason.

A footnote to Gary Aldrich's time in the Clinton White House: On *Rivera Live*, on January 28, 1998, Geraldo asked Aldrich whether he knew Linda Tripp and pressed him for the number of times the two had met. "Maybe 75," Aldrich answered.

* * * * *

The publisher of *Unlimited Access* is Regnery. According to Gary Aldrich's editor, Harry Crocker, the book was a huge success for the company, selling more than 500,000 copies. "The amazing thing," Crocker told the author, "is that there are no returns. It hasn't been brought out in paperback because it's still selling in hardback—it's really become a part of American folklore."

Crocker was the former editor-in-chief at Regnery but had been working in the division's book club. In the fall of 1995 he received a call asking if he wanted to edit a new book and jumped at the chance. It turned out, however, to be extremely frustrating because he wasn't allowed to see or read it. Aldrich had to submit his manuscript first to the FBI for clearance. Meanwhile, the publishing deadline neared. Finally, unable to delay any longer, it was decided to proceed without the FBI's clearance. In the rush to beat the deadline, Crocker moved into Aldrich's house. A couple of frantic weeks later, the book was ready for the printer. Some excerpts from the author's interview with Crocker:

On fact-checking:

Crocker: We relied on Gary's being an FBI agent for 30 years. We didn't do any ourselves.

As for David Brock's being the source of Clinton's alleged late-night trysts at the Marriott:

Crocker: Gary's chief source may have been someone other than Brock. It may have been another hotel other than the Marriott, but Gary stands behind the story.

Retter: Have you seen the pictures Aldrich claims he took of the obscene Christmas tree ornaments?

Crocker: Yes, but it was just a cheap home camera. You can't see much.

Retter: But didn't Aldrich say "without a photo, no one would believe there were pornographic ornaments?"

Crocker: There is one of a gingerbread man, but it's not good photographic evidence to prove anything. They just show him standing in front of a Christmas tree. It could be a Christmas tree anywhere.

Retter: Was it ghost-written?

Crocker: No, Gary wrote it all himself.

Two Regnery books on politics came out in the fall of 1997. Apparently frustrated by the failure to bring about the real thing, the *American Spectator*'s E. Emmett Tyrell Jr. was driven to fiction with the first book, *The Impeachment of Wm. Jefferson Clinton*. The second is *The Secret Life of Bill Clinton* by Ambrose Evans-Pritchard. (See Appendix C.) Editor Crocker promises that the former will "read like the real thing." Of the latter, he says that Evans-Pritchard has elaborated on "things about Clinton that he thinks are underreported."

The Southeastern Legal Foundation represented Aldrich regarding any possible legal action by the Justice

Department. The Foundation's Tony Young told the author that Aldrich was a client six months before *Unlimited Access* was published and is one still. The Southeastern Legal Foundation is supported by contributions. Richard Mellon Sciafe is a major contributor, having given more than $300,000.

TROOPERGATE

After Iran-Contra, the defeat of Supreme Court nominee Robert Bork, and the bloodying of Clarence Thomas—I viewed Troopergate as not only a good story—but as "an eye for an eye."
—David Brock, *Esquire* magazine,
July 1997

July 1993: Four Arkansas troopers contact Cliff Jackson about setting up a book deal. Jackson devised a media strategy that would have the story break first in the mainstream media.

August 1993: The troopers meet with the *Los Angeles Times* and David Brock of the *American Spectator*.

December 1993: The *Los Angeles Times* was not ready to publish, but the *Spectator* was. Not wanting the story to break in a right-wing publication, Jackson offers two of the troopers to CNN. ("We needed a mainstream 'hammer,'" he said.)

December 19, 1993: CNN airs the story.

December 20, 1993: The Associated Press picks it up from CNN.

December 21, 1993: The *American Spectator* publishes its 11,000-word story in a January 1994 issue. Then-Congressman Robert Dornan (R-Cal.) is the guest host on Rush Limbaugh's radio show, and Brock is the guest. The entire three-hour show is devoted to the troopers' story.

December 22, 1993: The *Los Angeles Times* publishes its troopers story. The *Washington Post* runs the story on the front page. The *CBS Evening News* leads with it. Brock discusses it on C-SPAN.

December 23, 1993: Cliff Jackson is in hog heaven. With the *Larry King Live* appearance, he had delivered the media "big hammer." Talk shows were consumed with tales of Bill Clinton using his troopers to fetch women for sex. Almost as a special bonus, it was the week before Christmas. The *Los Angeles Times* also reported that Clinton made a long-distance call from Virginia to a woman in Little Rock at a late hour. The woman told reporters that he was talking her through a personal crisis. This revelation ran on the front page.

In the intervening months, some aspects of the troopers' story were found to be false. For example, they claimed to have watched—via security camera—Clinton having sex in a parking lot of the governor's mansion. Arkansas reporters asked for a demonstration and discovered that the security camera had no zoom lens. They couldn't see a thing. Likewise, the troopers claimed that Hillary had ordered a visitors' logbook destroyed, ostensibly to hide Gennifer Flowers' visits. Reporters discovered there had been no such logbook.

Virtually the only one on the national scene to challenge the troopers' veracity was Geraldo Rivera. On February 15, 1994, troopers Roger Perry and Larry Patterson were guests on his show, and the following exchange occurred:

Rivera: Larry Patterson, did you ever commit adultery?

Patterson: Yes.

Rivera: Isn't it a fact that you're accused of beating your wife?

Patterson: That was an allegation, Geraldo. I never beat my wife.

Rivera: Now you fellas are in a bit of trouble over an insurance fraud, aren't you?

Perry: No.

Patterson: No, sir. No trouble at all.

Rivera: Didn't you lie about a car wreck you had?

Patterson: I did. Yes.

Rivera: Driving a state car?

Patterson: I did.

Rivera: You said you had an unavoidable car crash when, in fact, you were dead drunk. You two guys were out with some female state trooper. Isn't that the truth?

Patterson: I wasn't dead drunk. I had been drinking, yes.

Rivera: Wait a minute. You had six or seven Crown Royal doubles and a bunch of scotches later at some other joint?

Patterson: No scotches.

The discrepancies in the troopers' stories hardly received the attention their headline-grabbing charges about Bill Clinton had; nor did the discrepancies seem to seriously challenge their credibility. The *Los Angeles Times* and CNN, which were largely responsible for giving the story legitimacy among the mainstream press, were standing by the troopers' story.

Still, virtually unnoticed was that the troopers had not offered a single date or time for any of Clinton's alleged indiscretions, thus making it impossible for the president to defend himself. With this story, journalistic standards that once divided the "respectable" media from the tabloids had collapsed.

CNN's vice president for news, Ed Turner, later said, "The fact the troopers were willing to go on camera was what made us decide to do the story."

As Troopergate erupted, links were inevitably made to other scandals plaguing the White House. The *New York Times* and the *Washington Post* reported that Whitewater files had been removed from Vince Foster's office on the night of his death. The *Times* even called for a congressional investigation. On January 1, 1994, Representative Jim Leach (R-Iowa), in a *Post* commentary, called for the appointment of a special prosecutor. The *Times* echoed that call on January 4, as did the *Post* on January 5. And the embattled White House was backed into a corner, announcing on January 12 that the president would ask Attorney General Janet Reno to appoint a special prosecutor. On January 20, Reno announced the appointment of Robert B. Fiske Jr.

* * * * *

The case of the president vs. Paula Jones: Who is telling the truth? These days, the better question might be: Is anybody telling the truth? The latest revelation comes from one of the Arkansas state troopers who first corroborated rumors about then-Governor Clinton's alleged sexual escapades. Now he's talking again for the first time on television. And he tells Dateline *a very different and equally sordid tale.*

—Jane Pauley, *Dateline NBC*

In the beginning there were four. A united four: troopers Roger Perry and Larry Patterson, Danny Ferguson—he of Paula Jones fame—and Ronnie Anderson. Then, Ferguson got separate counsel, and in July 1997, Anderson met with *Dateline NBC*'s Chris Hansen.

> **Hansen:** Your name was in the *American Spectator* article?
>
> **Anderson:** Yes.
>
> **Hansen:** Did you confirm some of these stories?
>
> **Anderson:** Yes, I did. I was just sitting there and they'd say, "You remember this? You remember that?" And I'd say, "Yeah, I remember"—you know, confirming the stories.

Hansen asked if any of the troopers' charges had actually happened, to which Anderson replied, "Not in my presence, they didn't." Anderson said he was changing his story not because of presidential pressure but because of a guilty conscience and the tactics of new independent counsel Kenneth Starr, Fiske's successor.

*　　*　　*　　*　　*

A year after Fiske's appointment, Congress had passed legislation that gave a panel of federal judges the authority to appoint an independent counsel with broad powers to conduct nonpartisan inquiries. On July 1, 1994, Janet Reno requested that Fiske, a moderate Republican, remain in his position because he was in the middle of his Whitewater investigation. It was later reported by Eric Schlosser in the March 19, 1998, issue of *Rolling Stone* that "Senator Lauch Faircloth, a conservative Republican from North Carolina, attacked Reno's request, claiming that Fiske's reappointment would be 'highly improper.' Right-wing organizations were infuriated by Fiske's recent conclusion that Vincent Foster had indeed committed suicide. Faircloth argues that Fiske's work was tainted by conflicts of interest and that the panel should appoint 'a new, truly independent counsel that will enjoy the confidence of those who seek truth and justice, regardless of party.'"

Schlosser continued that "Two weeks later, Faircloth and his fellow Republican senator from North Carolina, Jesse Helms, joined the presiding judge on the Independent Counsel Panel for a private luncheon. Judge David Sentelle, also from North Carolina, had been appointed to the U.S. Court of Appeals by President Reagan at Jesse Helms' request.... A few weeks after these three Republicans had lunch, the Independent Counsel Panel fired Fiske and named Kenneth Starr to replace him."

According to Schlosser's article, Judge Sentelle said his luncheon with Faircloth and Helms had been dominated by talk about Western wear and old friends. "To the best of my recollection," Sentelle claimed, "nothing in these discussions concerned independent counsel matters."

*   *   *   *   *

Yet soon Starr was in Little Rock, putting a list of women's names in front of Ronnie Anderson, who was asked whether he'd seen any of them with Bill Clinton. He refused to cooperate. By talking to *Dateline*, he was going public with what he considers a political fishing expedition by Prosecutor Starr.

"The whole thing was set up for money from the beginning," Anderson said. He claimed the troopers were told they could make about $2.5 million on a book deal. Cliff Jackson was hired by the troopers to negotiate the deal. But, in 1994, Anderson had a change of heart and confessed all in an affidavit given to Clinton's lawyers; he thought that was the end of it.

Anderson was also going public about the role of Cliff Jackson, who—in order to do the maximum early damage to Clinton—did not want to wait on a book but wanted to get the story out as soon as possible. "I just think he wanted these stories out before Clinton got in office real good, and try to get him impeached from office," Anderson stated. Anderson added that Jackson offered to find the troopers high-paying jobs if they got fired because of telling their stories, all in exchange for postponing a book deal and going public immediately. Anderson said that Jackson told him, "I don't like [Clinton]. I have no use for him. I would like to see the man impeached."

Anderson spent nearly eight years in Clinton's presence, often around the clock, and was emphatic that he didn't witness any of the alleged activity.

> **Hansen:** When you boil all this down, is this just about Little Rock politics, Cliff Jackson taking on Bill Clinton, and some guys who thought they could make some big-time money by telling their story?

Anderson: That's it rolled up in a nutshell.

Ultimately, Troopergate was about credibility. By not following the most basic rule in journalism, which is to first check the facts, the mainstream press has resorted to the "New Journalism" of David Brock. Still, the troopers had one more story to tell. This one would be recounted by Ambrose Evans-Pritchard.

*   *   *   *   *

TROOPERGATE 2

April 9, 1995

Ambrose Evans-Pritchard wrote that the White House had possibly falsified both the time and place of Vince Foster's death. The story mentioned a phone call from Chelsea Clinton's governess, Helen Dickey, to friends back in the Little Rock governor's mansion, informing them of Foster's death. It bears repeating here, for at the center of it are the same two troopers involved in Troopergate.

The park police notified the Secret Service of Foster's death at 8:20 P.M. Yet, trooper Roger Perry told Evans-Pritchard that Dickey called the mansion at 6:15 P.M. and was "kind of hysterical, crying real upset. She told me that 'Vince got off work, went to his car in the parking lot, and shot himself in the head.'" For confirmation, Perry stated that he hung up the phone and called his fellow Troopergate trooper Larry Patterson.

Within days, a reprint of Evans-Pritchard's article was published in a full-page ad in the *Washington Times*, paid for by the Western Journalism Center. The *New York Post*, the *Wall Street Journal*'s editorial page, and Richard Mellon Scaife's *Tribune-Review* wrote articles about the story as well.

New York Senator Alfonse D'Amato's Whitewater Committee duly subpoenaed Dickey, who testified that she had indeed phoned the governor's mansion and spoken briefly to trooper Perry, but that the call was made after 10:00 P.M. She said nothing about a parking lot and further explained that "we lived next door to the Fosters in Little Rock. It was a very personal thing to me." She did not want Foster's friends in Little Rock to learn of his death on the news. Senator D'Amato said that having her appear before the Committee was all the Democrats' idea, thanked her for her testimony, and that was the end of it, until, within days, trooper Perry was telling his tale to a shocked Pat Robertson on the *700 Club*.

None of the papers that reported the trooper's story retracted it, and while Senator D'Amato called it a false alarm, it was well on its way to becoming conspiracy folklore, courtesy of troopers Perry and Patterson.

There was, however, more to the story. Days after Vince Foster committed suicide in Ft. Marcy Park, Virginia, on July 20, 1993, Larry Nichols told listeners of radio talk shows that "Foster had been murdered and his body had been moved to Ft. Marcy Park from somewhere else." Nichols claimed that a "secret contact" of his working on the White House staff had seen White House employee Helen Dickey sobbing uncontrollably in the middle of the afternoon on the day of Foster's death. Nichols said his contact reported that Dickey "told people she was sobbing because she had just learned that Foster had died." The body was not discovered by police for another couple of hours—which would allow time for the body to be moved and taken to the park.

In an interview in the March 1998 issue of *Salon* magazine, it was reported that "Nichols recalled that he had lost all hope of corroborating the story until he told it to [troopers] Roger Perry and Larry Patterson." Perry told Nichols that he remembered Dickey had called the Arkansas governors mansion early in the evening the night of Foster's death. Larry Patterson then remembered that Perry called him early in the evening with the news.

It was then that Nichols told the troopers that he had a business proposition for them. *Salon* reported that, "according to Roger Perry, 'If they would tell their sensational story about the Foster death on a video sequel to the *Clinton Chronicles*, he would share the profits from its sale with them.' Nichols, according to Perry, had complained that he had not been fairly compensated for his role as the narrator of the *Chronicles*, so he wanted to produce the next one by himself."

Perry and Patterson signed a contract with Nichols that called for "Nichols to pay both troopers a dollar for each video sold." In separate interviews with the magazine, Nichols, Perry, and Patterson "all confirmed the existence of the contract and corroborated other details originally provided by Perry."

After signing the contract, Perry and Patterson told their stories about Foster's death to investigators in independent counsel Kenneth Starr's office. Nichols promised hefty profits for the Foster video. The magazine reported, "He boasted, according to Perry, that Falwell had agreed to purchase between 50,000 and 75,000 copies of his video and promote it on television. Citizens for Honest Government also had agreed to buy a substantial number of the videos, Nichols said, as had several radio talk-show hosts on whose programs Nichols was a regular guest.

"Perry, however, never saw any money from the video sales. Nichols told him that the video made no profits. Nichols told other people, however, that he made more than $150,000 from the sales of the video, and Perry says he believes Nichols cheated him."

Roger Perry seems to be having second thoughts about his involvement, and told *Salon* that he was going through a "very painful experience.... When I learned about the kind of things that Larry Nichols and Pat Matrisciana were doing, I came to believe that what they were up to was wrong...and now there is going to be a price to be paid again for speaking out."

Salon also revealed that Matrisciana shared a joint bank account with Richard Scaife's reporter for the Pittsburgh *Tribune-Review*, Chris Ruddy, and that, as of September 1997, "the bank account controlled by Matrisciana and Ruddy had total assets of $3.069 million" and no liabilities.

WHITEWATER

I'm going to say that there are going to be some indictments that are going to stun you— some high officials are going to end up being indicted—sooner rather than later...you just see if I'm not right about this.
　　　　—Rush Limbaugh, February 14, 1996

There's something there—for the life of me I don't know what it is—but it must be something damaging.
　　　　—Rush Limbaugh, May 8, 1997

WHITEWATER POP QUIZ:

1. Had all the Whitewater lots been sold on time, how much would the Clintons have made?
   a. $1 million
   b. $500,000
   c. $250,000
   d. $47,500

2. How much did the Clintons lose on the Whitewater investment?
   a. Nothing.
   b. $5,000
   c. $20,000
   d. $45,000

3. How much did the Clintons "borrow" from Madison Guaranty Savings & Loan?
   a. $1 million
   b. $500,000
   c. $100,000
   d. Not a penny.

4. True or false: The Clintons were business "partners" with James McDougal in Whitewater.

Answers: 1-d; 2-d; 3-d; 4-False. Whitewater was a corporation, not a limited partnership. The difference is that, unlike a limited partnership, in a corporation one does not file joint tax returns or have anything to do with the daily running of the business. The Clintons were stockholders, not partners.

There is a point in the *Clinton Chronicles* that illustrates the problem the right wing has with Bill Clinton. It comes after the de facto narrator, Larry Nichols, has accused Bill Clinton of running a drug-laundering operation that netted him "$100 million a month." Nichols then stated, "But Bill Clinton was never interested in money."

Yet, the Wednesday Group's Grover Norquist said that "starting with the Small Business Administration loan, Whitewater, and everything," one sees Clinton's corruption. So, on the one hand, Clinton has $1.2 billion a year he doesn't want or care about, and on the other hand, he's facing impeachment over trying to hustle $47,500.

Where Whitewater presently stands: Clinton—having been accused of using Madison Savings & Loan as his own personal savings and loan (from which he took no loans)—puts everything on the line to get a $300,000 small business loan for a friend, a loan from which he personally gained nothing.

Initially, Whitewater was not the right wing's story. "Eighty to 90 percent of what the press knows about Whitewater," wrote the *American Journalism Review*, was contained in stories filed by *New York Times* reporter Jeff Gerth. It started March 8, 1992, in a story headlined "Clintons Joined S&L Operator in an Ozark Real Estate Venture."

The irony is it should have ended with a report from a Republican. Jay Stevens was a former U.S. Attorney who lost his job when Clinton took office. He was with an accounting firm—Pillsbury, Madison & Sutro—when the firm was tapped by the Resolution Trust Corporation to deal with the Whitewater Development Company and the Clintons' liability for Madison Guaranty losses. The Clintons gave sworn statements, 45 witnesses were interviewed, and 200,000 documents were examined. Two years and nearly $4 million later, the final report was completed. Released December 13, 1995, its conclusion: The president and first lady had told the truth about Whitewater all along. They were passive investors who lost money and were kept in the dark by Jim McDougal about the real status of the project. Every charge leveled was refuted.

Gerth's *New York Times* article contending the Clintons had a "sweetheart" deal in which they put up very little money and had no risk was wrong. The couple put up $45,000 (which they lost), and they were exposed to $200,000 in liabilities. Likewise, Gerth's assertion that Tyson Foods got $9 million in government loans was wrong. There was no such loan. "There is no basis to charge the Clintons with any kind of primary liability for fraud or intentional misconduct," the RTC report stated.

Yet, two special prosecutors and two congressional hearings later, more than $45 million has been spent investigating the deal, and to what result? Even Rush Limbaugh doesn't know what Whitewater is about.

Much of the fault lay with reporters who relied on two sources: Jim McDougal and David Hale. Until his recent death, the former was slowly and steadily going off the deep end; the latter ran the Small Business Administration in Little Rock and set up dummy companies to loan himself money. He bilked the SBA out of millions all by himself—with no help from Bill Clinton. Speculation is that by mentioning Clinton's name, he's trying to save himself.

Still, the Pillsbury, Madison & Sutro report was supposed to end wild speculation by laying out the facts, but the press and politicians ignored the conclusions reached.

In fact, major reporters and writers continued to get it wrong. For example, after Gerth's mistaken report of a $9 million loan to Tyson Foods, then-*Newsweek* columnist and later *Primary Colors* author Joe Klein wrote of the president's "multiple personality disorder." Using the *Times* report of the (nonexistent) $9 million loan as a springboard, he wrote that Clinton "snuggled up close to the Arkansas oligarch, the bond daddies, and chicken pluckers—and never quite escaped the orbit of the shadowy Stephens brothers, Witt and Jackson."

Little Rock reporter Gene Lyons was left scratching his head. For one thing, Witt Stephens had been dead for years, and his brother, Jack, was a Reagan Republican who had bankrolled nearly every Clinton opponent since the early 1980s. And the business about a $9 million loan was laughable. "This," Lyons wondered in amazement, "is the great Eastern-Establishment press?" Meanwhile, each bit of misinformation from the mainstream press was being heralded by Limbaugh and the right-wing media as confirmation that Clinton was indeed a crook.

Then came *Blood Sport*, the self-proclaimed definitive exposé on Whitewater by Pulitzer Prize–winning writer James B. Stewart. It was two years in the making. Lyons in turn wrote his own book, *Fools for Scandal*, and noted that Stewart claimed Clinton, "instead of Governor Frank White, as history records," had appointed David Hale to a judgeship, and that Stewart "makes no mention of the 13 dummy companies or the $2.04 million Hale pled guilty to scamming from the SBA." Lyons accused Stewart of "telling half the story," of siding with McDougal and Hale, and with leaving out key documents that show what really happened.

Even so, *Blood Sport* uncovered no big crimes in Whitewater, "just a lot of deceit, bad character, and political opportunism." At least that's what Stewart was saying in *Time* magazine and on his book tour. Then, on *Nightline*, Ted Koppel asked Stewart, "What is it you would say if you were obliged to summarize what is troublesome about Whitewater and what will still come back to haunt the Clintons?"

Stewart responded that what Whitewater came down to was the Clintons' refusal "to abide by financial requirements in obtaining mortgage loans...and it is a crime to submit a false loan document."

"But you can put a hold on the handcuffs and the one-piece his-and-her orange jumpsuits with the presidential seal," stated Lyons in his own book. "Because Joe Conason at the *New York Observer* was pondering this allegedly felonious document—thoughtfully reproduced in the appendix to *Blood Sport*—when he noticed something funny. At the bottom of the page, above the suspects' famous signatures, he noted this funny little notice: (BOTH SIDES OF THIS STATEMENT MUST BE COMPLETED.)"

Lyons continued: "Conason wondered about that. Surely not. It couldn't be. Curious, however, he made it his business to check it out. He put his hands on a copy of the original statement. And guess what? All the information Stewart accused Hillary Clinton of fudging was right there, in the first lady's quite legible hand. Stewart had simply neglected to check the second page." (See Appendix E.)

DAVID BROCK

The Paula Jones lawsuit against President Clinton, the tales that Clinton used Arkansas state troopers to procure sex, the rumor that the president sneaks out of the White House at night for secret sexual trysts, all derive from the work of one man, conservative writer David Brock.

—Lars-Erik Nelson, syndicated columnist

David Brock's feelings were hurt. Several times he played back the message on his answering machine just to be sure, but there was no mistake. Each time his friend's voice said the same thing: It would be better if he did not come to her party. Brock knew exactly what it meant, for this was not just any party; this was one for conservative movers and shakers. The "right-wing road warrior" had just become roadkill, and for that he could thank Gary Aldrich and Hillary Clinton (*Esquire*, July 1997).

Yet, he had so recently been on top. From the moment his book *The Real Anita Hill* hit the stands in 1993, Rush Limbaugh and the other radio-talk shows could not praise him enough. Then, with Christmas week 1993 came the troopers' story in the *American Spectator*, which Brock gleefully described in *Esquire* as "perhaps the most humiliating portrait of a sitting president and his wife ever published." In the article, he mentioned a woman named "Paula," who two months later filed sexual harassment charges against the president. "I kill liberals for a living," Brock boasted.

After the 1994 Republican takeover of Congress, Brock crafted a book proposal on the "most tempting" target he could think of—Hillary Clinton—and grabbed a reported $1 million advance.

However, several months before his book on the first lady was published, Gary Aldrich's *Unlimited Access* hit the stands with its report that Bill Clinton was sneaking out of the White House for trysts at the D.C. Marriott. "I called Aldrich, who verified that I, in fact, was the sole source for his supposed scoop," Brock wrote in *Esquire*. Brock said that he had asked Aldrich about this piece of gossip, which he'd heard while researching his book on Hillary.

"Aldrich told me that he knew nothing about the rumor," Brock stated. When the "revelation" made front-page headlines, he responded "viscerally." Unwittingly, Brock had become the source for the most sensational charge in Aldrich's book and tried to set the record straight by telling the truth. Yet, the *Washington Times*, the *Wall Street Journal*'s editorial page, and virtually all of right-wing talk radio ignored his disclaimer and let Aldrich "perpetuate a hoax on the public by celebrating *Unlimited Access* as legitimate and well-researched," Brock contended. It was a precursor of what would happen with Brock's book on Mrs. Clinton.

* * * * *

There is no "liberal movement" that blackballs journalists in the sense that there is a self-identified, hardwired "conservative movement" that can function as a kind of neo-Stalinist thought police."
—David Brock, *Esquire,* July 1997

When Brock started his book on the first lady, his frank intention was to "butcher" his prey. Then something happened. "For the first time in my experience, my partisan prejudices were substantially dispelled rather than reinforced," he revealed in *Esquire*.

Brock's ax to grind with Hillary conflicted with the reality he was discovering. He questioned whether he should continue, and finally decided to let the chips fall where they may. "If the image of Hillary as a greedy influence peddler was confounded by the evidence—she made about $20 a month on the controversial representation of Jim McDougal—that's what I would write. If the paper trail substantiated Hillary's much-doubted claim that she had little involvement in sham deals at the Castle Grande trailer park development...so be it. There was no dirt down the lesbian trail, either," he wrote in the *Esquire* story.

Brock concluded that Hillary was not the "corrupt, power-mad shrew of conservative demonology." *The Seduction of Hillary Rodham* hit the stands and was greeted by the right-wing press with venom. The *Washington Times* called it a "whitewash," and talk-show hosts Oliver North and G. Gordon Liddy wouldn't book Brock on their shows. Bay Buchanan told Brock that "if only I had taken the 'right perspective' on Hillary," the conservatives would have gotten on board. Cato Institute's David Hoaz was more to the point: "People who hate the Clintons are supposed to write books about how evil they are," he said in *Esquire*. "If you don't find any evil, you're not supposed to write the book."

All of which led Brock to conclude that conservatives have "come to so revile Hillary Clinton and everything she represents that they have lost their moorings." On the June 22, 1997, edition of *Meet the Press*, he said that in the conservative culture there is a "kind of mentality that values loyalty above critical thinking, and that equates dissent with betrayal...the stupidity of questioning motives rather than debating the ideas on their merits."

> *With his lurid stories, Brock has been the source of more glee for conservatives, more fodder for radio talk shows and barroom jokes—and more heartache for the First Family—than anyone in America.*
> —Lars-Erik Nelson, syndicated columnist

David Brock is gay. He admitted his sexual preference in the *Washington Post* shortly after writing the troopers story. Yet, he worked for the *American Spectator* and received awards from the Western Journalism Center, both of which are virulently antigay. "When I came out, I made a leap of faith that my conservative friends were not the bigots portrayed by the liberal typecasters," he wrote in *Esquire*. That it turned out not to be the case surprised him. But why? Was it that Brock didn't know how deeply homophobia runs in the right wing, or was it that he felt it didn't apply to him?

All of which begs the question: What else has Brock failed to notice about his right-wing benefactors? For example, does he know that the *Washington Times*, the *American Spectator*, the *New York Post*, and *Weekly Standard* are all money losers, subsidized by wealthy conservatives because they print ideologically reliable propaganda for them? Was he aware that Richard Mellon Scaife gave $175,000 to the *Spectator* in 1992 for "special projects" and may well have financed Brock's story on the troopers?

Several years ago, Brock appeared on C-SPAN. Also on the program was a historian who challenged Brock's tendency to print rumor as fact, asking whether he thought it was "good journalism." Brock hissed, "It's the New Journalism." By complaining that the right wing turned against him because they wanted "red meat, not serious biography," and that they "should debate ideas on their merits" obscures the fact that heretofore it was Brock himself who brought home the red meat that fed the right wing's personal hatred of the Clintons.

> *Troopergate was started and financed by the right wing. Paula was started and financed by the right wing.*
> —David Brock, *Larry King Live*

In an "open letter" in the April 1998 issue of *Esquire* magazine, David Brock apologized to Bill Clinton. "I want to tell you how it all began," Brock wrote. "I didn't go searching for the story. It found me." A man who was a "major contributor to Newt Gingrich's GOPAC" telephoned and put him in touch with Cliff Jackson, "your Arkansas friend turned nemesis." Of the four original troopers, two—Ronnie Anderson and Danny Ferguson—"peeled off." Roger Perry and Larry Patterson were left, and they wanted money.

"The big stumbling block was the troopers' insistence that their story was worth money...there was talk about how to structure a future book deal, and there were several rounds of negotiations between Cliff Jackson and the GOPAC moneyman about guaranteeing the troopers' income and legal expenses," if they lost their jobs.

The name of "Paula" appeared as an "...oversight. I should have removed it," Brock wrote. "Surely, this will go down as one of the more fateful oversights in the history of your presidency." As a result of his story, "It was now open season on you: Anybody could say just about anything they wanted about the president. A virulent scandal culture was spawned that eventually drew in not only your conservative critics, but also the mainstream press." Brock adds, "*Newseek* has become the *American Spectator*.

"I made Paula Jones famous. And whatever happens with her case, in a way, the people who hate you have already won, and we have all suffered not only from their malice toward you but also from their contempt for the office of the president. When one of Jones' key legal advisers told me that he didn't necessarily believe her story of sexual harassment, my worst fears were realized. 'This is about proving Troopergate,' he told me gleefully. Troopergate had come full circle."

During a March 15, 1998, appearance on *Meet the Press*, Brock was asked if he still believed the troopers' story. "No," he said, "I don't."

RUSH LIMBAUGH

Talent on Loan From God

Nietzsche said, "Sometimes convictions are more dangerous foes of truth than lies." When it comes to broadcasting conviction, the New Right has many pretenders to the throne but only one king: Rush Limbaugh.

Limbaugh, sitting before a TV monitor, gave the "straight" line: "Could we see the cute kid? Let's see who's the cute kid in the White House."

A close-up photo of a dog flashes on the TV monitor. No audience reaction. Limbaugh in mock horror: "No, no, no—that's not the kid!"

A close-up photo of Chelsea Clinton flashes on screen. "That's the kid!" blurts Rush. Explosive audience laughter. Camera shot of audience clapping and laughing.

Rush Limbaugh had broken new ground in broadcasting. He had humiliated a 12-year-old girl on national television—a distinction that would prove to be a defining moment for the man, his humor, and his honesty.

Limbaugh is the New Right's biggest cannon in the

frontal assault on the Clintons. Ronald Reagan called him the most important conservative in America. Jack Kemp said, "He's leading public opinion, and Lincoln said, 'You can accomplish anything you want if you've got public opinion behind you and you can't get anything done without it.'" In 1994, before the convening of the 104th Congress, the new Republican members gathered to plot strategy. Limbaugh was the guest of honor and was made an honorary member.

With more than 20 million listeners on 643 radio stations, including Armed Forces Radio, there has never been anyone like him. In his heyday, Walter Winchell was on the radio only 15 minutes a week; Limbaugh is on 15 hours a week. The cornerstone of his appeal, he has said, is that he tells the truth. In a December 1993 *Playboy* interview, Limbaugh stated: "I am a profound success because I relentlessly pursue the truth, and I do so with the epitome of accuracy. That sets me apart from mainstream journalists."

The Chelsea Clinton segment occurred during the first year of his television show. At least once a year thereafter, a caller or a critic would note the incident. Limbaugh always offered the same explanation: It was all a mistake. "We were doing an 'in-and-out' list for the White House. We said 'in' White House cat or dog, and up came a picture of Chelsea Clinton by mistake. It was not something done on purpose...for the express purpose of commenting on Chelsea's looks."

On November 11, 1996, Representative David Bonior (D-Mich.) cited the incident as an example of the kind of person Limbaugh is. Limbaugh again maintained that it had all been a mistake and asked the audience to "spread" the story. He then added that the person who had supposedly put up Chelsea's picture had been fired.

"There are those who to this day claim that we did

it on purpose for a cheap laugh," he continued, "and that's not the case...it's just amazing that it keeps cropping up. It's comforting that [critics] have to go back four years to find something that they think is horrible and vicious and mean, when in fact it was a mistake from the get-go, it was a mistake that we regret making. We didn't try to cover it up, though."

Why wasn't the scene simply edited? "We could have stopped tape and done it all over again," he explains, "and nobody would have ever known. I'll take the blame on this one—I decided to let it go." The show, he continues, is "live-to-tape," and he didn't want the reputation of someone who "stops down every minute to fix something."

Limbaugh's explanation has problems. If the scene had played without the dog photo, what's funny about showing a close-up photo of Chelsea with the line "cute kid"? Moreover, Limbaugh's explanation for not redoing the scene because it was "live-to-tape" doesn't make sense. What else could a taped show be? His show is scripted. Where's the script? Who was fired over the incident?

The Chelsea episode was covered in a *Frontline* program on February 28, 1995, titled "Rush Limbaugh's America." Coproducer Steve Talbot tried to get answers to the above questions. "It was a complete stonewall," he told the author. "Limbaugh refused to be interviewed, as did people associated with him and his show."

This author, likewise, had no luck. The closest person to Limbaugh contacted was John Fund, who collaborated with Limbaugh on his book *The Way Things Ought to Be*. A reporter for the *Wall Street Journal*, Fund could offer no encouragement, only advice: "I never saw it," he said, "and no one will talk to you about it."

Limbaugh frequently mentions Chelsea. He has discussed her pierced ears and speculated that her decision to attend Stanford was to join a boyfriend. When she spent the night at Yale in a girl's dorm, Limbaugh cracked that she was no doubt "following in her father's footsteps." Commenting on how "lovely" Nixon's daughters, Tricia and Julie, looked at their father's funeral, Limbaugh said, "so unlike another First Family—and you know who I mean." When the Carters were in the White House, Rush got an on-air rebuke from his own mother for calling Amy Carter ugly.

Picking on young girls is one thing; spreading rumors is another. There was, of course, the reporter L.J. Davis, who went to Little Rock to do a story for the *New Republic*. As the *Wall Street Journal* reported, Davis entered his hotel room and woke up four hours later with a lump on his head and four "significant" pages of his notebook missing, which prompted Limbaugh's comment, "In Arkansas, they're dropping like flies."

Davis was horrified. Something had gone terribly wrong in the retelling of the time in question. "I told [*Wall Street Journal* reporter] Paul Gigot about waking up on the hotel room floor," he told the author, "but never said that four pages of my notebook were missing." He did say they appeared to be somehow "loosened" but were never out of his possession. Davis said that the story was "hijacked by the hard right." He asked the *Journal* to print a correction. "[Editors] said they would but did not." Limbaugh too would not relent. "I had some very heated conversations with his people about getting the story corrected," Davis laments, "but nothing came of it."

Limbaugh's coauthor Fund said, "It would not surprise me that Clinton's people got to a bartender," adding that the hotel owner is a Clinton supporter. (The bar, Filibuster's, had a tab for Davis that showed he had had six double martinis.)

When told of this, Davis was surprised. "I do not dispute the bartender's account," he told the author. "I also have the bar bill. I did have six martinis; they were doubles. I admit I like to drink, but I was not drunk."

Another person who Limbaugh treated similarly was Manuel Johnson. His Johnson Smick International newsletter was the source for the following announcement by Limbaugh about the death of Vince Foster (See Appendix D.):

> Okay, folks, I figure I got enough information here to tell you the contents of this fax that I got. Brace yourselves. There's a Washington consulting firm that is scheduled to release a report this afternoon that will appear, that will be published, that claims that Vince Foster was murdered in an apartment owned by Hillary Clinton and the body was taken to Ft. Marcy Park.

After he returned from a commercial break, Limbaugh claimed that "the Vince Foster suicide was not a suicide."

Returning from lunch the day of the broadcast, Johnson encountered a crush of reporters waiting outside his office. When he learned what Limbaugh had said, he too was horrified. His newsletter had printed nothing about a murder and nothing about Hillary and an apartment. "We are a consulting firm," he told the author, "and have no interest in partisan politics. Our job is to service our clients with information affecting the markets." To make matters worse, the next day the *Wall Street Journal* ran an article citing Johnson Smick as the source for the information about Foster.

In the newsletter, then-senate Finance Committee Chairman Patrick Moynihan's office was credited as the source for the story, which detailed the Clintons' problems with the Whitewater investigation. Lawrence

O'Donnell, staff director of the Finance Committee when Moynihan was chairman, denies anyone in the senator's office provided information.

"We only ran it because it came from the office of the finance chairman," Johnson explained to the author. Stressing that the newsletter is circulated only to the company's paying clients, Johnson can only speculate about who faxed it to Limbaugh. "I can only assume that it was an opportunity to stir up the markets," he said. The most satisfaction Johnson got from the *Wall Street Journal* was the publication of his letter to the editor. (See Appendix D.) Johnson's attempts to set the record straight with Limbaugh have also been futile. The radio personality has never explained how he came to be in possession of a newsletter that reads in part: "Warning: This telecopy transmission contains confidential and proprietary information for use by clients of Johnson Smick International only." (See Appendix D.) Nor has he revealed why he added that Foster was murdered in a Clinton-owned apartment and his body moved to Ft. Marcy Park, giving the erroneous impression that the information came from the newsletter.

When asked about this by the author, Limbaugh's coauthor Fund replied, "See the *Frontline* video." The *Frontline* segment cites the episode as an unfounded rumor spread by Limbaugh, and notes that a 23-point drop in the market happened on the day of the broadcast.

* * * * *

Rush

Rush Hudson Limbaugh III, called Rusty, was born in 1951 in Cape Girardeau, Missouri, into a family of

Republicans and lawyers. His father, Rush Jr., and grand-father, Rush Sr., were both Republican county chairmen. His uncle was a federal judge. In a December 1993 *Playboy* interview, Limbaugh described his grandfather as a man who "never cursed, never smoked, never drank, never lied, never cheated. A man whose image is impeccable. Living up to that threw my dad through some loops. It threw a lot of us."

Rusty's father was formidable. His opinions were loud and long and always right-wing. Communism, Democrats, and liberals were the enemy and treated with equal bombastic contempt. As Rush Jr. got older, he became even more convinced the country was going to hell in a handbasket. The Vietnam War and the peace movement drove him even further to the right.

On his November 5, 1996, show, Limbaugh said of his father, "Being a liberal was not an option. I owe that to my dad. My dad is the smartest person I've ever known, and it was never, never even a possibility—even at my rebellious stage—for me to be a liberal.... I never rebelled in opposing his views or his world view. Not one thing that I read turned on the light—my light was always burning brightly, and it came from my dad."

"I never heard Rush cross his dad," Rush's mother, Millie, said on the "Rush Limbaugh's America" episode of *Frontline*. "Never did. He was quiet. Rush always wanted to be an adult. In fact, I think from 10 on, he was an adult. He did not want to be bothered with child things. He was a loner."

Limbaugh may have sat passively through his father's harangues, but in high school history class, he's remembered as a vocal "hawk" on Vietnam, who forcefully defended escalation. After graduation, Limbaugh reluctantly entered Southeast Missouri State University. After one summer and two semesters, he dropped out and found work as a deejay in Pittsburgh, much to his father's chagrin. Limbaugh loved the job. It was his chance at the big time and to show his father that college wasn't necessary after all. However, after being fired from one station after another, in 1979 he ended up in Kansas City in the sales department of the Kansas City Royals. He was 28 years old and making $18,000. It was, however, the first job of which his father approved.

"I was married twice when I was with the Royals," Limbaugh revealed in *Playboy*. "The first time my divorce took place about six months after I started there. Then I remarried two years later. Kansas City was the site of profound failure for me."

After five years with the Royals, Limbaugh was fired. "I had already failed at the one thing I really love, radio," he said in *Success* magazine. "Now I'd failed at the 'real job' which was supposed to make me a 'real person.' I was looking into the future, and I saw absolutely nothing. I had no idea what I was going to do, who I was going to call.... I was 32 years old, making less money than I'd earned at 21. I was empty, directionless, and futureless. So I decided to go back to what I loved."

After a month without work, KMBZ in Kansas City hired him to do reporting and commentary. But management changes and Limbaugh's strident political bias caused problems. He was making more enemies than friends, and he was fired.

His career was saved by Norm Woodruff. While Limbaugh was at KMBZ, Woodruff had briefly been a consultant. He moved on to KFBK in Sacramento, where Morton Downey Jr., the resident shock jock, had just gotten himself fired for refusing to apologize for an on-air ethnic slur. Woodruff remembered Limbaugh and pressed the station's management to give him a shot. Woodruff felt that a radio personality should look the part, and he gave Limbaugh a few fashion pointers. The interview went well, and he got the job. This time it was going to be his way. Unlike talk-show host Don Imus, who welcomes guests of almost any stripe, there would be no two-way dialogue. Limbaugh's would be the only voice heard. He was going to be Rush Limbaugh.

He became a hit by saying things like, "Feminism was established so that unattractive, ugly broads could have easy access to the mainstream. A bunch of cows!" Environmentalists were "whacko tree-huggers," and unwanted callers were dispatched with "caller abortions"—a vacuum cleaner sound followed by a scream. "Gays," he said, "deserved their fate." Especially popular was his "AIDS Update," which maintained that gay men "like to stimulate themselves with small rodents," and that in great numbers they are "reporting to hospital emergency rooms needing gerbils surgically removed from their rectums." The way not to get AIDS was simple, according to Limbaugh: "Do not ask another man to bend over and make love at the exit point!"

Ironically, Norm Woodruff was gay. What he thought of Limbaugh's comments isn't known; he died of AIDS in the mid-1980s. Limbaugh does not mention the role Woodruff played in his career. He is not cited in the many tributes Limbaugh has given to those who contributed to his success, nor is he listed in the index of *The Way Things Ought to Be*.

Unlike Downey Jr., who was loud and shrill and insulted minorities, Limbaugh was loud and shrill with a sense of humor and one goal: ripping liberals. Sacramento loved him. His picture appeared on billboards. While Downey had been getting a 5 rating, Limbaugh was getting better than a 14. This caught the attention of Edward McLaughlin, former president of the

ABC Radio Network, who was striking out on his own with a radio-syndication company. He made Limbaugh an offer he couldn't refuse, and in August 1985 Rush was ensconced at WABC in New York.

Limbaugh was not an immediate success. Some changes had been made to his show. "Caller abortions" and "AIDS Update" were gone. Limbaugh briefly tried taking bets on the number of Haitian boat people washed ashore on a given day, but that too was dropped. His attacks on liberals and Democrats eventually found an audience, however, and his soon became the most-listened-to commercial radio program ever. Money and celebrity rained down.

But it was a somewhat melancholy Limbaugh who told *Playboy*, "If all you ever do is radio, you know your job is to go into a tiny room that's encased by glass and sit behind a microphone. And in order to have an attitude of confidence, bravado, and positiveness, you have to talk into that microphone and envision everybody listening to you—actively listening to you. Not passively. If you sit in there and say, 'Why am I doing this?' you are not going to succeed. You have to create an illusion. You must. And I think that is the beginning of the ego problems and self-esteem problems that radio performers have...people who do nothing but radio are not nearly as successful as those who have done something else in their lives or are doing something concurrently."

Rush's second wife, Michelle, had left him. He was rich, famous, and alone. "I succeeded because I've been able to immerse myself totally [in work]. However, that has created a void that, at the age of 42, I've only recently contemplated. I look at other people who are just as committed to their careers, and yet they still manage to have a family and a relationship and other things that are not related to what they do. With my sudden realization of this void, I've found myself desiring to fill it," he said in *Playboy*.

To fill the void, he went online and met Hazel Staloff, who became a regular caller on his show. "We used to do a sort of schtick together, and it worked well. He likes to be flattered by listeners, and I was glad to do it," Staloff said on "Rush Limbaugh's America." She has saved all of Limbaugh's messages, including one that reads: "I remain in an interminable funk, no end in sight, listless, uninspired, and self-flagellating."

"What a sad thing to write to somebody you didn't even know," she said.

Later, in 1990, he met his third wife, Marta, via E-mail. Although she was married at the time and living in Florida, they made arrangements to meet. After Marta's divorce in early 1992, she and Limbaugh wed in May of that same year. Supreme Court Justice Clarence Thomas presided over their wedding vows. In addition to a Park Avenue penthouse, they have a mansion in Palm Beach near the former Kennedy winter White House.

Politically, Limbaugh was an early supporter of Pat Buchanan's '92 presidential bid. Then George Bush invited him to spend the night at the White House. On *Frontline*, Limbaugh said: "After everybody else had gone to bed, it's about one o'clock in the morning and I'm just sitting there at the desk where Abraham Lincoln wrote the Gettysburg Address.... I just want to make sure I savored it." He shifted his allegiance to Bush and had him as a guest on his show. Along with Pat Robertson, Rush sat next to Marilyn Quayle in the vice president's box at the 1992 Republican convention. With his presidential nominee preference clear, he was free to focus on his main goal of pummeling Bill and Hillary Rodham Clinton. He did so by casting aspersions and spreading rumors on a number of issues.

Rush and Pot

When George Bush's campaign manager, Mary Matalin, called Clinton a "pot-smoking, draft-dodging, womanizer," she was doing more than employing pollster Frank Luntz's admonition to, as he told the author, "turn Clinton's generation against him"; she was saying a mouthful. Matalin herself has been married three times, has admitted to smoking pot, and presumably could have joined the protest against the war in Vietnam had she so desired. Her words were widely used by the right wing to "define" Clinton, and no one used it to greater advantage than Rush Limbaugh.

Limbaugh has admitted to smoking pot twice. In the *Playboy* interview, he said, "I never enjoyed it. I got sick to my stomach. Didn't throw up, but I felt nauseated. I never got high on it." The admission in itself is surprising, particularly considering a depiction Limbaugh gave of Clinton in *Frontline*'s "Rush Limbaugh's America." "This is the White House now with the Clintons. We've elected a guy who drove around a VW bus with the peace signs all on it. He's now president. One of these peaceniks." Certainly, Limbaugh wasn't one of the peaceniks, but one can wonder why he didn't "just say no" to the symbol of '60s rebellion.

Randy Raley disputes Limbaugh's claim that he tried marijuana only twice. Raley was at KYYS in Kansas City when he met Limbaugh at a party shortly after the latter left the Royals. "A group of us were passing a joint around," Raley told the author. "If you're with a bunch of guys who are smoking dope and you don't know what you're doing, you stand out. He knew what he was doing. I got on the radio and said, 'How can you call Clinton a dope smoker when you did the same thing?' He just kept beating up on Clinton—'He's a dope smoker!' I got on the radio and said, 'Well, Rush, so are you.' This guy's such a hypocrite. Don't tell people you got sick doing this when you didn't. He's never mentioned this party. I know what I saw, and I saw him smoking a doobie, and if that's getting sick, give me some of it!"

Limbaugh hated everything about the '60s, telling his audience that if a son of his ever came home sporting an earring, "I'd make him go upstairs and put on a dress." David Crowe, a boyhood friend, said, "All of us rebel to some extent or another when we're adolescents. But Rush didn't rebel politically. He didn't rebel philosophically, like so many in our generation did."

Limbaugh loved the Establishment. It meant opposing things like the civil rights movement and the Voting Rights Act of 1964. He told David Letterman, "The only thing I rebelled against in the '60s was going to college."

Rush and Welfare

The poor in this country are the biggest piglets at the mother pig and her nipples. The poor feed off the largess of this government and give nothing back.... We need to stop giving them coupons where they can go buy all kinds of junk. We just don't have the money. They're taking out, they put nothing in. And I'm sick and tired of playing the one phony game I've had to play and that is this so-called compassion for the poor. I don't have compassion for the poor.
—from The Way Things Ought to Be

On May 10, 1995, Rush Limbaugh said something startling on his show: "I was without income once when I was married, and my wife made me go and file for unemployment, and it was the most gut-wrenching thing I've ever done." He was responding to a call from May, a

Hispanic woman whose husband had abandoned her with two small kids, a toddler and a three-year-old.

Limbaugh told her of his plight: "I have been without work six times in my life. At age 28, when you're supposed to be climbing the ladder, I was making less money than ever in my life, and I was married.... I was not earning enough to have cash in my pocket—grocery stores then didn't take credit cards—I literally, for a couple of years, was going to snack foods kinds of places that did take credit cards, and buying junk, potato chips and so forth.... I got by, I was not in poverty, but I'm telling you I know exactly what it's like to have no money in your pocket."

He continued: "I was able to afford shelter, but that was it. I wasn't able to afford the upkeep on the shelter. If it weren't for the fact that I had a friend whose boys would mow my yard, then I would have had weeds instead of a yard.... I eventually had to sell [the house] and lost money in the process.... But at no time did I ever think—it never crossed my mind—to go to some federal building or state building, and say, 'I need some assistance.' I ended up having my credit card suspended."

May replied, "Well, we don't have credit cards." Limbaugh responded that he wanted to "do radio" so badly that he was willing to stick with it "even if it wasn't going to pan out," and that he eventually had to take a job that he didn't like.

"But it was paying your bills," May interrupted.

"But it wasn't," Limbaugh said. "I was in debt. I know exactly how you feel.... If you need money to feed your kids, then there are jobs out there that you can find. And if it takes working two or three for a while, then that's what you have to do. But you're going to be far better off putting effort into that than putting effort into finding a government program to help you. We don't have the money." He closed by telling May to "look to yourself."

All this struck writer-comedian Al Franken as pretty strange. Franken is a confessed liberal who has never met Limbaugh. In 1992, he did try to get him as a guest on a show he was hosting for Comedy Central called *Indecision '92*. Limbaugh, however, had demands. "No one could be on camera with him, and no one could comment on anything he said," Franken told the author. "Screw that," was Franken's response, and Limbaugh did not appear.

Still, Limbaugh's "I-filed-for-unemployment-but-my-wife-made-me-do-it" was something Franken pursued for his book *Rush Limbaugh Is a Big Fat Idiot*. In it he wrote, "Given his feeling about the poor, you might find it surprising that Limbaugh has himself fed off the largess of the government. In the form of unemployment insurance. Was Rush temporarily disabled? No.... This self-described 'rugged individual' and scourge of government handouts had the gall to file for unemployment at a time when he was able-bodied and spending his days sitting around the house eating junk food, too lazy to even mow his own lawn."

Franken told the author that he tried to reach Limbaugh for comment. "I called Limbaugh's producer, Kit Carson, and asked him if Rush would supply the dates that he was on the dole. Kit was very nice and said he'd talk to Rush. The next day, Kit called back and said, 'Rush doesn't want to provide the information.' I said that I could see why."

"Then I tried to take legal means," Franken continued. "I checked in Kansas City, which I surmised was where he was talking about. Missouri state records couldn't locate the time period that Rush was probably talking about. After that I just quoted what he'd said himself. He told a woman with no resources, two preschool kids, to get two jobs if she had to, but don't get help from the government. Yet, he went on unemployment when he was married with no kids."

Franken issued a challenge to Limbaugh for a debate on Comedy Central. Calling Franken a "gap-toothed moron," Limbaugh declined. One thing more on Limbaugh's house: He bought it with a loan from the Federal Housing Authority (FHA).

Rush and Sex

Whenever the "character" issue is discussed with Clinton, folks, make no mistake about it, it's his sexual forays that are being discussed—when they talk about his "character," that's what it is.
                              —Limbaugh radio show, May 22, 1996

The panelists on CNBC's *Equal Time* were discussing the right of the press to poke around a politician's bedroom. The debate surrounded Michael Isikoff's *Newsweek* article about attempts by Paula Jones' lawyers to establish a "pattern" of sexual misconduct by Clinton.

According to the ethos of Rush Limbaugh, infidelity equals lying equals bad character equals one is unfit to be president. "The Dole campaign should heed my advice: Connect personal character to personal leadership— that's what has to be done. You have to connect the lack of character to the kind of leadership you're gonna get," Limbaugh said on his June 20, 1996, show.

Clinton's sex life is important to Limbaugh. "Who cares if any married man with children cheats on his wife, right? Didn't Clinton get reelected—or elected—even though the public knew he was an infidel?" was the question on his May 19, 1997, broadcast.

Defining personal character by fidelity—or infidelity—and then using it to prejudge leadership would seem to leave few presidents in this century fit to serve and therefore begs the question: Is this really a good idea? Should someone who had two wives walk out on him, and who is alleged to have started dating his third wife while she was still married, be calling people infidels?

Rush and the Draft

The issue with Clinton is not that he didn't serve—you must understand this—there are a lot of people who didn't serve. The issue is what he did in order to get out of it. And then, what he did after he got out of it.
—George Bush

On September 21, 1992, George Bush appeared on Limbaugh's show and denounced Clinton's "total failure to come clean with the American people" on the draft issue. "He has not told the whole truth," Bush said. He accused Clinton of having "condemned the whole military as immoral" in his 1969 letter to the Arkansas ROTC director. Clinton's letter made no such reference.

This was not the first time the subject of the draft had come up. Limbaugh had described the New York draft riots in 1864, recounted the loss of life and property, and concluded that the moral was: "Never trust a draft dodger." Limbaugh failed to point out that one of the causes of the riot was the computation fee, whereby a person of means with $600 could buy his way out of the draft.

Limbaugh has cited Clinton's draft record as a major reason to question his character. And on his June 9, 1995, show Limbaugh called Clinton a "coward and a draft dodger who had no right to be at the D-Day ceremonies."

That day, something unusual happened. Instead of a string of sycophantic callers, a woman got through and demanded to know how Limbaugh had avoided the draft. "Every reporter in America," he stammered, "has had a crack at this. I had a student deferment and a high lottery number."

Actually, that isn't true. Virtually no one had looked into Limbaugh's draft record. After Bush's appearance, *New York Observer* reporter Peter Donald felt that since Limbaugh was such a boisterous critic of Clinton's draft record, Limbaugh's own draft story was relevant. "Mr. Limbaugh," Donald reported in an October 5, 1992, article, "first invited such scrutiny a year or so ago when he told a national radio audience that he had nothing to hide about the draft. He [claimed he] had been scared of going to Vietnam, so his father, a prominent Republican attorney, had taken care of the matter at the local draft board in Cape Girardeau, Missouri. He wasn't sure whether there had been a payoff, but whatever happened, it kept him from going to Vietnam."

The story produced a flood of irate calls. One was from his father. "Later," Donald notes in his article, "as he often does, Mr. Limbaugh reversed himself and claimed he had only been joking." Donald tried to reach Limbaugh. Kit Carson, his producer, told the reporter, "He had a high lottery number. He was 4-F. It's public record. He had a pilonidal cyst. If he had been called, he wouldn't have had to serve. In point of fact, he was never called." When asked for documentation of Limbaugh's medical condition and draft status, Carson told Donald, "Find it."

Limbaugh has claimed the following as reasons for his draft deferment: a "football injury," "a student deferment," an "inoperable pilonidal cyst," a "high lottery number," and a 4-F classification.

One thing is certain: When Limbaugh graduated from Cape Central High School in Cape Girardeau in 1969, the war in Vietnam was raging. Peter Donald reported that Rush Hudson Limbaugh III registered for the draft two days after he turned 18, on February 12, 1969. Two weeks later he was granted a 1-SH status, a student deferment given to young men still in high school. He graduated that June.

In November 1969, two months after enrolling at Southeast Missouri State University, Limbaugh received a 2-S college student deferment. Barely making it through his freshman year, he dropped out in 1970, and moved to Pittsburgh to be a disc jockey. The July 1970 draft lottery gave Limbaugh his number—152—not particularly high. Donald reported, "The previous year's draftees had gone as high as number 195. And by leaving Southeast Missouri State, he would automatically lose his student deferment."

"On November 24, 1970," Donald wrote, "Limbaugh was reclassified I-Y, a partial medical deferment that made him eligible for military service only in a declared war—which Vietnam was not—or in a time of 'national emergency.' This deferment was apparently based on the pilonidal cyst mentioned by Limbaugh's producer."

The cyst is described as an "anorectal disorder that usually occurs in young hirsute whites. The lesion is usually asymptomatic unless it becomes infected." It is a congenital incomplete closure of the neural groove at the base of the spinal cord in which excess tissue and hair may collect and cause discomfort and discharge. It can be corrected by surgery.

A doctor contacted by Donald described a pilonidal cyst as a "reasonably common and really benign condition. It doesn't seem like anything that would keep someone out of the military. It's easily healed, and antibiotics keep it from coming back."

Was Limbaugh joking when he said his father had "paid someone off to get him out of the draft?" Donald concluded his article by quoting Willie Bryan, the KGMO radio personality who gave Limbaugh his start, as saying: "He said he was joking, but my gut feeling is—I don't think he was joking. I think he was telling the truth. This family, you're talking about political clout."

Limbaugh's *Playboy* interview tried to get to the truth:

> **Playboy:** There have been several stories about how you avoided the Vietnam conflict.
>
> **Limbaugh:** Well, first thing, there was no avoidance. You imply that I undertook action.
>
> **Playboy:** Escaped the war.
>
> **Limbaugh:** Well, I didn't do anything. I did have a student deferment because I was in college for that one year. And I had a medical deferment for what is called a pilonidal cyst. It's a tailbone cyst. I don't know if it's still something that disqualifies you, but it did then. If the thing flared up, which they are wont to do, it required major surgery. So I didn't do anything to avoid the war. And had I been called, I would have gone.
>
> **Playboy:** And politically you were then as you are now?
>
> **Limbaugh:** I was a hawk.

Another writer who looked into Limbaugh's draft situation was *Newsday*'s Paul Colford. While writing his book *Rush*, Colford dug extensively into Limbaugh's past. "I spent more time on it than anything else for the book,"

Colford told the author. He found out that as of July 1, 1970, Limbaugh and all other 19-year-olds faced the draft lottery that was to determine their order of military call-up in 1971. Colford, like Peter Donald, also found out that Limbaugh's lottery number was not especially high.

"Four months after the lottery, Board No. 16 effectively spared Limbaugh. Records indicate that the panel acted on medical information obtained at Limbaugh's own initiative, most likely from his physician, and classified him I-Y on November 24, 1970. This meant that Limbaugh was conditionally acceptable for military duty but would be called up only in the event of a declared war or national emergency, neither of which applied to Vietnam.

"The I-Y protected Limbaugh," Colford continued, "against having to join the military. But Limbaugh did not mention the I-Y classification to his radio callers amid reports of Clinton's own evasiveness. Limbaugh also omitted reference to his I-Y during a subsequent public appearance, even though he had held I-Y for more than a year—until all I-Ys were changed to 4-Fs as American involvement in the war waned."

Did Limbaugh, fearing that number 152 might not be high enough to avoid Vietnam, latch onto the pilonidal cyst—after the lottery was held—to make sure he was sidelined from the draft? Colford found that there was no notation that the draft board ordered its own examination, nor do the records indicate that one was administrated by the military. "In other words," Colford concluded in his book, "Limbaugh presented a medical report obtained on his own before the draft board might have reclassified him I-A or, at the very least, ordered him to undergo a military physical as a preparatory step toward a possible draft."

The records Limbaugh submitted to the board were

destroyed after the draft ended in 1973. As for Limbaugh's "football knee from high school," the coach during his lone year of play told Colford that he did not remember any injury.

Rush and the Military

Everybody who's called here has called to defend the honor of what they did, and to express disgust and outrage that they have been insulted. It's just a short version of what liberals think of the average American. What she's really saying is that we didn't send any rich people there; we only want dirt-poor, average dummies. That's what she really thinks.
—Limbaugh radio show, April 16, 1996

In April 1995, Department of Health and Human Services Secretary Donna Shalala was on CNN's *Capitol Gang* and said: "We sent not 'the best and the brightest' sons to Vietnam. We sent men from small towns and rural areas, we sent kids from the neighborhoods I grew up in, and we exempted the children of the wealthy and of the privileged and it tore this country apart, and we must never do that again."

Eleanor Clift, another panelist on the show, said: "Actually, the people who went there were the best and the brightest," to which Shalala responded, "Absolutely."

The term "the best and the brightest" was coined by David Halberstam and was the title of his book, which excoriated the men in the Kennedy and Johnson administrations who led the country into the Vietnam war.

Shalala's comment was picked up and reported as "the best and the brightest sons didn't go to Vietnam."

Out of context, the comment led many to believe Shalala was saying that the men who fought in Vietnam were stupid. Limbaugh, Oliver North, and G. Gordon Liddy all called for Shalala's resignation.

In *Rush Limbaugh Is a Big Fat Idiot*, Al Franken reported the following: "Now my friend Josette Shiner, the managing editor of the conservative *Washington Times*, was on *Capitol Gang* that day with Shalala. So Josette calls Liddy's show, and they put her on the air with him. She explains what Shalala said. Liddy agrees that Shalala has been misinterpreted, and explains to his audience that he was wrong. Meanwhile, Clift goes on North's show, and North, like Liddy, admits that he was wrong.

"Then Josette calls one of Limbaugh's top people. She explains that Shalala was completely misunderstood, and Limbaugh's guy responds: 'That's her problem.'"

In the June 1995 issue of the "Limbaugh Letter," Limbaugh continued the attack: "'We sent not the best and the brightest sons to Vietnam.' This was the declaration on CNN's *Capitol Gang* by Donna Shalala.... My friends, there is no better demonstration of the liberal view of the country than this. Ordinary American kids who fought and bled and died in Southeast Asia—or their parents—were too stupid to know any better. These were not the talented ones, the ones with great promise, the future national leaders, the coming movers and shakers. These were mere working class, the patsies, the chumps, the losers."

From Rush's April 19, 1996, broadcast:

Caller: You said "people in the know—people who know—know that Clinton loathes the military." That is a bald-faced lie, the most stupid thing anybody's ever said.

Limbaugh: You've never heard the president say that?

Caller: That he loathes the military? Of course not.

Limbaugh: Have you ever heard of the letter he wrote to Colonel Holmes begging him to make it possible for him to escape being drafted? He wrote in the letter that he and his friends loathed the military.

Caller: That was at a time when the military leaders deserved to be loathed.

Limbaugh: Wait—I thought your original charge was that I made it up? That I lied about it. So now you admit Clinton said it?

Caller: You said present day, June 1994 of last year, you said, "People in the know—people who know—know that Clinton loathes the military."

Limbaugh: I have people who are friends in the military who have made such an observation. It's no mystery to the people of this country; it's no secret how he feels about the military.

Limbaugh added, "Who would have thought that a guy who's had more affairs than any politician in the history of this country, with the exception of JFK, and had protested against his own country in a time of war, would be elected president? Who would have ever thought that?"

But then, who would have thought that Robert McNamara—the architect of the Vietnam War—would come out with a book titled *In Retrospect*, in which he said that it was a tragic mistake? On February 15, 1996, Limbaugh agreed with a caller that the book might be a conspiracy to help Clinton. "Because," he said, "this would allow the antiwar mob—of which Clinton was a proud leader—to say: 'Hey, we were right...we should have listened to people like Bill Clinton, who in his youth knew the truth, blah, blah, blah...'" He lumped all protesters together and concluded: "The people of this country do not want to hear that the longhaired, tie-dyed, maggot-infested, dope-smoking types that were blowing up buildings and throwing rocks through windows were right!"

Rush and Foreign Policy

During the 1994–95 U.S. intervention in Haiti, a heated debate raged on Rush Limbaugh's show over his claim that American troops about to be sent to the island did not have enough ammunition. It was resolved only after a commander for the operation called to assure the radio host that this was not the case. Dismissing the operation as sheer folly, Limbaugh openly questioned Clinton's ability as commander-in-chief before, during, and after troops had landed. Similarly, when Iraq challenged the "no fly" zone and Clinton ordered a nighttime retaliatory strike, Limbaugh sniffed, "We're attacking the cleaning staff."

An American president's authority to conduct foreign policy was being challenged during hostilities by a partisan whose vitriolic comments were broadcast instantly and simultaneously to American soldier and enemy alike—a partisan widely considered to be speaking the views of the Republican party. The silence of Republicans of any stripe condemning Limbaugh's inflammatory rhetoric was deafening. To the contrary, it grew even more heated. Clinton was called a "draft-dodging coward"; callers referred to the president as "coward in chief."

Limbaugh was no more supportive of the president's Balkans policy. "I don't give a rat's behind about

Bosnia," Limbaugh said, revealing his feelings about American involvement in trying to stop the slaughter of innocents. "Just wait until Americans start coming home in body bags," he warned.

However, the body bags that came home during the Vietnam War did not move him to similarly question U.S. involvement. To the contrary, then as now, he attacked the protesters, calling them, "not antiwar but anti-American." When the conflict's most famous war protester, Jane Fonda, went to North Vietnam, there were demands that she be tried as a traitor—that she was giving aid and comfort to the enemy. Yet, in her heyday Fonda did not have three hours a day on 643 radio stations to broadcast her antiwar views. Nor were her views aired on Armed Services Radio directly to American troops stationed around the world.

A caller to Rush's June 20, 1995, show reminded the host that under Clinton, the killing had stopped in Bosnia and that no Haitians or Cubans were washing up on our shores. "Sadly, you're gonna go through these things and to the average American who pays scant attention, you're gonna 'nail' every one of these things and you're gonna be right," Limbaugh replied. "But the bottom line is, this is a horribly incorrect precedent to set for the use of U.S. troops...I love the way you applaud Clinton and his courage in sending other people into harm's way in Bosnia while he remains barricaded in the White House—how typical to anoint this man with courage."

Rush and Hillary

Our society is such that you're supposed to be gentle and kind to the girls—you're not supposed to beat up on the girls.
> —Limbaugh radio show, June 27, 1996

Putting Hillary in charge of the health-care proposal was a bold move for the Clinton administration and a challenge to Limbaugh. A popular and trusted first lady identified with the plan was more threatening than the details of the plan itself. Hillary needed to be labeled, to be "defined," to be stopped. It would be ugly, but then so much was at stake. Limbaugh, however, was more than up to the task.

But then, all first ladies have been pilloried to some degree. Nancy Reagan was criticized about White House china and designer evening gowns. It got especially nasty over her role in the firing of chief of staff Donald Regan, and a book claimed that she "entertained" Frank Sinatra when her husband was out of town.

With Eleanor Roosevelt, however, the motive was politics. Jokes and parodies made the rounds, and the consensus was that she was treated as savagely by the right wing as was her husband. The reason was simple: As first lady she was pushing an agenda more liberal than that of her husband. People to the manor born resorted to the gutter for humor. Unable to comprehend Eleanor's concern for the plight of minorities, stories circulated that she was part black. Eleanor's sex life was another favorite topic and, years later, the role J. Edgar Hoover played in spreading stories that she preferred women would be revealed. However, none of these stories were carried by the "respectable" media. No radio station or newspaper or personality would publicly repeat them.

*   *   *   *   *

Question: What do you get when you cross a draft dodger with a lesbian?

Answer: Chelsea.

Times have changed. The above "joke" is from a newsletter called "Slick Willy Times," available at most newsstands. On a segment of *Politically Incorrect*, host Bill Maher proclaimed that Hillary's love before she met Bill was in the audience. As the camera zoomed in, a woman stood up. After comedienne Ellen DeGeneres announced she was gay, Limbaugh suggested that if a movie were made about the Clintons, DeGeneres would be perfect to play Hillary. So rife is the allegation of Hillary's sexual preference that right-wing author David Brock decided to explore it in his book *The Seduction of Hillary Rodham*. His findings that the report was baseless did little to stop the rumor mill.

From the beginning, Rush Limbaugh seemed to make taking down Hillary a priority. Ignoring her earlier support for Republican Barry Goldwater and her middle-class background, Limbaugh went to work defining her. When a torn note was found in Vince Foster's briefcase, he suggested that it was Hillary's prenuptial agreement. On his June 27, 1996, show, he explained his feelings about her: "She attempts to portray herself as something she's not.... There are some people who think that co-opting someone else's power is a cheap end run and certainly not worth making a symbol of.... I really believe we're dealing here with a mean woman."

He held an on-air contest on June 19, 1995, asking: What does Hillary Clinton think when she's inside the mansion of one of [the Clintons'] supporters or friends? I want to know what you people think she thinks." After a couple of hours of salacious speculation, Limbaugh gave his answer: "I'm gonna tell you—it's a series of things, [one being] envy—'Gee, I could have had this if things would have turned out differently'—but I don't think that's the big one. I think she walks into these mansions and says: 'What'd these people really do to get this?

Nobody makes this kind of money legitimately. I'll go ahead and take their contributions, I'll use them all I can—but you don't just earn this kind of money!' Then I think it's, 'We've got to find a way to take these homes away from these people.' And then, I think she thinks, 'You know, this would make a great public housing project!' I think those are the things that go through her head." When a caller said that with Bill's roving eye, he felt sorry for her, Limbaugh snapped back that he didn't, because "she's not a normal woman."

In spite of everything Limbaugh threw at her, Hillary didn't wilt.

Rush and Education

How reliable is Limbaugh for information? Kathleen Hall Jamieson of the Annenberg School for Communications at the University of Pennsylvania conducted a study of the different radio talk shows and their hosts. In her report, "Call-in Political Talk Radio: Background, Content, Audiences, Portrayal in Mainstream Media," she concluded that "Limbaugh's focus differs substantially from that of the other shows. His topics are more likely to focus on domestic politics and business. In addition Limbaugh spends more time than other hosts urging his audience to assume personal responsibility and insisting they can make a difference. Limbaugh's priorities are as different from the mainstream media as from conservative talk shows."

Limbaugh touted Jamieson's findings as proof that his show does inform and that the mainstream media are biased against him. What he did not tell his audience was the following, which was also in Jamieson's report: "We just concluded a study of 360 people, whom we watched watch the health-care reform debate for nine months.

And at the end of that period we took the people who said they relied on talk radio, and by this, we mean primarily Rush Limbaugh...and we asked them how well informed they felt.... Of all the people we watched, they said they were the best informed. And of all the people we watched, they were the least informed."

Rush and Ted Koppel

The subject of this particular episode of Nightline *was a discussion of the Vince Foster suicide, and how this was being played in the media. The "setup" piece by John Martin was about all the people who believe President Clinton has been responsible for a lot of deaths in Arkansas.*
—Limbaugh radio show, August 17, 1994

Limbaugh was livid. The *Nightline* segment had accused him of spreading the "smear," taken from the *Clinton Chronicles.* As Limbaugh told it: "Here came a clip of me, sitting in this studio, in which they had me saying, 'My gosh, look at 'em—they're dropping like flies out there!'—right after John Martin talked about all the people who think there have been a bunch of murders associated with this president." At the very least, the *Nightline* piece made Limbaugh look like a rumormonger, undermining his promise: "A fact is a fact and I'm about facts."

The next morning a puzzled Limbaugh got together with his chief of staff, H.R. "Kit" Carson, and tried to figure out what *Nightline* was talking about. "It wasn't death when I said 'They're dropping like flies.'" He figured it out: "I made that comment at a time when subpoenas were being issued left and right for the White House by Robert Fiske about Whitewater."

"At this point," Limbaugh continued, "we called the *Nightline* people and informed them that we thought we'd been taken out of context—and they knew it from the get-go—and immediately apologized." He said Koppel himself called and told Limbaugh: "I knew the minute we played it that it was wrong. I was listening to your show that day, Rush, and you were talking about those subpoenas. You have my personal apology. You have my utmost, profound apology for doing this." Koppel added that Limbaugh could "rip me a new one if he wanted to."

Limbaugh accepted Koppel's apology and concluded that "it was totally out of context and was not even within the same discussion. It was just as big an error as one can make."

There was an error alright, and it wasn't John Martin's or *Nightline*'s. Limbaugh has used "they're dropping like flies" on numerous occasions. For example, the comment followed his account of [trooper Danny Ferguson's ex-wife] Kathy Ferguson's suicide and writer L.J. Davis and his "missing" pages. Of the February 1993 raid on the Branch Davidian compound in Waco, Texas, he said: "Three of the four agents killed had been assigned to Bill Clinton's security detail in Little Rock. And you know who ordered the assault? Janet Reno! They're dropping like flies!" Referring to writer Chris Ruddy, Limbaugh said: "This guy in the *Philadelphia Inquirer* has got it right—the worst place in America to be right now is in this category called Friend of Bill's. They're dropping like flies!"

In a more oblique reference, Limbaugh asked of Clinton on June 20, 1996, "Just ask yourself this question: How many people do you know who are indicted, subpoenaed, unindicted coconspirators, or dead because of their proximity to you?"

As for being associated with the Foster "murder" story, Limbaugh broke it on national radio. He has continued to comment on it: "Vince Foster—did he die at somebody else's hand?" Rush asked. "Why, in any case, is he dead? Two, maybe three, years ago, I said, 'If you want to know what's going on in the White House, find out why Vince Foster is dead.'" And, "There is far, far more to this than we are being led to believe—as everybody knows."

Still, Limbaugh told his listeners: "I have never said on this program that I believe that [Clinton has been responsible for a lot of deaths in Arkansas].... I have never stated that I believe it; I've never touched it; I've never gotten close to it."

Whether Koppel apologized as Limbaugh claimed and whether *Nightline* was right or wrong are almost unimportant. There are reasons why Koppel or anyone else might want to think twice before incurring Rush Limbaugh's wrath. One reason was demonstrated on the same *Nightline* broadcast. Reporting on the health-care debate, ABC reporter Tom Foreman concluded that both liberal and conservative talk shows have "spent more time talking about health-care reform than newspapers or television. But most often it is talk of conflict, not compromise. And for both sides in the health-care debate, that may be worse than no talk at all."

Limbaugh started by informing his audience that ABC wanted to film him for the report, but he refused. "They pulled quotes of me from a radio show, put [them] in their newscast, and attempted to position me as the symbol, the champion, the essence of talk-radio misinformation. This was an entire effort to discredit all of talk radio, with me as the monster head of it." He added that journalists were about "personal-life prying," and that their reports were not "fact based" but "simply based on criticism because of my ideology." Limbaugh's objective was "the next time that some reporter is assigned by an editor or a producer to do a profile of me that they get scared to death."

Rush and Newt

Oh Lord, deliver us from all evil. Look upon us with thy favor. Bless our GOPAC family and all its work. Bless Speaker Gingrich, Rush Limbaugh, and their families. And now, almighty God, we thank you for the food that is before us. May it strengthen us to do thy will.
—Prayer before GOPAC meeting

Former Representative John Bryant (D-Texas) learned about Gingrich and Limbaugh the hard way. For 18 months, he had worked on a lobby-reform bill that was finally ready to go to the House floor for a vote. Not only was Gingrich a supporter, but he had specifically asked for a grassroots lobby provision, and he wanted it in writing. The night before it went to the floor, however, Gingrich sent Limbaugh a fax.

The next day, Limbaugh began attacking the bill. Referring to it as "Hush Rush," he said: "I want to read to you now a paragraph from a letter that Newt Gingrich sent to all Republican members, advising them of the elements of this legislation. It is theorized that if you listen to me or watch this show or listen to any talk-show host and, as the result of hearing what you hear, are motivated to call Washington, that we could all be considered lobbyists, and you'd have to report this. It's an effort to try to get people to shut up out of fear!" The fine, Limbaugh warned, could be "$200,000 for calling your congressman!"

By 11:00 A.M. the next day, telephones were ringing

off the hook with people calling their representatives about this horrible provision. Gingrich went on Limbaugh's show and proclaimed that "buried in this so-called lobbying bill is a deliberate grassroots gag rule designed to kill precisely the pressure from back home that has been so effective in this Congress," adding, "Let's be honest, liberals hate grassroots pressure."

Representative Bryant was stunned. He explained that he'd been blindsided by Gingrich and it was all a lie. No one, it seemed, was listening. What the other congressmen were listening to, however, were angry phone calls and the letters and faxes that were pouring in. The entire talk-show network and the Christian Coalition weighed in as well. The lobby reform bill died.

"Frankly," Limbaugh told his audience, "everything Mr. Newt says makes 100 percent sense."

With Limbaugh, Gingrich virtually had his own radio talk show, and together they set out to "make Bill Clinton the enemy of normal Americans," according to Gringrich. To do so, Gingrich would rely on family values and his vaunted "new ideas." It would prove to be a volatile mix.

In November 1994, the world saw Susan Smith tearfully plead for the return of her two "kidnapped" sons, then watched in horror as she eventually confessed to killing them. Gingrich proceeded to blame Smith's terrible act on the Democrats' countercultural ethics (until it was revealed that her stepfather, a leader of the local Christian Coalition, had molested her). Gingrich did this to prove a point: Democrats and their policies are not only bad, they are immoral.

Life, Gingrich believes, should be like it was in the 1950s. However, as journalist Margaret Carlson pointed out in the August 21, 1995, issue of *Time*:

Births to teenagers reached record highs in the mid-'50s that are unsurpassed even now, and a third of marriages ended in divorce, but it especially wasn't like that for Newt. His grandfather was born out of wedlock and raised in a household in which his real mother posed as his sister. His father was a Navy man who left right after Newtie was born and who later allowed him to be adopted by his stepfather in exchange for not having to pay child support. Newt's mother, Kit, said in *Vanity Fair* that she is manic-depressive and that Newt's stepfather, Bob, comes across as cold and silent. The senior Gingrich proudly recounts smashing Newtie against the wall when he was 15. Gingrich's half-sister, a lesbian activist, is writing a book about all this for Scribner's.

When he was a high school senior, Gingrich started dating his geometry teacher, 24-year-old Jackie Battley. He married her after his freshman year in college. They had two daughters. She put him all the way through school to his Ph.D.—Newt never worked.

L.H. "Kip" Carter, who was Gingrich's campaign treasurer in 1974 and 1976, said on *Frontline*'s "The Long March of Newt Gingrich," "Jackie was supposed to be getting alimony and child support and Newt refused to pay. So at the First Baptist Church and some other places in town, we collected some money and some canned food and took it down to the house so that she could keep the lights on and keep the kids fed."

Carter added, "How could I have been so focused on the campaign that I wouldn't say to him: 'You know, this is not right. You don't need to be doing this. You got two small children.' I thought it was a kind of passing fancy and there were so many of them [women] it couldn't possibly have meant anything. You know, it's just some sort of psychological problem he's got."

Anne Manning became romantically involved with Gingrich, while he was married, during his 1976 campaign. The September 1995 issue of *Vanity Fair* reported that she is "repelled by Newt's stance as Mr. Family Values. He is morally dishonest. He has gone too far, believing that 'I'm beyond the law.'" She said that he prefers oral sex "because then he can say, 'I never slept with her.'"

When asked about this, Limbaugh said on his August 9, 1996, show, "That's all the press is anymore— 'He alleges this and somebody responds.' The whole *Vanity Fair* story on Mr. Newt is 'alleged.'"

Gingrich took over GOPAC in 1986 and transformed the committee into his personal marketing and money-raising machine. Between January 1, 1993, and December 31, 1994, GOPAC raised $5.2 million. Every Republican candidate for state or local office got a new audiotape once a month. These tapes transmitted the conservative gospel straight from the mouth of Gingrich to the ear of every young, ambitious true believer behind the wheel of a car traveling the back roads of politics.

Gingrich said the GOP's "great problem" was in not being "nasty." In the August 25, 1991, issue of the *Los Angeles Times Magazine*, he advised a group of young Republicans to "do things that may be wrong, but do something." Accordingly, GOPAC published a how-to textbook that Gingrich calls "absolutely brilliant." It advised candidates to "go negative" early and "never back off. Use minor details" to demonize the opposition. GOPAC supplied 6,000 Republican candidates with word lists to teach them how to "speak like Newt." The words used to define Democrats included "pathetic," "sick," "traitors," "corrupt," "bizarre," and "criminal rights."

Richard Mellon Scaife, a GOPAC charter member who had given $60,000 to the organization from 1989 to 1995, gave $35,000 more in the second quarter of 1995. Shortly thereafter, Gingrich became the first mainstream politician to raise doubts about Vince Foster's suicide. He told a group of reporters, "I don't question [his suicide], I just don't accept it."

On Bob Grant's July 6, 1995, radio show, Gingrich elaborated: "I was very struck by an article in *Investor's Daily* that I thought was stunning, raising question after question after question about Foster and what happened there."

The Gingrich quotes on Foster's death have been published three times by organizations funded by Richard Mellon Scaife. Scaife's *Tribune-Review* featured Gingrich's quote in a story by Chris Ruddy headlined: "Gingrich Calls Flaws in Foster Case 'Stunning.'" The Western Journalism Center then paid to have Ruddy's story reprinted in the July 19, 1995, issue of the *Washington Times*. The July 24, 1995, issue of *Dispatches*, a monthly newsletter published by the Western Journalism Center, ran a front-page reprint of the Ruddy story.

Previously, however, Gingrich had said on CNN's *Capitol Gang* (July 24, 1993) that "if an independent investigation...ends up concluding that whatever happened was entirely personal, then I think that ought to be sealed. I think human beings and their families deserve some level of decency in which to live their lives out, even in this town."

THE UNWITTING ACCOMPLICES

The Tabloidization of the Mainstream Media

All I know is what I read in the newspapers.
—Will Rogers

When Alexander Hamilton was charged with using public money to support his mistress Maria Reynolds, the issue of sex and politics shifted from one of titillation to one of criminality. The press closed in, claiming the public had a right to know. But didn't the public also have a right to know that the man making the charge against Hamilton was a poison pen for hire named James Callender, and that the man stuffing checks into Callender's pocket was Hamilton's rival Thomas Jefferson? Will Rogers notwithstanding, when it comes to sex and politics, just how good is the press's record?

Politics and the Press

I have on this paper the names of people who are traitors.
—Senator Joseph McCarthy

Senator Joseph McCarthy may be remembered as a liar and a bully, but he rose to power by making unsubstantiated accusations against numerous U.S. officials and citizens. The publicity resulted in an extreme sense of paranoia and ruined the lives and careers of many.

Distorting the truth was not new to McCarthy. During World War II, he was an intelligence officer in the Pacific. McCarthy, however, claimed that he was a tail gunner who had taken part in 31 combat missions in the Pacific. "Tail-Gunner Joe" rode the lie all the way to Washington and was elected to the U.S. Senate in 1946.

On February 9, 1950, McCarthy was invited to speak before a group of Republican women. Communism was a hot issue at the time, and McCarthy chose it as his topic. He charged that Communists were working inside the U.S. government. The local newspaper picked up the story, and the rest, as they say, is history. Within months, McCarthy was making the front pages of newspapers all over the country. He had gone from being a relative unknown to one of the most familiar public figures in America.

From his soapbox, McCarthy ranted and raved about "Reds" occupying government positions. He would hold up a list containing what he claimed were the names of Department of State employees who were agents of the Communist Party. The enemies were not overseas, McCarthy explained, they were here, on our own soil, in our own government. McCarthy claimed there were at least 25,000 traitors in the government. Witch-hunts and blacklists ensued.

Yet, as he traveled from city to city, waving this list in front of reporters, there was a problem. McCarthy had the headline-grabbing issue—Communists in government—but what he didn't have were Communists. His famous paper, with the list of names, was blank.

But McCarthy did have the press. It hung on his every word and was his accomplice in the charade that terrorized the country. The press's role in creating Joseph McCarthy was the real dirty secret. However, by 1957, McCarthy's tactics of wild charges and guilt by association were exposed on national television by news reporter Edward R. Murrow and Army lawyer Joseph Welch. Suddenly, the man who had petrified everyone from laborer to president became irrelevant.

With the public's dramatic shift, the press reversed itself. There was no postmortem on McCarthy and the media's role in creating him. He was simply ignored, which—for a publicity hound like him—was the final blow. He died at the age of 48.

Joseph McCarthy was a cash cow for the mainstream press's bottom line. He stands as a bell-ringing example that headlines can be made and public opinion formed regardless of the facts. When it comes to Bill Clinton, is today's press an unwitting accomplice in the right wing's goal to make him the "enemy of normal Americans"?

June 13, 1993. It was the haircut heard around the world. When Clinton paid $200 for a haircut by a one-name Hollywood stylist and held up air traffic at Los Angeles International Airport, it was front-page news. The *New York Times*, *Washington Post*, *Boston Globe*, and *Dallas Morning News*, to name a few, felt it was major news—regardless of Clinton's protestation that he was told no flights were inconvenienced. John McLaughlin, host of *The McLaughlin Group*, told viewers that the haircut had tied up "ground and air traffic, putting as many as 37 planes in a holding pattern."

Likewise, when then-Press Secretary Dee Dee Myers announced the White House travel office firings, the members of the fourth estate were in an uproar. At one briefing they asked 169 questions about the firings. Neither Bosnia nor the president's deficit-reduction package, both major news stories, received a fraction of that attention. The travel office story made page one of the *Washington Post* six times. It also made the front pages of the *New York Times*, *Los Angeles Times*, and *Chicago Tribune*.

Were the haircut and travel office stories really news, or was the White House pressroom really—as one pundit put it—the only day-care center in America Ronald Reagan hasn't closed?

In a September 15, 1993, article titled "Covering Clinton," which examined how the president was being treated by the press, *Los Angeles Times* reporter David Shaw wrote that six weeks after the haircut, *Newsday* used the Freedom of Information Act to acquire Federal Aviation Administration records that showed no planes had been forced to circle the airport, no runways had been backed up, and only one plane was delayed—for two minutes.

Newsday, *USA Today*, and the *Houston Chronicle* gave that corrective story prominent attention. However, Shaw discovered that virtually every other news organization in the country had either ignored or buried it. Shaw's own paper, the *Los Angeles Times*, which had run the original account on page one, buried the corrective story in the local news roundup on page two of the Metro section. The *Washington Post* ran one paragraph. The *New York Times*, which had editorialized about the "haircut that tied up two runways," ran not a word. The three major network evening news shows were also silent.

It wasn't always so. Before the New Hampshire primary, Clinton was the press corps' pinup boy. *Time*, the *New Republic*, and *New York* magazine all ran cover stories on him, and he was anointed the Democratic front-runner before a single primary ballot had been cast. Then came Gennifer Flowers.

Twelve days after Clinton took office and after a series of false moves, ABC's Sam Donaldson was on a weekend talk show saying: "This week we can talk about 'Is this presidency over?'" That same day, a page-one story in the *New York Times* stated: "The president desperately needs a victory, as soon as possible." Al Hunt, then Washington bureau chief of the *Wall Street Journal*, said: "I'm not sure he's going to recover from the problems of his presidency." *Time* magazine published a tiny photo of Clinton on its cover beneath the large-type words "The Incredible Shrinking President." David Broder called Clinton's "presidential meltdown" a "calamity," adding, "that this is happening to the man who will remain as president for the next 43 months is an international disaster."

The Center for Media and Public Affairs showed that through the first six months of Bush's presidency, 61 percent of the network news' evaluations of his performance were positive; for Clinton, in a similar period, the figure was 34 percent. Writer Shaw concluded: "Never in our nation's history has a president so early in his term been subjected to a greater barrage of negative coverage than Bill Clinton's first 239 days in office."

Shaw offered some possible reasons, including everything from the closing of the White House press door to reporters to increased competition from various media outlets to Watergate envy. Whatever the reason, Bill Clinton was the first president in memory who was denied a "honeymoon." The press had changed. The governing reporters were gone and were replaced by political reporters who judged everything in purely political terms.

For example, when U.S. warships launched cruise missiles on Baghdad in June 1993, panelists on *Capitol*

Gang were analyzing the political fallout before the White House even knew if the missiles had hit their targets. Pundits and talking heads were competing with each other for the boldest statement of the week, in what Jim Lehrer of the *Lehrer News Hour* referred to as "the stench of contempt. My colleagues and I, like journalistic Dr. Strangeloves, are ready to nuke Mr. Clinton at the slightest provocation. All politicians are scum. Only journalists are smart enough to know what to do about each and every problem facing the body politic," he said.

It was becoming more difficult to tell where opinion stopped and news began. Just who are these reporters, and how did they get to be so "pure"?

* * * * *

> *Probably outside professional wrestling there is nothing more deliberately phony than the way that the Washington roundtables are manipulated.*
> —Christopher Hitchens, *Frontline*: "Why America Hates the Press," October 22, 1996

A writer for *Vanity Fair*, Christopher Hitchens told *Frontline*: "These shows are all pre-rehearsed, and they're all fixed. The questions are known in advance by the participants. The topics are decided in advance. The answers to the questions are often known in advance. The share-out of time is determined in advance. There's usually a conference call a couple of days before you go on, everyone talks about what we're going to do this week."

To prove it, Hitchens let *Frontline* film the preparations for his appearance on *The McLaughlin Group*, always billed as an unrehearsed program.

Roberts (on phone): Chris Hitchens? John Roberts of *The McLaughlin Group*. I wanted to tell you first we're going to tape tomorrow at WRC. The four issues are—the first one is on the Saudi Arabia bombing. Question going into that is "Why wasn't the Pentagon ready?"

CUT TO PROGRAM

McLaughlin: Question: Why wasn't the Pentagon ready? Michael Barone.

BACK TO HITCHENS

Roberts (on phone): Issue two is Richard Lamb's announcement to run for the Reform Party nomination and the question is: "How seriously should the Lamb candidacy be taken?"

CUT TO PROGRAM

McLaughlin: Question: How seriously should we take the Lamb candidacy?

Hitchens: The bleating of the Lamb not at all. But there was one reason Perot acted so fast: Mr. Lamb is in favor of letting the oldsters die off, if not actually stepping on their oxygen lines. I wonder, what did happen to General Stockdale? And shouldn't Perot worry...?

McLaughlin: (laughs)

Hitchens adds: "That's what makes it so farcical. That the audience get[s] the impression of a no-holds-barred food fight, when in fact the reverse is the case..."

Hitchens cited what he thought was the most notorious instance of media cross-dressing. It involved George Will:

"Will helped to prep Ronald Reagan for a presidential debate with papers that had been stolen from Jimmy Carter's campaign. Having helped in that scene prep, he then went on the air as an objective commentator later that night to say that he thought Reagan—viewing it objectively, dispassionately, fair-mindedly—had done best in the debate."

"Rehearsed" news programs, in which reporters have the questions in advance, giving them a running start at sounding well informed, harken back to the rigged game shows of the 1950s. Is the public any more informed about this practice than it was in the 1950s? What does this say about the morals and ethics of the press who participate? And what about the journalists who know about it but do and say nothing? Shouldn't this be the subject of a roundtable discussion on *The McLaughlin Group*?

Also pointed out by *Frontline* was that in the middle of the health-care debate, correspondents Sam Donaldson and Cokie Roberts moonlighted before hospital and insurance lobbying groups, reportedly getting fees of $30,000. Roberts in particular has been criticized for speaking to groups that do important business in Washington. James Warren of the *Chicago Tribune* told *Frontline*:

> Someone told me Cokie Roberts was to speak at a private Phillip Morris executive gathering in Palm Beach, Florida, and it was something I checked out and it was absolutely true. And then when I called ABC, their response was that Cokie didn't know what they were talking about—this had to be a mistake. It was her husband, Steve Roberts, a reporter for *U.S. News & World Report*, who had been invited.

Well, I sort of did a double take, called Phillip
Morris back, and the response that came back to
me a day later was, unequivocally, that Cokie
Roberts had been invited, and called at the last
minute to say that she was ill. And her husband
went in her place and took Phillip Morris' money.

Frontline reported that Cokie and Steve Roberts
declined to be interviewed. Yet had Roberts and her husband been politicians, wouldn't ABC News have covered
the story, undercover cameras and all? The Roberts'
refusal to appear on a fellow news program is curious,
especially in light of what has been her and the press's
mantra when it comes to anything involving the
Clintons: "Why don't they just tell the truth?"

Still, any tabloidization of the mainstream media as
it applies to Bill Clinton begins and ends with his presumed sex life. In that regard, there are three reporters
who have had much to say: Cokie Roberts, Michael
Isikoff, and Joe Klein.

Cokie Roberts

*If you break your marriage vows, how can you
be trusted?*
—Cokie Roberts, *This Week With David Brinkley*

The topic on *This Week* was General Joseph Ralston.
He'd had an affair while he was separated from his wife,
and though it had happened 13 years before, it was still
causing him grief, enough so that he withdrew his name
from consideration as chairman of the Joint Chiefs of
Staff. Roberts thought the withdrawal was wholly appropriate, particularly since she was the first national
reporter to raise the issue of Bill Clinton's sex life.

In 1992, Paul Begala was a top aide to then-candidate Clinton. He was with Clinton in New Hampshire at a debate sponsored and broadcast by WMUR. It was the first big major candidate's debate. "The question," Begala told the author, "posed to each candidate was about their greatest weakness. There, Cokie Roberts dropped a bombshell: 'Since women are so important to the Democratic Party, how can you reassure them, given questions about your womanizing?'" No other candidate was asked such a question.

Hints as to Roberts' bias have cropped up before. Appearing on the *Tonight Show* with Jay Leno shortly before the 1992 elections, she opined that while people may not think much about character, "it matters when they get in the voting booth." Since the Republicans were making the "character" attack on Clinton, it's unlikely that she was referring to candidate George Bush. But what did Roberts know, and when did she know it? Did she personally investigate the womanizing charges against Clinton?

When Roberts questions the character of presidential candidates, she does not seem to be altogether consistent. In the heat of the 1996 presidential campaign, a tabloid story broke that the standard-bearer for a major political party had an affair while still married. The former mistress was willing to talk. Her story checked out; there was proof. Yet, no one in the mainstream media acted on it.

In its September 24 issue, the *National Enquirer* stated that Bob Dole had a mistress in 1968 while still married to his first wife. The woman, Meredith Roberts, said the affair lasted two years and that she was coming forward because Dole's harping about being the candidate of character and family values struck her as more than a little disingenuous. She thought the public should know.

The press, however, thought otherwise. Aside from the New York *Daily News*, no other mainstream newspaper or magazine picked up the story. The *Washington Post*, it would later be revealed, had the story but—along with every other publication and all of talk radio—decided it wasn't important. The public really didn't need to know.

Equally silent was Roberts. This time she had no questions to ask the candidate and no moralizing comments to make. Suddenly, sex outside of marriage was not a test of character after all.

Bill Clinton, however, wasn't so lucky. The person who has done his best to convince the public that Clinton's sex life does matter is a reporter for *Newsweek*.

Michael Isikoff

Michael Isikoff began reporting on the Paula Jones scandal when he was given the "exclusive" on Jones' story. Isikoff was a reporter for the *Washington Post* at the time. At *Newsweek*, he continues to cover the story and makes the rounds on news shows, where he is introduced as the "expert" on Paula Jones. Isikoff on Paula Jones and Bill Clinton:

> **Retter:** Why did you feel Paula Jones' story was important?
>
> **Isikoff:** It was a story of specific misconduct by the president, and there were corroborating witnesses. I felt the story deserved to be heard by the public. How important it is in the larger scheme of things? Who knows? It was a specific, on-the-record allegation of misconduct. I felt to not publish the story amounted to suppressing and censoring the news.

Retter: How do you explain Jones' relationship with the right wing and the fact that Ambrose Evans-Pritchard was with her before she filed her lawsuit?

Isikoff: I didn't know he was. If he was, why didn't he write about it?

Retter: He did. The right-wing mantra goes: Infidelity equals lying equals bad character. Do you agree?

Isikoff: Infidelity per se is not of interest to me. Paula Jones is news because she filed a lawsuit.

Retter: Was that your opinion about Gennifer Flowers? Did you listen to her tapes?

Isikoff: Yes, and I thought there were some pretty damning things—he told her to "just deny, deny"—some of the troopers confessed that they took Clinton to the Quapaw Towers. I don't see the troopers making this whole thing up.

Retter: What about the *National Enquirer*'s story about Bob Dole's mistress?

Isikoff: In that case it was a long time ago, for all accounts consensual.

Retter: Is that the standard? After enough dust collects...?

Isikoff: We do have a statute of limitations, even for criminals.

Retter: Even when the press says fidelity is an important issue and when the former lover comes forward to say she objects to Dole's presenting himself as this family-values guy? Why is it important for the public to know about Clinton's accuser but not Dole's?

Isikoff: Dole never did raise the issue of women. He never discussed fidelity. Had he raised it, it would have been a different issue.

Retter: You don't think Dole's "a man you can trust" line was about the character issue?

Isikoff: With Clinton, that could mean a whole lot of things—Troopergate. Look, you'd have to be a Clinton loyalist to not believe that the troopers are telling the truth.

Retter: Why? Because Jones is not that kind of girl?

Isikoff: Oh, come on! Clinton's trying to present it that Paula was hitting on him, and the helpless Bill Clinton had no choice but to meet her up in the hotel room. It's almost preposterous on its face.

Isikoff added that it was a fact that Clinton had "charges brought and convictions—they have been proven about Clinton." He did not say what the charges were. His "facts" are that neither Jones nor the troopers could be lying.

Joe Klein

Life may be a journey; but character, most assuredly, is not.
　　　　—Joe Klein, *Newsweek*, May 9, 1994

Joe Klein thrilled the right wing when he was driven to write his work of "fiction," called *Primary Colors*. Writing an anonymous roman à clef about a president may have been a brilliant marketing strategy, but the need to keep up the ruse exposed Klein.

In retrospect it's hard to imagine why Klein wasn't immediately "outed" as the author of *Primary Colors*. It should have been obvious to anyone who had read his four-page article, "The Politics of Promiscuity," which appeared in the May 9, 1994, issue of *Newsweek*. What Rush Limbaugh and the right wing were doing daily to Bill Clinton—equating marital infidelity with character—Klein brought to the pages of *Newsweek*.

It has been called the most savage attack ever by a mainstream journalist on a sitting president. It read, in part:

> It seems increasingly, and sadly, apparent that the character flaw Bill Clinton's enemies have fixed upon—promiscuity—is a defining characteristic of his public life as well. It may well be that this is one case where private behavior does give an indication of how a politician will perform in the arena.

By creating the illusion that *Primary Colors* was written by an "insider" who knew the real Bill Clinton, Klein sold a lot of books. He also sold that perception that he knew what went on behind closed office and bedroom doors. A fictional Gennifer Flowers made an appearance in the book:

> "Governor," I said, "I was just on the phone with Libby. She says that Cashmere McLeod has tape recordings of you and her talking on the phone, and she's going to play them at a press conference tomorrow."
>
> —*Primary Colors*, p. 122

But the book's real shocker comes when Clinton's character impregnates a 14-year-old black girl. As with

Cokie Roberts, the question becomes: What did Joe Klein know, and when did he know it? Klein on Clinton:

> **Retter:** As someone who was around Clinton on the campaign trail, did you see anything that indicated the promiscuity you're accusing him of?
>
> **Klein:** No.
>
> **Retter:** Rush Limbaugh and Grover Norquist make the link between infidelity and character.
>
> **Klein:** That is an argument that I have never bought. In fact, if you do a Nexis search, look at the pieces I've done on Jim Wright, John Tower, Barney Frank, Clarence Thomas, Bill Clinton. In every last case, I said, "This is ridiculous; we should not be poking around in this sort of thing." I think it's disgraceful.
>
> **Retter:** As far as Gennifer Flowers and Paula Jones and their sex claims about Clinton and whether their stories are true?
>
> **Klein:** I have no interest in the details. I haven't asked about them because I haven't been interested in them. Likewise with Whitewater.... I think these things are overblown and are extremely damaging to public discourse.
>
> **Retter:** Yet you wrote *Primary Colors*.
>
> **Klein:** The perception of why I wrote the book has been the subject of some of the stupidest, the most ridiculous, and least informed interpretations imaginable. Very few people have asked me why I did. There were a lot of assumptions and most of them wrong.
>
> **Retter:** Why did you write it?

Klein: I saw it as a comment on the craziness that politicians have to go through. If *Primary Colors* was an attack on anything, it was an attack on the feverish inanity of the whole political process. I have no idea whether Clinton ever slept with Gennifer Flowers. But I wanted to take a politician who was in that situation and show that those kind of character flaws could coexist with tremendous strengths—like empathy and great political skills. Having an interesting sex life has been a leading indicator of success in the presidency.

Retter: Are you saying you saw [an interesting sex life] as sympathetic?

Klein: I saw it as neither sympathetic nor unsympathetic—it certainly wasn't the hatchet job that some of the stupider people who have written about it have alleged. The characters in my mind were not the Clintons. They were characters whom I invented.

Retter: Yet in an interview, John Travolta described how he was trying to imitate Clinton.

Klein: That's John Travolta. I had nothing to do with the movie.

Author: How does what you're saying jibe with your article "The Politics of Promiscuity"?

Klein: That was an exception. When I began to look at the lack of discipline, I thought it might be an exception to the rule—it might be a case where Clinton's private lack of discipline was reflected in his public lack of discipline. Turns out I was wrong. Turns out he's become one of the most disciplined public figures that we've seen.

LENO, LETTERMAN, AND MAHER

STAND-UP POLITICS: MOVE OVER, WILL
ROGERS. BILL MAHER REVIVES SATIRE AS
COMEDY'S SHARPEST WEAPON
—Cover story, *U.S. News & World Report*,
January 20, 1997

For Bill Clinton, the mainstream press is one problem; the popular culture is another. As defined by talk-
show hosts Jay Leno, David Letterman, and Bill Maher, it
is a different but equally potent opinion-maker with
which the president has had to contend.

Will Rogers: The Real Thing

In the early 1930s, Will Rogers was the nation's
most influential political and cultural voice, reaching 40
million Americans with his columns and radio commentaries. Using wit and common sense, Rogers emphasized
pulling together and extending a generous hand to those
down on their luck. With unemployment at 25 percent,
he said: "There is not an unemployed man in the country
that hasn't contributed to the wealth of every millionaire
in America."

Rogers mastered one medium after another: Wild
West shows, vaudeville, radio, newspaper, and movies. In
the early '30s, he was the most widely read columnist and
the number one box-office draw in the nation. Appealing
to the best things in the American character, he had no
patience for hypocrisy, and felt that the decent thing to do
was to help those who most needed it. His signature line,
"I only know what I read in the papers," belied the fact he
could destroy a politician or a celebrity with a quip.

He defined mainstream American humor and satire

for decades and seemed to mean it when he said, "I never met a man I didn't like." Regardless of how dark the nation's psyche or how long the bread lines, Rogers assured Americans that we were all in it together. In 1933, he said about FDR's inauguration: "No money, no banks, no work, no nothing, but they know they got a man in there who is wise to Congress, wise to our big bankers, and wise to our so-called big men. The whole country is with him. Even if he does wrong, they are with him."

Times have changed. Bill Maher, the man who *U.S. News & World Report* feels is Rogers' successor, freely comments on Bill Clinton and the voting public. During the 1996 campaign, one guest on Maher's *Politically Incorrect* was Roger Stone, who was introduced as "a political strategist [who] has just been named senior adviser to the Dole campaign."

> **Maher:** Roger, you told me a story—can I tell what you told me that day when we were on C-SPAN about the Nixon funeral?
>
> **Stone:** Yes.
>
> **Maher:** We were talking, and you said that the president hit on your wife at Nixon's funeral.
>
> **Stone:** Absolutely true—and he's got good taste—but he didn't get anywhere.

Stone added that the way Clinton hit on his wife was to tell Mrs. Stone, in front of a battery of TV and press cameras, "Here's my private phone number, if you're ever in Washington, give me a call."

All of which led Maher to conclude: "We used to call Reagan the Teflon candidate, but Clinton is like a cockroach—you can't kill him. My question here is, it doesn't seem to affect anybody. His ratings have never been higher. If Americans care more about their own selfish pocketbooks than about the fact that Clinton's screwed around, how good are they?"

Two weeks later, an article in the September 24, 1996, *National Enquirer* called into question not Bill Clinton but the lifestyle and character of Mr. and Mrs. Roger Stone.

The headline read:

TOP DOLE AIDE CAUGHT IN GROUP-SEX RING

While Bob Dole campaigns on the "moral crisis in America" issue, one of his top advisers has been caught in a sleazy scandal—he and his wife frequent a group-sex club and post notices on the Internet and in swingers' magazines seeking others to join them in orgies!

The article published revealing photos of Mrs. Stone from swinger's magazines and from the Internet, which advertised for couples and single men to join them for sex. When Roger Stone protested their innocence, the *Enquirer* noted that it had copies of swingers' magazine bills that were paid by Stone's wife's credit card, as well as handwritten letters and graphic photos of the couple engaging in sex.

After the *Enquirer* story ran, Maher did nothing to question his own judgment for his part in spreading the rumor about Clinton and Mrs. Stone. In fact, Roger Stone's assertion was used in spot promotions for *Politically Incorrect*.

When Clinton injured his knee, Maher speculated: "We live in an age of conspiracies. Now yesterday, President Clinton, the report was, fell down the stairs at

1:30 in the morning at Greg Norman's house in Florida. Now, c'mon, what really happened? I mean, I think it's interesting that the president is such a golf groupie that in the middle of all his problems, he's staying with a golfer in Florida." To a guest who expressed disbelief at Gennifer Flowers' claim, Maher snapped: "What do you mean, you don't believe her?! She had tapes!"

"Will we in this country ever allow a politician to be a normal person?" Maher asked on one show. This, after his monologue in which he announced that Hillary Clinton's lover before she met Bill was in the audience and, as the camera zoomed in, a woman stood up.

Maher has provided insight into who he thinks today's downtrodden are: "I have a theory—bullfighting. We think it's barbaric in this country. They stick swords in a dumb animal's back. How awful. They torture the animal. In this country we would not do it to an animal— we do it to celebrities!"

It isn't that Maher never asks thoughtful questions. The following exchange occurred between Maher and Jay Leno on *Politically Incorrect*.

Maher: Jay—you are in the news—you, me, and Mr. Letterman, because they say too many people are getting their news from monologues. They say that 40 percent of people under 30 get their news that way.

Leno: They get some news. What you do as a comic—you watch a person say something. A comic listens to what that person is saying and puts his or her joke on it. He is saying what the average person is thinking.

Maher: Is the image correct?

Leno: You don't change anyone's mind with these jokes. All you do is reinforce what they already believe.

Maher: But that can be just as detrimental.... If you don't watch the news or read the paper, but you watch late-night talk shows, then you're getting your news from the monologues—half the people in this country are getting their idea of who these politicians are by what we're saying on television.

Leno commented that he "calls CNN two or three times a day," asking whether a politician said this or that. One of Leno's jokes got the author to wondering what facts Leno did know. "Today down in Little Rock, jury selection got under way for the first Whitewater trial. I guess that's going to be tough finding 12 people in the country who don't know anything about Whitewater. Actually, you know what? Two people who don't know anything about Whitewater are Bill and Hillary Clinton—that's about it. Everybody else knows about it."

Responding to what he knew about Whitewater, Leno told the author that he didn't know enough about the deal to discuss it. He observed that Americans are interested in only three things: "sex, taxes, and a neighbor's barking dog. You have to understand. I watch the 4:30 afternoon news with a notepad and pen. My job is to deliver a joke."

In his monologues, Leno makes light of serious topics: "A gunman got to the White House," the host said one night, "but was told he'd have to wait in line. There were five other gunmen ahead of him... God forbid Clinton should get shot. They'd take him to the hospital and he'd be turned away—no health-care plan."

The sex jokes continue with numbing frequency. A

photo of the Clintons is captioned: "Two people who aren't having sex." If Leno sounds a bit like Rush Limbaugh, it is probably because the national president of Limbaugh's fan club, Ken O'Rourke, is a contract writer for Leno.

However, for sheer audacity, it's hard to top David Letterman's "Top Ten" reasons why Republicans should hold their convention in New York: "Excellent babysitting service for Reagan."

U.S. News & World Report concluded its cover story on Maher by stating: "It's this idea of political humor emerging from a combination of outsider thinking with real issues that is in the best tradition of Will Rogers." The talk-show hosts have defined for the popular culture new standards for judgmentalism, nastiness, and rumor-mongering, representing with a vengeance the credo "anything for a laugh."

*   *   *   *   *

When Thomas Jefferson sued a newspaper editor for writing that he'd called George Washington a traitor, Jefferson's concern wasn't facts, for truth was with the editor. Rather, Jefferson was thinking politics. His motive was revenge; future precedent was not a concern.

However, the future was Alexander Hamilton's concern, and in defending the newspaper editor, he won a major victory for a free press and free speech. He worried, though, about that freedom, that a "press unchecked, free to publish whatever the highest bidder demanded, would destroy public and private confidence and overawe and corrupt the impartial administration of justice. In the hands of unprincipled men, it would be a terrible engine of mischief, used for private malice and revenge."

EPILOGUE

There is a vast right-wing conspiracy...
—Hillary Rodham Clinton, January 27, 1998

"I should know; I was part of it," said former right-wing hit man David Brock on *Crossfire*. It had been a years-long open season on Bill Clinton, and that was before Monica Lewinsky and Kathleen Willey erupted. Within days of the Lewinsky allegations, pundits were predicting, ad infinitum, that Clinton's ouster was imminent. It was a familiar pattern, and the details got murkier as the "facts" began to change and the accusers were subjected to closer examination. But it reinvigorated Kenneth Starr's investigation and subpoenas flew far and wide.

It was dismaying to the man responsible for starting the whole mess. "It was no longer enough to defeat your opponent fair and square on issues," Brock wrote in his March 1998 Letter to the President. "You had to destroy him as a human being…. When I published Troopergate, I didn't much care. Now I do, and many other people don't seem to."

Yet it was much too late for apologies. The genie had been let out of the bottle and no one can say where the furies that have been unleashed will end. Still, the man who bemoans starting it all had turned philosophical and observed that, "If we continue down this path, if sexual witch-hunts become the way to win in politics, if they become our politics altogether, we can and will destroy everyone in public life."

The mainstream press rushes to judgment even as stories emerge undermining the credibility of witnesses, including the Reverend Jerry Falwell and the *American Spectator* funneling money to the troopers; money going to David Hale and other Whitewater witnesses; Gary Aldrich having 75 meetings with Linda Tripp while the two were in the Clinton White House; Sheffield Nelson taking *New York Times* reporter Jeff Gerth to meet with James McDougal; and Gennifer Flowers managing to keep under wraps her employment at two state jobs. Virtually unnoticed behind an alarming number of these "scandals" looms the financial and political influence of Richard Mellon Scaife. It is an amazing state of affairs.

Equally amazing is that—for all the ink and truckloads of videos devoted to Bill Clinton's financial and private life—the country would have been spared this unseemly trauma had the press shown some skepticism and asked some simple questions like, "Where was Bill Clinton at 2:30 in the afternoon on the day in question?" From Whitewater to the Paula Jones case, sloppy journalism has allowed the perpetuation of a monumental hoax.

David Brock, in a response to the lament of journalists that a president's sex life is news, wrote, "If a reporter is determined to make a name for himself by publishing a sexual exposé, he can usually find some high-minded reason to do it. The pieties of the press know no bounds."

In a March 20, 1998, appearance on CNBC's *News With Brian Williams*, Brock was asked by reporter Chris Hansen for his response to newly released legal filings that question the reliability of the troopers and Paula Jones. His response was telling. "You have all three troopers—Roger Perry, Larry Patterson, and L.D. Brown—saying that they have no personal knowledge of what happened with Paula Jones. And you have the fourth trooper, Danny Ferguson, saying that Paula Jones—not Bill Clinton—instigated that meeting at the Excelsior Hotel. Furthermore, there was a deposition of the troopers' supervisor—Buddy Young— released today in which he says...the troopers were using their position on the governor's security detail to procure women for themselves rather than for Clinton. I think that's important. I think that there's a lot of material just released on the motive, politics, and money behind this story from day one. There's further evidence today of a $2.5 million book deal that was discussed among the troopers before I arrived in Little Rock. That all goes to their credibility."

Still, what is this assault by some very flawed members of the right wing on Bill Clinton's character really about? A clue can be found in something the then-governor said in his May 7, 1991, address before the Democratic Leadership Council. "The centrist banner will have to be embraced if the Democrats want a chance to win back the presidency they failed to capture in five of the last six elections." To the right wing, Clinton's successful capture of the "center" was not only a stunning surprise, but perhaps his one great sin.

As for the press, in *Breaking the News,* James Fallows writes, "The institution of journalism is not doing its job well now. It is irresponsible with its power. The damage has spread to the public life Americans all share. The damage can be corrected, but not until journalism comes to terms with what it has lost."

The question is: Will it?

Appendix A

1. A January 1991 letter from Gennifer Flowers' attorney to the president and general manager at KBIS, stating that a talk-show host "wrongfully and untruthfully alleged an affair between my client and Bill Clinton."

2. A 1986 letter to Gennifer Flowers from Judy S. Gaddy, special assistant in the Office of the Governor.

3. A February 1991 letter from Gennifer Flowers to Bill Clinton.

MCHENRY, CHOATE AND MITCHELL
ATTORNEYS AT LAW

UNION NATIONAL BANK BUILDING
SUITE 850
LITTLE ROCK, ARKANSAS 72201

ROBERT M. McHENRY
JOHN S. CHOATE
DAVID B. MITCHELL

TELEPHONE
801-372-3623

January 30, 1991

Mr. Phillip Johnson
President & General Manager
KBIS Radio
2400 Cottondale Lane
Little Rock, AR 72202

Dear Mr. Johnson:

On October 16, 1990, a radio announcer employed by KBIS and acting within the scope of his duties as a "talk show host" caused to be published a portion of a press release which wrongfully and untruthfully alleged an affair between my client, Gennifer Flowers, and Bill Clinton, Governor of the State of Arkansas.

This defamation has not only caused my client great emotional and physical distress, but it has resulted in her inability to find gainful employment.

I have been instructed to file a legal action in this matter unless you are willing to compensate Ms. Flowers for her losses. I will, however, refrain from filing such lawsuit for two weeks; however, if we have not begun a meaningful discussion about Ms. Flowers compensation at the end of that two week period from the date of this letter, we will immediately commence litigation.

Please contact either me or David Mitchell at my office.

Sincerely,

Robert M. McHenry

RMM/bm

STATE OF ARKANSAS
OFFICE OF THE GOVERNOR
State Capitol
Little Rock 72201

Bill Clinton
Governor

January 27, 1986

Gennifer G. Flowers
9030 Markville Dr. #4116
Dallas, TX 75243

Dear Gennifer:

Governor Clinton gave me your resume and asked that I
help you with your job search. I would be glad to do
anything I can to assist you.

In order to assist you better, I need some further
information. Please call me at 371-2345 so that I can
discuss possibilities in state government with you.

I look forward to hearing from you.

Sincerely,

Judy S. Gaddy
Special Assistant

JSG:vm

THE
Gennifer Flowers
COMPANY

2/23/91 RECEIVED FEB 25 1991

Daddy
$5500

Ro
Job

Dear Bill,

Since we've been unable to connect by phone, I thought I should drop you a note.

July has not been very successful in the job hunting area.

I've been to one interview at Ark. Historical Heritage. It only pays $15,200.00 a year, but, as of yet, I haven't been offered the position. When I asked Judy if there were anymore prospects, she said no. It took three weeks to come up with that one.

Bill, I've tried to explain my financial situation to you and how badly I need a job. Enclosed, is some correspondence that will be of interest to you. Unfortunately, it looks like I will have to pursue the law suit to, hopefully, get some money to live on, until I can get employment.

Please, be in touch.

Gennifer

700 EAST 9th, SUITE 2J • LITTLE ROCK, AR 72202 • (501) 376-4442

Appendix B

The following is an article titled "No Exegesis" by Mickey Kaus, which ran in the May 8, 1995, issue of the New Republic.

Guess who just won the National Magazine Award for "Excellence in Public Interest"? We did! We won it for Elizabeth ("Betsy") McCaughey's articles on the Clinton health plan. McCaughey "waded through all 1,364 pages of the health care reform package," the judges said, then she "tore it apart." Her "carefully researched" pieces "transcended the coverage in most of the press. More than any other single event in the debate, what she wrote stopped the bill in its intellectual tracks."

So why don't I feel more like celebrating? Is it because, as a *New Yorker* editor publicly complained, the McCaughey articles seemed to have been "nominated for buzz"? Perhaps. But does *The New Yorker* not care about buzz? (Tell it to the Easter Bunny.) Is it because my colleague Michael Kinsley, in this space, denounced the initial McCaughey piece as a "screed," and James Fallows, writing in the *Atlantic,* said its claims were "simply false" and Theodore Marmor, professor of public policy at Yale, told me his fellow health experts of left, right and center consider McCaughey's articles "risible"?

Maybe all these people are just jealous. If they aren't, though, the award to McCaughey has not only validated a misleading view of the Clinton health plan, but also a peculiar idea of how journalists should affect public debate. To help resolve this issue, I have waded through all 9,000 words of Betsy McCaughey's critique and tens of thousands more words of controversy that followed. Here is what I found out:

Did Clinton offer "no exit"?: "If you walk into a doctor's office and ask for treatment for an illness, you must show proof that you are enrolled in one of the health plans offered by the government," McCaughey wrote, describing Clinton's proposal. "The doctor can be paid only by the plan, not by you." In other words, in the Clinton scheme you'd be at the mercy of your insurance plan. Unless it approved, you couldn't pay Doctor Welby to diagnose your stomach pain, even if you were willing to pay him yourself. In her second article, McCaughey specifically reaffirmed that "the bill prohibits doctors from accepting payments directly from you for the basic kinds of medical care" covered by insurance. Hence, "No Exit," the title of her cover story.

It turns out McCaughey misread the bill. It did ban Doctor Welby from accepting both a payment from an insurance plan and extra payment from a patient. (The idea was to control costs by forcing doctors to accept insurance money as payment-in-full.) But if you paid Doctor Welby entirely from your own funds, you could pay him to do anything you wanted. A clause on page 16 of the bill guaranteed this. The White House press office, in its ham-handed response to McCaughey, implied that this escape hatch worked only for medical procedures "outside" the basic services covered by insurance. But the press office misread the bill, too.

The obvious analogy, notes Clinton adviser Paul Starr, was to education. Everybody pays taxes to support public schools. Likewise, everyone in Clinton's scheme would have to pay for mandatory insurance. But if you don't like the public schools, you can use your own money to send your kid to private school. And if you didn't like the doctors your insurance company paid for, in Clinton's plan you could go out and hire your own doctors.

You can argue that Clinton should have offered more choice, enabling the affluent to pay physicians with a mix of insurance and their own money (though we don't let a rich man pay a public school teacher extra to give his kids special attention). But McCaughey's argument wasn't that Clinton didn't offer sufficient choice. The force of her articles derived from her claim that there was "no exit" from his mandatory insurance plans. She was wrong. Clinton's plan also opened a brand new "exit" for patients trapped in health maintenance organizations, giving them the right to see doctors outside their HMO. McCaughey simply ignored this feature.

Would the plan doom fee-for-service medicine? In "No Exit," McCaughey said "fee-for-service (choose-your-own-doctor) insurance" would be doomed because the Clinton bill "outlaws" plans costing more than 20 percent above average. But the bill didn't outlaw such plans. It said the government didn't have to offer them. In practice, Starr points out, fee-for-service plans aren't that much more expensive, and government officials would have a hard time dropping even an expensive plan that nevertheless attracted a big clientele willing to pay for it. (The government could cancel Social Security benefits, too, but it won't.)

Did the plan ominously threaten privacy? McCaughey made a big to-do over the bill's requirement that doctors report "clinical encounters" to a "national data bank containing the medical histories of all Americans." The White House answered: "Not true." An honest—and better—response would have been: "So what?" Virtually all Republican and Democratic reform plans provide for reporting such information, which is sloshing around the current private insurance system already. Clinton's bill actually had stronger privacy protections than its competitors. But individual records of treatment are necessary to help patients, who may have multiple insurers, get their benefits. Besides, wouldn't it be nice to have the national data that would enable doctors and consumers to determine, say, whether pallidotomy, the controversial new Parkinson's disease treatment, actually works? McCaughey's "data bank" hysteria illustrates the pitfalls of the I-know-nothing-about-this-subject-but-I've-read-the-whole-bill methodology. A more comical example was her horror at discovering that the Clinton plan would pay only for "medically necessary or appropriate" treatment—as if all insurance policies don't contain a similar restriction now. A more damaging example was her attribution to the Clinton plan of all the horrors of HMO life— as if Americans weren't already being forced into HMOs and other managed care plans by the millions because that is all their employers offer. Clinton, by providing a menu of plans, would at least have opened up some choice.

McCaughey herself doesn't need journalism awards. The "buzz" from these two articles was enough to propel her into a successful Republican candidacy for the lieutenant governorship of New York. There she has been busy helping to herd Medicaid recipients into the heartless HMOs she denounced in her [*New Republic*] pieces.

I don't mean to leave the impression that McCaughey's efforts were worthless. She did unearth some juicy provisions, like one steering medical training slots to "racial or ethnic minority groups" (though, like a good GOP apparatchik, she called this inchoate preference a "quota"). She got some things right. But she got a lot wrong. In the process, she completely distorted the debate on the biggest public policy issue of 1994. Give her a medal.

Appendix C

The following is a sampling from Ambrose Evans-Pritchard's articles in the London Sunday Telegraph *for the period from March 1994 to December 1994, and a review by Gene Lyons of Evans-Pritchard's book,* The Secret Life of Bill Clinton, *published in the December 23, 1997, issue of* Salon.

March 13 – "Little Rock's Mean Machine"
Evans-Pritchard quotes Larry Nichols: "Bill Clinton destroyed me. He took away my reputation, and the only way I can get it back is to destroy him."

March 27 – Evans-Pritchard states that he appears on at least one talk show a day: "It is an eye-opener. The callers talk about the president in an undisguised contempt.... Clearly, there is a very effective grapevine out there beyond the capitol, a network of tens of millions of people."

March 27 – "Clinton Accused of 'Grotesque' Sex Harassment"
Reports that Paula Jones is ready to sue.

April 3 – "Despots Line Up to Test Clinton Mettle"
Evans-Pritchard: "What can the Clintons be thinking now that their high-minded act has been exposed as a venal sham?"

May 8 – Discusses Paula Jones.

May 12 – Discusses Paula Jones.

June 19 – "Hawks Hammer at White House Door"
Reports that Pyongyang is exposing Clinton's lack of foreign policy.

July 17 – "Clinton Took Cocaine While in Office"
"Exclusive" interviews detail his drug use.

July 31 – "Doubts Linger Over Death of Clinton Aide"
Reports that talk radio shows have challenged the official verdict of Vincent Foster's death as suicide.

September 11 – "Clinton Plays His Green Card"
Reports that Clinton's sympathy for the Irish nationalists was formed at Oxford.

September 25 – "Carter's Haiti Hijack"
Claims the consequences could be political and military disaster for Clinton.

October 9 – "Bill Clinton and the Chicken Man"
Claims that Mike Espy's career was destroyed by Clinton.

November 20 – "Clinton Unfit for Office"
Evans-Pritchard quotes Jesse Helms as saying that Clinton is unfit to be commander-in-chief.

November 23 – "It's America First"
The United States accuses the British of planting stories about a U.S. covert operation in Bosnia.

December 4 – "Patriot Games Turn Deadly"
Glowing coverage given to the militia movement; describes them as "the shock troop and enforcement arm of the 1994 American Revolution."

On November 7, 1993, Evans-Pritchard "predicted" that a host of scandals would erupt around Clinton.

On January 23, 1994, Evans-Pritchard "predicted" that escalating scandals would drive Clinton from office by the end of the year.

The Pied Piper of the Clinton Conspiracists

British journalist Ambrose Evans-Pritchard thinks the president is guilty of everything. And he has the twisted facts and distorted reporting to prove it.

By Gene Lyons

In the past, whenever lunatic Clinton-haters were accused of being beyond the pale, they would point to one particular journalist—a veteran foreign correspondent who wrote for a respected British newspaper and whose dispatches from Washington and Arkansas, they proudly claimed, bore out their most incendiary charges.

The correspondent's name is Ambrose Evans-Pritchard. Much to the regret of our home-grown kooks and conspiracists, he has since departed these shores to become the *London Daily Telegraph's* "roving European correspondent." As a parting gift, however, Evans-Pritchard has bequeathed us a book, *The Secret Life of Bill Clinton*, just published by Regnery.

The temptation, in addressing so manifestly absurd and error-filled a piece of work, is to raillery. In form, Evans-Pritchard's book is a feverish concatenation of what his countryman, *Guardian* Washington correspondent Martin Walker, calls "the

Clinton legends" into one vast, delusional epic. In effect, *The Secret Life of Bill Clinton* is a militiaman's wet dream. Evans-Pritchard nowhere advocates violence against the president or the United States government, but he does provide the impressionable True Believer with a rationale. Publishing this book is the moral equivalent of leaving a loaded revolver in a psychiatric ward. And that, perhaps, requires an approach other than satire.

Accompanied by pseudo-scholarly "documentation," Evans-Pritchard's disarming narrative essentially portrays the president as a criminal psychopath. There is no evidence so contrary, nor tragedy so solemn that Evans-Pritchard will not distort it to this end.

The book's first 100-odd pages accuse federal agencies of knowing complicity in the 1995 Oklahoma City bombing that took 169 lives. According to Evans-Pritchard, it wasn't just the work of terrorist freelancers like the convicted Timothy McVeigh and his alleged accomplice Terry Nichols: It was, he suspects, an ATF/FBI "sting" gone bad, followed by a Justice Department cover-up. He doesn't directly accuse Clinton of being part of the plot, but does hint darkly that he has profited politically from the tragedy.

That truckloads of actual hard evidence have been produced at the McVeigh and Nichols trials impresses him very little. He spends page after page amplifying the baseless canard that ATF agents were warned against reporting to work in the Murrah Building that terrible morning. In reality, several were badly injured in the blast. That none died was purely fortuitous. Their offices lay on the side of the building opposite the bomb. A reporter for the *Daily Oklahoman* interviewed two ATF agents as they staggered out of the still-smoking rubble.

At his best, Evans-Pritchard practices journalism the way creationists interpret science. Was the "Piltdown Man" a hoax? Very well then, Darwin and a century's worth of supporting evidence stand refuted, and creationism is proved. Do inconsistencies exist among the hundreds of eyewitness accounts of the Oklahoma City tragedy? They do. Were there ongoing investigations of other white supremacist, anti-government extremists in the region at the time of the bombing? Absolutely. To Evans-Pritchard, these constitute all the evidence he needs to posit a massive government conspiracy. In the real world, of course, eyewitness accounts of so devastating an event are often confusing and contradictory, and wild rumors inevitable. The hard work of law enforcement (and journalism) comes in sorting things out. Seamless consistency is a state achieved only by conspiracy theorists, assisted by the twisted reporting of an Evans-Pritchard.

The real energy in this opus, however, is devoted to the more traditional themes of Clintonphobia: sex, drug-smuggling, money laundering and murder. Of the many homicides he lays at the president's feet, "the Rosetta Stone" is what Evans-Pritchard calls the "extrajudicial execution" of White House counsel Vince Foster. He sees in this "murder," allegedly carried out at the behest of the White House inner circle and possibly on the direct orders of first lady Hillary Rodham Clinton, a sign of "incipient fascism" in the United States.

Never mind that the sprawling, Arkansas-based criminal conspiracy Evans-Pritchard purports to have uncovered would require the complicity of the Little Rock Police Department, numerous county sheriffs and district attorneys, the Arkansas State Police, the FBI, DEA, CIA, several Republican-appointed U.S. attorneys and federal judges, Arkansas Sens. David Pryor and Dale Bumpers, not to mention Oliver North, the late William Casey, Iran-contra independent counsel Lawrence Walsh and Whitewater independent counsels Robert Fiske and Kenneth Starr (dubbed by Evans-Pritchard the "Pontius Pilate of the Potomac"). His methodology remains everywhere the same. If two dozen witnesses, crime scene photographs and an autopsy attended by a half dozen investigators confirm the existence of, say, an exit wound made by a .38 caliber slug in the back of poor Vince Foster's skull, this intrepid reporter can be counted upon to track down an ambulance attendant who failed to see it, and from that failure deduce that all the others have perjured themselves and the cover-up has been exposed. In the footnotes, that source turns out to be a "confidential informant."

When necessary, Evans-Pritchard resorts to even more questionable methods. He quotes a Little Rock funeral director named Tom Wittenberg asking, "What if there was no exit wound at all? ...I'm telling you it's possible there wasn't." By way of support, in yet another of the book's roughly 500 footnotes, Evans-Pritchard claims to have a tape recording to that effect, surreptitiously made by an unidentified Arkansas private eye. Puzzled, I phoned Wittenberg, an old friend and neighbor for more than 20 years. To my knowledge, the Tommy Wittenberg I know has never spoken to any reporter about a body entrusted to his care. Sure enough, Wittenberg insisted vehemently to me that Evans-Pritchard made the whole thing up. He not only refused to be interviewed, but told the reporter that out of personal feelings for the deceased, he'd never looked at Vince Foster's body at all.

Rookie reporters and probationary cops quickly learn that anybody can say absolutely anything about anybody else. If Evans-Pritchard ever absorbed this cautionary lesson, it's one he has strived successfully to overcome. He wanders the remote and fabulous land of Arkansas like some credulous Gulliver at large among the Houyhnmhnms. (On Swift's island of philosophical talking horses, it will be recalled, no word existed for the concept of falsehood.) Evans-Pritchard treats the wild inventions of Arkansas penitentiary inmates like Holy Writ. The concluding chapter linking Foster's "murder" to Iran-contra drug dealing, to the president's alleged cocaine use, to his sexual abuse of teenage girls and to three unsolved Arkansas homicides, consists almost entirely of double and triple hearsay from two dead men. One of those men is apparently Foster himself, with whom Evans-Pritchard's source claims once to have shaken hands. "At times the moral imperatives of reportage," the author proudly announces, "require one to violate the Columbia School codex."

Speaking of moral imperatives, it's time to unmask. Evans-Pritchard has designated this reviewer a "collaborator" in the Evil Clinton Empire, claiming to discern the dread hand of the White House in my *Arkansas Democrat-Gazette* columns. (For the record, I had no knowledge of this when I agreed to write about his book.) Oddly, he cites no particulars, not even in a footnote. He does, however, expound at modest length about articles I've written elsewhere. It turns out that our conscientious friend not only misrepresents others' work as it suits him, but, as need be, even his own.

Central to Evans-Pritchard's scenario about Foster's death is an unlikely tale he first broke in the *Sunday Telegraph* on April 9, 1995. His sources were a pair of Arkansas state troopers named Roger Perry and Larry Patterson. I summarized Evans-Pritchard's account in what he calls the "ultraserious" *New York Review of Books* as follows: "Perry and Patterson...[said] that a White House aide named Helen Dickey phoned the Arkansas Governor's Mansion hours before Foster's body was discovered in a Washington park. Supposedly Dickey told them Foster had shot himself that afternoon in a White House parking lot, which could only mean—so deduced the *Telegraph* reporter, Ambrose Evans-Pritchard—that the body had been moved and a White House cover-up begun."

Based upon a U.S. Senate hearing transcript, I went on to add that "when Perry and Patterson were subpoenaed to appear before Sen. Alphonse D'Amato's Whitewater committee on February 16, 1996, they suddenly decided they didn't want to repeat that story under oath. D'Amato even apologized to Ms. Dickey for the pain and embarrassment his own credulousness...had caused her." I continued: "It's the timing that's significant here. Because if such a phone call had, indeed, come from the White House on July 20, 1993—the day Foster died—then you'd think the troopers would have mentioned it to [the *American Spectator*'s David] Brock and the others who reported the 'Troopergate' stories five months later. But either they kept it to themselves, or the reporters did. Either way, it gives the troopers something of a credibility problem."

My summary of his story incensed Evans-Pritchard. In a scathing letter in the November 28, 1996, issue of the *NYRB*, he contended that I'd "traduce[d]" his original article, which he claimed concerned itself only with the timing of Helen Dickey's alleged call. "The article," he huffed, "did not examine the question of where Foster died...It should have been clear to anybody reading the *Telegraph* that the focus of our investigation was the timeline."

Evans-Pritchard also (correctly) pointed out that the troopers hadn't refused to testify before D'Amato's committee. Minority counsel Richard Ben Veniste had misspoken. What actually happened, I acknowledged in a response to his letter, was that the troopers' lawyers kept postponing their deposition until the absurdity of their story became sufficiently evident that even Republicans on the Whitewater committee no longer wished to hear it. Possibly to imply that I am indifferent to facts, Evans-Pritchard now contends that far from correcting the error, I repeated it in *Harper's* magazine. He cites the alleged incident as "an interesting insight into the way that consensus is manufactured in the Washington media culture."

Problem is, no *Harper's* article of mine exists regarding the Dickey episode. As for traducing Evans-Pritchard's meaning, all that was necessary by way of response was to quote his original text. What made Dickey's alleged call significant, he'd written, was its close similarity to an erroneous Secret Service memo that night that reported that "the 'U.S. Park Police discovered the body of Vincent Foster in his car.'" Then, Evans-Pritchard asks ominously: "The memorandum was wrong, of course, or was it? When rescue workers and park police found the body...Foster's corpse was deep inside a Washington park."

In reality, the actual Secret Service memo and the troopers' apocryphal tale aren't very similar at all. But why quibble? The point is that Evans-Pritchard's insinuation that Foster's body had been moved could hardly have been clearer. What puzzled me then was why he denied it. What amazes me now is that he's turned the tale inside-out all over again. In "The Secret Life of Bill Clinton," Evans-Pritchard couldn't be more explicit. "The hard evidence," he writes, "indicates that the crime scene was staged, period." Whether or not Foster suffered from depression, he argues, "somebody still inflicted a perforating wound on his neck, his body still levitated 700 feet into Fort Marcy Park without leaving soil residue on his shoes, and he still managed to drive to Fort Marcy Park without any car keys" (page 226).

Almost needless to say, every one of these allegations has been conclusively proved false in independent counsel Kenneth Starr's final report on the Foster suicide, reaching precisely the same conclusions as Robert Fiske did in his 1994 investigation. The Starr report disposes of the troopers' allegations about the timing of the Dickey call in a footnote, citing telephone records and the testimony of other witnesses.

Oddly, Starr's sleuths neglected to interview the ultimate recipients of Dickey's message, former Gov. Jim Guy Tucker and his wife, Betty, who remember the call coming at roughly 9 P.M. in Little Rock. This accords with all the available evidence that Dickey telephoned the Governor's Mansion with the terrible news some time after 10 P.M. Washington time, more than three hours later than the two troopers claimed.

Since then, of course, the Whitewater independent counsel has convicted Jim Guy Tucker of making a false statement on a 1986 loan application, making him a convicted felon. Maybe that's why Starr's investigators neglected to interview the couple—although Betty Tucker hasn't been charged with any crimes. Or just maybe Kenneth Starr has reasons of his own for not wishing to state plainly that so pliable a witness as Trooper Patterson, who has testifed before Starr's Whitewater grand jury, lied about so grave a matter. That's merely a suspicion, not a fact. Nevertheless, I offer it free of charge to Evans-Pritchard. He will know exactly what to do with it.

Appendix D

Documentation regarding the way in which Rush Limbaugh distorted the role of Johnson Smick International, Inc., in reporting the death of Vince Foster as a murder rather than a suicide:

1. Letter from Manuel H. Johnson, and David M. Smick, senior partners, to the *Wall Street Journal*

2. Text of the newsletter article Limbaugh used as his source ("Dog Days for Bill and Hillary")

3. Johnson Smick mission statement

From the *Wall Street Journal*, Letters to the Editor, Friday, April 29, 1994

Our Role Distorted in Whitewater Rumors

Our firm was mentioned in recent articles in this and other newspapers about the effect of Whitewater developments— and their related rumors—on financial markets. In some cases, including in this newspaper, our firm's role was so distorted that a correction of the record is necessary. On March 8 our firm, which concentrates largely on analyzing issues of interest to foreign-exchange markets, issued a private memorandum to about four dozen financial clients in response to questions from them concerning Congressional reaction to Whitewater. Ironically, while the memorandum was reported to have caused a market reaction, it actually made rather modest observations, including a prediction that changing White House tactics on Whitewater could bring a return to business as usual. Buried in the middle of the report was a brief mention that for months rumors had circulated among Republicans on Capitol Hill regarding the location of the suicide death of Deputy White House Counsel Vince Foster. The point of interest: The rumors were now bipartisan, having originated also from a staff aide to an important Democratic senator who is responsible for health-care reform and other important legislation. The obvious question: how Whitewater might affect the president's legislative agenda.

Only the most imaginative of minds would conclude after reading the memorandum that a small economics consulting firm had stumbled upon the largest scoop since Watergate and then buried it in the middle of a private memorandum. Any logical reading could not help but conclude that the political source was the issue.

The memorandum circulated to clients for 24 hours without incident until is was misappropriated and loosely interpreted by a popular conservative talk-show host, among others. It was at this point the memorandum drew broad-based attention.

Your article on March 11 was particularly troubling. It inaccurately gives the impression that an interview had been done by the reporter. Moreover, it could easily lead the reader to the conclusion that our firm gleefully mass-marketed erroneous information in order to disturb financial markets as a means of marketing a retail-subscription newsletter. That impression is contrary to the facts, as our firm has a legal track record in trying to protect the confidentiality of the proprietary nature of our product. We also do not sell a broad-based newsletter. While apparently it isn't irregular for byline reporters to get input from other sources, the process by which this story was prepared leads to confusion.

When we informally discussed market developments with your Washington bureau chief on March 10, he didn't make us aware that a reporter was preparing an article on our firm, so we didn't have an adequate chance to present our case.

The article's use of the quotation, "If you're 55% to 60% right, you're gold," was taken from a two-and-a-half-year-old *Journal* article on our firm, and its context has long been in dispute. The quotation was referring to the most successful traders and investors, not to the field of economic consulting.

Manuel H. Johnson
David M. Smick
Senior Partners
Johnson Smick International, Inc.
Washington

DOG DAYS FOR BILL AND HILLARY
A Johnson Smick International Report (Copyright, 1994)

Wednesday, March 9, 1994

Normally, at such an early date, we would hesitate to say much about something as sensitive as the Whitewater affair currently plaguing the White House. After all the betting of many Clintonites is that by avoiding the prolonged public drama of Congressional hearings and simply allowing Special Prosecutor Fiske to do his job (the lease on Fiske's investigative office in Little Rock runs for three years) Whitewater could be moved off the front pages for months or years, allowing the White House to return to business as usual. Without a doubt, the Clintonite's wish could come true.

Be that as it may, we have been inundated with questions about Whitewater and what follows are some quick observations, many of which have not yet been reported in the popular press. We would warn, however, that this is a preliminary glimpse of Whitewater and not some definitive statement on our part.

At this point, the person most important to watch is Republican House Banking Committee Member Jim Leach. Remember, Leach is not some partisan firebrand. In fact, he is considered the most statesman-like of GOP House members and he has specialized in matters involving S&L abuses. We offer this as a preface because Representative Leach has been telling other members of the Congressional leadership that he has, through House Banking Staff investigations, uncovered a series of "very explosive" information regarding the Clintons' financial dealings in Arkansas. Indeed, Senate GOP leader Bob Dole has used the descriptive phrase "nuclear warhead" in describing Leach's bombshell, although Dole goes on to admit that he does not know the specific details.

What's happening at this moment is a fight over whether Leach will be allowed to make the information public at a House Banking Committee hearing currently set for March 23rd and 24th involving oversight of the Resolution Trust Corporation (RTC). Congressional insiders say it is important for Leach to make the information public during the hearings and not simply at his own press conference because while some witnesses have already signed sworn statements voluntarily, others would have to be subpoenaed by Congress. Not surprisingly, House Banking Committee Chairman Gonzalez is suddenly facing big pressure to postpone or cancel the hearings.

This afternoon we spoke with a member of the House GOP leadership, asking what he thought of the Leach situation. His response: "No one knows what Leach is up to, but I wouldn't want to bet against him at the poker table. I've never seen him so confident. He's walking around with a cool smile acting as if he has four aces in his hand and one up his sleeve.

This individual went on to describe how Leach is not the normal kind of political bluffer roaming the halls of Capitol Hill. He described how Leach seems more motivated if anything by sentiments toward George Bush. Leach was one of the few House Republicans with real admiration for the former President. "I think Leach really resented what the Clinton crowd did to Bush," the same House leader said, adding, "and he was particularly incensed at what they did to the President's sons over S&L matters knowing that they were doing far worse around the same time."

Again, we would warn that no one in Washington knows if Leach really has much by way of incriminating evidence against President and Mrs. Clinton. It may be that Leach is bluffing but such a move would be highly uncharacteristic according to close associates.

Safe House. As if this situation were not problematic enough for the White House, there are now serious questions about exactly where White House Deputy Counsel Vince Foster committed suicide. Again, we usually ignore Washington's regular stream of rumor mongering every time a President gets into trouble because the rumors are almost always untrue. In this case, however, the offices of Senate Finance Committee Chairman Moynihan are getting the word out that Foster in fact committed suicide in a private apartment in Virginia. That apartment (the Moynihan crew refers to it as a "safe house") was said to be used frequently by many of the senior White House staff as a place to wargame long term problems without the normal distractions of the West Wing.

According to Moynihan staff information, which is making its way through Capitol Hill, Foster's body was somehow later transferred to Fort Marcy Park along the Potomac River. Obviously, if this is true it complicates the situation for the White House to a significant degree.

RTC Briefing. Another mystery involving Whitewater is how Senate Banking Committee Member Phil Gramm knew that Deputy Treasury Secretary Roger Altman had taken the provocative step of briefing the White House on the RTC implications of scandal (Altman is acting head of the RTC). According to White House insiders, only a small group of individuals would have known that Altman was engaged in such private briefings. "That means one thing," a White House aide said, "Roger was assassinated. He was taken down by someone who clearly was not pleased with all the Deputy Treasury Secretary's positive press in recent months suggesting that he would be the certain next Treasury Secretary."

Of course, the problem for the White House was that when Altman admitted to the briefing (which later turned out to be more than one briefing) the entire situation exploded. Special Prosecutor Fiske suddenly saw his investigation compromised. He immediately blanketed the entire White House and Treasury operation involved with individual subpoenas. Be assured, this move has essentially paralyzed the top echelon of the United States government. Now, every senior Clinton official involved in Whitewater has retained individual legal counsel. And you can bet the first word of advice in each case was, "tell everything you know. Remember the Nixon guys."

New Agenda. This morning the top Clinton team met to discuss how to move the national agenda away from Whitewater. Indeed, communications advisor Dave Gergen pointed out how the White House needed a "circuit breaker"—an event to diffuse the current situation much the way Vice President Gore's debate with Ross Perot diffused the opposition last year to NAFTA and instantly changed the climate for the President. Vice President Gore in fact is said to have joined in in suggesting that the health care be the circuit breaker. In other words, the President at this point, with the help of the Democratic leadership, needs to strike an immediate compromise on health care so as to divert media attention away from Whitewater and create the impression of business as usual.

Clearly, this would be a sound strategic move were it not for the fact that these appear to be unlucky times for the President and Mrs. Clinton even in the case of their most prized legislative issue. We say "unlucky" because while a health care compromise would make sense, it is not a certainty at this point. The reason is that while the Clinton health care plan itself is all but dead on Capitol Hill, there is no logical compromise. For example, Democrats on both the Ways and Means and Commerce Committees are actually now moving toward compromise plans which incredibly are to the Left of the Clinton health care plan. White House aides worry that if a compromise were reached this week among the committee Democrats in the House, the actual outcome might be defeated when it came to the House floor. The reason: many moderate and conservative Democrats would bail out and support the certain Republican effort to kill the bill. "That's why we might have to begin in the Senate but even there Moynihan is not our friend and nothing would be easy," a Clintonite said.

But perhaps Bill Clinton's biggest obstacle in reaching a quick diversionary compromise on health care is Hillary Clinton herself. Top Clintonites say that the President would have compromised on health care a long time ago. Indeed, they say that Hillary's power was slipping quickly and a compromise with the more moderate Democratic position in the House was likely over the First Lady's objections. "But then something important happened," a Clinton insider told us this week, "the state trooper sex scandal hit the President like a ton of bricks. It was at that point that you could almost feel Hillary's power coming back in full force. She now had the moral high ground and the compromising spirit on health care evaporated."

The bottom line is that these are dog days for President and Mrs. Clinton. Of course, the climate could change rather quickly more to the positive. But for that to happen, the President above all needs Congress out of the picture on Whitewater plus some type of circuit breaker to divert attention. As one Clintonite put it, "Where is Saddam Hussein when we need him."

These are just some quick thoughts.

We will keep you posted.

JOHNSON SMICK INTERNATIONAL, INC.
1133 CONNECTICUT AVENUE, N.W.
SUITE 901
WASHINGTON, D.C. 20036

Telephone: (202) 861-0770
Telefax: (202) 861-0790

Johnson Smick International (JSI) is an international economic and financial consulting firm that specializes in major developments among the G7 and developing countries. JSI's central focus is both analyzing the potential for various policy actions and the impact such actions might have on international currency, credit, and equity markets. JSI services include client meeting with the partners and associates, telephone contacts, and telefaxed written reports.

Formed in 1985, JSI's first client was currency trader, George Soros. Since that time, JSI has worked closely with many of the world's leading hedge funds and major international financial institutions.

Since 1985, JSI has sponsored a number of high-level international economic policy conferences. Until becoming Chairman of the Federal Reserve System, Alan Greenspan served as moderator of the conferences. Participants have included heads of state and the finance ministers and central bank governors of every major industrialized country.

Appendix E

The following is Mortimer B. Zuckerman's editorial "The Real Whitewater Report" which ran in the January 29, 1996, issue of U.S. News & World Report; plus a breakdown of New York Times reporter Jeff Gerth's Whitewater allegations.

Have you no sense of decency, sir, at long last? Have you left no sense of decency? Forty years ago, Joseph Welch, a venerable Boston lawyer, thus rebuked Joe McCarthy in the Army-McCarthy hearings and stopped his reckless persecution of a naive but innocent young man. How one longs for a Joseph Welch to emerge in the middle of the extraordinary affair now known as Whitewater! The parallels between Sen. Alfonse D'Amato's investigation of a land deal in Arkansas and McCarthy's investigation of communism in the Army are hardly exact, but there is an uncanny echo of 1954 in the fever of political innuendo we are now experiencing and in the failure of an excitable press to set it all in proper perspective. Then, as now, the public found itself lost in a welter of allegation, reduced to mumbling the old line about "no smoke without fire."

It would be foolish to expect a congressional investigation to be above politics. But at what point, in a decent democracy, does politics have to yield to objectivity? At what point does rumor have to retreat before truth? In Whitewater that point would seem to have been reached when we have had an independent, exhaustive study of the case under the supervision of a former Republican U.S. attorney, Jay Stephens, a man whose credibility is enhanced by the fact that he was such a political adversary of the Clintons that his appointment provoked Clinton aide George Stephanopoulos to call for his removal. Yes? No. That official report is in, but hardly anyone who has been surfing the Whitewater headlines will know of it. It has been ignored by both the Republicans and a media hungry for scandal. The Stephens report provides a blow-by-blow account of virtually every charge involved in the Whitewater saga. Let us put the conclusions firmly on the record. The quotes below are directly from the Stephens report.

■ **Question 1:** Were the Clintons involved in the illegal diversion of any money from the failed Madison Guaranty Savings & Loan, either to their own pockets or to Clinton's 1984 gubernatorial campaign? "On this record, there is no basis to assert that the Clintons knew anything of substance about the McDougals' advances to Whitewater, the source of the funds used to make those advances, or the source of the funds used to make payments on bank debt...for the relevant period (ending in 1986), the evidence suggests that the McDougals and not the Clintons managed Whitewater."

■ **Question 2:** What of money diverted to the campaign? No evidence has been unearthed that any campaign worker for Clinton knew of any wrongdoing pertaining to any funds that might have come out of Madison into Clinton's campaign.

■ **Question 3:** Did taxpayers suffer from Whitewater through Madison's losses on the investment? No. Whitewater did not hurt Madison, the possible exceptions being a couple of payments involving James and Susan McDougal. The report says the Clintons knew nothing about the payments.

■ **Question 4:** Did the Clintons make any money? The report says they did not; instead, they borrowed $40,000 to put into Whitewater and lost it.

■ **Question 5:** What of the charge from David Hale, former municipal judge and Little Rock businessman, that Bill Clinton pressured him to make an improper Small Business Administration loan of $300,000 to Susan McDougal? As to the $300,000 loan to Mrs. McDougal, "there is nothing except an unsubstantiated press report David Hale claims then-Governor Clinton pressured him into making the loan to Susan McDougal." The charge lacked credibility in any event. It was made when Hale sought personal clemency in a criminal charge of defrauding the SBA.

What's left? Nothing. The report concludes: "On this record there is no basis to charge the Clintons with any kind of primary liability for fraud or intentional misconduct. This investigation has revealed no evidence to support any such claims. Nor would the record support any claim of secondary or derivative liability for the possible misdeeds of others."

Stephens's firm—Pillsbury, Madison & Sutro—spent two years and almost $4 million to reach its conclusions and recommended "that no further resources be expended on the Whitewater part of this investigation." Amen.

So when you cut through all the smoke from D'Amato's committee and almost hysterical press reports such as those emanating from the editorial page of the *Wall Street Journal,* what you have is smoke and no fire. No Whitewater wrongdoing to cover up, no incriminating documents to be stolen, no connection between the Clintons and any illegal activities from the real-estate business failure and the web of political and legal ties known as Whitewater.

But wait. What about the time sheets showing the amount of legal work that Hillary Clinton performed for the failed S&L? Surely we have some flames there? Again, no. Her role, says the Stephens report, was minimal. Mrs. Clinton did perform real-estate work in 1985 and 1986 pertaining to an option for about 2 percent of the land, but as the report says, that was at most related only tangentially to the acquisition itself. Mrs. Clinton did not play a legal part in the original acquisition of the land, known as Castle Grande, although the Rose Law Firm did. Both sides pointed out that the principals, as opposed to the lawyers, put together the deal. The lawyers did only the scrivener work, and if this transaction was a sham, there is "no substantial evidence that the Rose Law Firm knowingly and substantially assisted in its commission."

As for the option, the report says there is no evidence that Mrs. Clinton knew of any illegalities in this transaction: "The option did not assist in the closing of the acquisition. It...was created many months after the transaction closed. The option...does not prove any awareness on the part of its author of Ward's [Madison's partner] arrangements with Madison Financial...While Mrs. Clinton seems to have had some role in drafting the May 1, 1986, option, nothing proves that she did so knowing it to be wrong, and the theories that tie this option to wrongdoing or to the straw-man arrangements are strained at best."

Rep. James Leach's spokesman asserts that Hillary Clinton's minimal work on the option put her "at the center of a fraudulent deal," and D'Amato says that her billing records show tremendous inconsistencies with her previous statements on the time she spent on Whitewater. Fraud? The only fraud lies in these congressional statements; they are a political fraud on a credulous public. On the role of real-estate lawyers, I must endorse the Stephens judgments here from my personal business experience of thousands of real-estate transactions. Never, not once, have my lawyers drawing up legal documents determined the business terms or the appropriateness of the price.

It is appalling that the smoke and smear game has been played so long by the Republicans and the media that everyone is tagged with some kind of presumption of guilt rather than a presumption of innocence. The double standard of judgment is well illustrated by the performance of those standard-setting newspapers, the *New York Times* and the *Washington Post*. The *Times* originally broke the Whitewater story on its front page with a jump to a full inside page. What did it do with Stephens's report? Ran it on Page 12, in a 12-inch story. The *Post's* priorities were so distorted that it mentioned the findings in only the 11th paragraph of a front-page story devoted to a much less important Whitewater subpoena battle. Most other major papers ran very short stories on inside pages, and the networks virtually ignored the report.

The press has slipped its moorings here. It seems to be caught in a time warp from the Nixon-Watergate era. The two questions then—what did the President know and when did he know it?—

were at the very heart of the matter. The two questions now—
what did the president's wife know and when did she know it?—
seem a childish irrelevance by comparison. The time, money and
political energy spent barking up the wrong tree are quite amazing. The press gives the impression that it has invested so much
capital in the search for a scandal that it cannot drop it when the
scandal evaporates. The Republicans give the impression that if
one slander does not work, they will try another. No wonder the
nation holds Congress, the White House and the media in such
contempt; the people know that the press seems to be acting like
a baby—a huge appetite at one end and no sense of responsibility
at the other.

We have a topsy-turvy situation here. The Republicans win the
case on merit over balancing the budget but are losing it politically on the basis of public perception. The Clintons have the
better case on Whitewater but are losing it politically because of
smear and slander, a situation compounded by their defensive
behavior. The media seem unwilling to focus on the substance of
either issue. So much for a responsible press!

"The theory implicit in Gerth's Times *stories may be summarized as follows: when his business partner and benefactor McDougal got in trouble, Bill Clinton dumped the sitting Arkansas securities commissioner and appointed a hack, Beverly Bassett Schaffer. He and Hillary then pressured Bassett Schaffer to grant McDougal special favors—until the vigilant feds cracked down on Madison Guaranty, thwarting the Clinton's plan. This is the Received Version of the Whitewater scandal as it first took shape in the pages of the* New York Times—*what all the fuss is ultimately about. And it bears almost no relation to reality."*

— From "Fools for Scandal: How the *New York Times* Got Whitewater Wrong," Gene Lyons, *Harper's*, October 1994, p. 55

Jeff Gerth	Gene Lyons
Headline from Gerth's initial story—March 8, 1992: CLINTONS JOINED S&L OPERATOR IN AN OZARK REAL ESTATE VENTURE	This headline was misleading because when Bill and Hillary Clinton entered into the misbegotten partnership to subdivide and develop 230 forested acres along the White River as resort property in 1978, Jim McDougal wasn't involved in the banking and S&L businesses at all. He was a career political operative—a former aide to Senators J. William Fullbright and John L. McClellan. In the meantime, McDougal had done well in the Ozarks land boom of the '70s. But it wouldn't be until five years later—by which time the Whitewater investigation was already moribund—that he bought a controlling interest in Madison Guaranty.

Gerth	Lyons
Gerth wrote that McDougal quickly built Madison Guaranty "into one of the largest state-chartered associations in Arkansas."	Wrong again. Among 39 S&Ls listed in the 1985 edition of Sheshunoff's *Arkansas Savings and Loans*, Madison ranked 25th in assets and 30th in amount loaned. These errors in detail might be forgiven if Gerth had in fact uncovered a conspiracy between the Clintons and the Arkansas securities commissioner to treat Jim McDougal leniently. The appearance of conspiracy, however, was created not by the actions of the alleged parties but by selective reporting.
Of the appointment of Beverly Bassett Schaffer as Arkansas securities commissioner: "After Federal regulators found that Mr. McDougal's savings institution was insolvent, meaning it faced possible closure by the state, Mr. Clinton appointed a new state securities commissioner..."	The clear implication is that *in response* to a Federal Home Loan Bank Board report dated January 20, 1984, suggesting that Madison might be insolvent, Clinton in January 1985 installed Bassett Schaffer as Arkansas securities commissioner. So how come he waited an entire year? In reality, the timing of her appointment had nothing to do with the FHLBB report, which there's no reason to think Clinton knew about. (The Clintons had no financial stake in Madison Guaranty, although that, too, has been obscured.) The fact is that Bill Clinton *had* to find a new commissioner in January 1985 because the incumbent, Lee Thalheimer, had resigned to re-enter private practice.

Gerth	Lyons

[In 1984], Madison started getting in trouble. Federal examiners studied its books that year, found that it was violating Arkansas regulations and determined that correcting the books to adjust the improperly inflated profits would "result in an insolvent position," records of the 1984 examination show.

Arkansas regulators received the Federal report later that year, and under state law the securities commissioner was supposed to close any insolvent institution.

As the Governor is free to do at any time, Mr. Clinton appointed a new securities commissioner in 1985. He chose Beverly Bassett Schaffer...

In interviews, Mrs. Schaffer, now a Fayetteville lawer, said she did not remember the Federal examination of Madison, but added that, in her view, the findings were not "definitive proof of insolvency."

The title page of the document from which Gerth took the one brief passage he cited stipulated that it had "been prepared for supervisory purposes only and should not be considered an audit report," although Gerth neglected to point this out.

The Arkansas Securities Department's power to close ailing S&Ls was mostly theoretical. Basset Schaffer's office had no plenary authority to shut S&Ls down and seize their assets.

True. In a letter dated September 11, 1984, the FHLBB gave Madison formal approval of a debt restructuring plan that "negat[ed] the need for adjustment of $564,705 in improperly recognized profits" and dropped all references to insolvency. Arkansas officials also called Gerth's attention to an independent 1984 audit that also refuted Madison's insolvency. In his story, the reporter neglected to mention either document.

Gerth	Lyons

From the March 8, 1992, article:

In 1985, Mrs. Clinton and her Little Rock law firm, the Rose Firm, twice applied to the Arkansas Securities Commission on behalf of Madison, asking that the savings and loan be allowed to try two novel plans to raise money.

For Hillary Rodham Clinton to have ventured anywhere near Madison in any capacity was a damn fool thing to do. But the fact is that her entire involvement in the "novel" stock issue consisted of the mention of her name in a letter written by a junior member of the Rose Law Firm expressing the opinion that it would be permissible under state law for Madison Guaranty to make a preferred stock offering.

And from his December 15, 1993, story with the fellow *Times* writer Stephen Engleberg:

Just a few weeks after Mr. McDougal raised the money for [Governor Clinton] Madison Guaranty won approval from Mrs. Schaffer, Mr. Clinton's new financial regulator, for a novel plan to sell stock.

Now, what made Madison Guaranty's plan "novel" is hard to say. The vast majority of state-regulated S&Ls in 1985 issued stock. Even so, the adjective, with its implication of wrongdoing, has recurred mantra-like in virtually every Whitewater roundup article since.

March 8, 1992, article:

Mrs. Schaffer wrote to Mrs. Clinton and another lawyer at the firm approving the ideas. "I never gave anybody special treatment," she said.

Madison was not able to raise additional capital. And by 1986 Federal regulators, who insured Madison's deposits, took control of the institution and ousted Mr. McDougal. Mrs. Schaffer supported the action.

After studying the applicable statutes and consulting with her staff, Bassett Schaffer agreed [with the legal opinion expressed by the junior member of the Rose Law Firm mentioned above]. "Arkansas law," she wrote in a two-paragraph letter dated May 14, 1985—the now-famous Dear Hillary missive—"expressly gives state-chartered associations all the powers given regular business corporations... including the power to authorize and issue preferred capital stock."

Gerth	Lyons

The perception that Gerth most resents is the one most talked about in Arkansas: his reliance upon the hidden hand of Sheffield Nelson—Clinton's 1990 Republican gubernatorial opponent and a legendary political infighter. The *Times* reporter insists that Nelson did no more than give him Jim McDougal's phone number and later introduce him to former Judge David Hale, whose defense attorney is Nelson's associate.

Nelson, the Republican nominee for governor again in 1994, tends to be coy about his role. But he has given other reporters a 38-page transcript of an early 1992 conversation between himself and McDougal, then embittered by what he saw as Clinton's abandonment. Indeed, Jeff Gerth, Sheffield Nelson, and the *New York Times* go way back. As long ago as 1978, Gerth ran a well-timed exposé of Nelson's mortal foes Witt and Jack Stephens—the billionaire natural-gas moguls and investment bankers who ran Arkansas like a company store back in the Orval Faubus era (1955–67).

The same faults that mar Jeff Gerth's reporting on Whitewater—mis-
leading innuendo and ignorance or suppression of exculpatory facts—
also showed up in the Times *accounts of Hillary Rodham Clinton's com-*
modity trades with Springfield attorney Jim Blair and her husband's
dealings with Tyson Foods.

Gerth	**Lyons**
March 8, 1994, front-page account: During Mr. Clinton's tenure in Arkansas, Tyson benefited from a variety of state actions, including $9 million in government loans, the placement of company executives on important state boards, and favorable decisions on environmental issues.	The alleged $9 million in loans was the implied quid pro quo for old pal Blair's generous tips to Hillary in the 1970s that helped her turn $1,000 into nearly $100,000. Following Gerth's report, the incriminating $9 million figure appeared virtually everywhere [*Times* editorial, the *Baltimore Sun*, *Newsweek*]. There's just one problem with this chorus of self-righteous denunciation: the $9 million figure that inspired it never existed. Especially attentive readers of the *New York Times* may have noticed an odd little item in the daily "Corrections" column on April 20, 1994:

An article on March 18 about Hillary Rodham Clinton's commodity trades misstated benefits that the Tyson Foods company received from the state of Arkansas. Tyson did not receive $9 million in loans from the state; the company did benefit at least $7 million in state tax credits, according to a Tyson spokesman.

Gerth blames a chart misread on deadline. |

Gerth	Lyons

In the journalistic equivalent of double jeopardy, the *Times* editors, having convicted Hillary Clinton on a spurious charge, decided she was guilty of a new charge: helping Tyson Foods to get that $7 million in tax credits. No sooner had she held her April 22 press conference on Whitewater-related issues than the *Times* fretted that the first lady's performance had been smooth but cleverly evasive. Particularly suspicious, an April 24 editorial found, were her dealing with Jim Blair, "a lawyer for Tyson Foods, a large company that was heavily regulated by and received substantial tax credits from the Arkansas government." [Emphasis added.] And people call the President slick!

The truth is far less lurid. The $7 million in investment tax credits Tyson Foods claimed against its Arkansas state tax bill after 1985— that is, between 7 and 14 years after Hillary's commodity trades— were written into the state's revenue code and were never Bill Clinton's to bestow or withhold.

Gerth	Lyons

Besides the imaginary $9 million in loans, Gerth cited several other suspicious transactions, among them a bitter court battle over polluted ground water in which the Clinton Administration "failed to take any significant action," and a pair of seemingly failed appointments—including renaming a Tyson veterinarian to the state Livestock and Poultry Commission and Jim Blair to the University of Arkansas board.

An objective account of the court battle would have pointed out that the city of Green Forest was itself a defendant in the same lawsuit. Bill Clinton was not. Officials of the Arkansas Department of Pollution Control and Ecology testified for the plaintiffs against Tyson Foods. So much for yet another dark Clintonian conspiracy.

Reappointing a Tyson veterinarian to the Livestock and Poultry Commission? Clinton is guilty as charged. Except that the fellow happens to be the state's ranking expert on chicken diseases, the prevention and treatment of which is the commission's principal task.

As for naming Jim Blair to the University of Arkansas Board? Well, it's a great honor, and Blair can undeniably score great Razorback tickets. Otherwise, where's the scandal? At any rate, Blair wasn't a Tyson employee back when he and Hillary did their cattle trades. He was in private practice as one of Springdale's most prominent corporate attorneys, representing banks, trucking companies, insurance firms, and poultry interests.

Gerth	Lyons
All of this raises the really interesting question at the heart of the Whitewater scandal: Why, with representatives of the vaunted national press camped out in Little Rock for weeks at a time, squinting over aged public documents and pontificating nightly at the Capital Hotel Bar, has nobody blown the whistle on Gerth and the *New York Times*?	There are several reasons, ambition and fear among them. It is always safest to run with the pack, and editors who invest thousands of dollars on a scandal don't normally want to hear that there's no scandal to be found. Reporters who have challenged aspects of the official version, like Greg Gordon and Tom Hamburger of the Minneapolis *Star Tribune* and John Camp of CNN, have not found their celebrity enhanced.

Regional bias and cultural condescension play a part, too. How could the New York Times *be wrong and the* Arkansas Times *be right? But even if Bill Clinton had been governor of Connecticut instead of Arkansas, in the post-Watergate, post-everythinggate culture no reporter wishes to appear insufficiently prosecutorial—particularly not when the suspects are the president and his wife. By definition they've got to be guilty of something; it may as well be Whitewater.*

Appendix F

The following is an article titled "Now It's Starr Who Needs to Be Investigated: The counsel's witnesses, friends and benefactors appear involved in an anti-Clinton 'project'" by Robert Scheer, which ran in the March 31, 1998, issue of the Los Angeles Times.

Leads that Kenneth Starr would pursue if he were the least bit nonpartisan:

Did convicted felon David Hale, while providing testimony as Starr's key Whitewater witness, receive cash payments funneled through the *American Spectator* magazine from foundations controlled by right-wing billionaire Richard Mellon Scaife, who had established a project to discredit Clinton? Was Hale influenced by free use of a car and a fishing cabin provided by an Arkansas man who was being paid by the *American Spectator* to provide the magazine with information on the Whitewater case?

These are among allegations reported recently by the Associated Press, the *New York Observer* and the online magazine *Salon*. According to news reports, Scaife funded a nearly $2-million "Arkansas project" over four years to dig up dirt on Clinton. Parker Dozhier, a Hot Springs, Ark., bait shop owner, admitted to AP reporter Karen Gullo that during the time he received about $35,000 from the Spectator to supply information on Whitewater, he provided free use of a car and a cabin to Hale, who was then supplying information to Starr. FBI agents reporting to Starr accompanied Hale on trips to the cabin, where he reportedly met with representatives of Scaife's anti-Clinton project.

Funeral home assistant manager Caryn Mann, who was Dozhier's live-in girlfriend and bookkeeper, told Salon she witnessed Dozhier making cash payments to Hale. Mann's 17-year-old son, Joshua Rand, said he also observed the payments. According to Salon, Dozhier denied making the payments and said the boy was "destined to be a chalk outline somewhere." Mann told *Salon* that Dozhier also threatened her "if I ever talked about what he was doing against Clinton."

Mann told reporters that while she kept Dozhier's books, there were regular checks coming in to him from David Henderson, vice president of the American Spectator Educational Foundation, which runs the magazine, and from attorney Stephen Boynton, who received $1.7 million from the foundation. According to the *Observer*, those funds can be traced back to Scaife.

Mann told AP that Hale frequently discussed the Whitewater case with her, Boynton, Henderson and Dozhier outside the presence of the FBI agents accompanying Hale. Dozhier denied that Hale provided him with Whitewater information. Dozhier told the AP that he began to give Hale use of his cabin in 1994. That's when Hale emerged as a key witness in the Whitewater case.

The AP reported Saturday that Mann has been interviewed twice recently by FBI agents dispatched not by Starr but by the U.S. attorney in western Arkansas and was asked to turn over documents. Mann told the AP these agents focused on whether Dozhier or *Spectator* officials gave Hale money or sought to influence his testimony. Boynton denies facilitating payments to Hale but concedes he struck up a relationship with him in 1993 when the ex-judge ran into legal trouble.

The connections between *Scaife*, the *Spectator*, Boynton and the Arkansas project were explored by reporter Joe Conason in the *New York Observer*, which obtained the *Spectator's* tax returns. According to those records, the *Observer* reported, the magazine received $2.4 million from Scaife foundations between 1993 and 1996. Boynton's $1.7 million was listed as legal fees, but the Spectator's financial statements recorded less than $500,000 for "professional services," which included legal fees.

The *Observer* reported that Ronald Burr, *Spectator* publisher for more than 30 years, grew concerned that spending tax-exempt money on the Clinton project could jeopardize the magazine's tax-exempt status and requested an outside audit of the Boynton funds. Burr was abruptly ousted and paid a settlement on the condition that he remain silent about the situation. Some *Spectator* writers, including P.J. O'Rourke, resigned over Burr's treatment, the *Washington Post* reported.

Instead of the outside audit, the Spectator undertook an internal review headed by one of its own board members and its legal counsel, Theodore Olson. Olson, a longtime friend and former law partner of Starr, was hired by Hale to represent him in Washington on Whitewater matters.

Scaife contributed more than $1 million to establish Pepperdine University's new Public Policy School, which Starr will head when he finishes with Clinton. Asking Starr to look into this complex web surrounding his key witness and involving his friends and benefactors is asking him to investigate himself.

It's obviously time for a new independent counsel to investigate the independent counsel.

Copyright 1998, *Los Angeles Times.* Reprinted by permission.

INDEX

A

ABC, 74, 77, 120, 181, 242–43, 252–53
Accuracy in Media, 80, 152
Aldrich, Gary, 181–88, 204–5, 272
Alter, Jonathan, 167–68
American Journalism Review, 200
American Lawyer magazine, 78
American Spectator magazine, 30, 73, 117, 123, 188, 189, 204, 207, 272
Americans for Tax Reform, 122
Anderson, Ronnie, 73, 192, 194, 208
Annenberg School for Communications, U. of Pennsylvania, 239–40
Anthony, Beryl, 147
Anthony, Sheila, 147
Arkansas Appeals Tribunal, 29–30, 36–41
Arkansas Democrat-Gazette, 16–18, 23, 81, 99, 159, 160
Arkansas Department of Corrections, 41–42
Arkansas Department of Finance and Administration, 41–42
Arkansas Development Finance Agency, 155–58
and Clinton, Bill, 18–19
and Contras, 14
and Nichols, Larry, 14–19
Arkansas Historical Heritage, 37–38
Arkansas Industrial Development Commission, 72
Arkansas State Troopers, 22, 26–27, 30, 50–51, 73, 123, 188–92, 194–98, 272
Associated Press, 15, 47, 166, 189
Atwater, Lee, 117–20

B

Bad Boy: The Life and Politics of Lee Atwater, 119
Baird, Zoe, 147
Bakker, Jim, 165
Ballantine, Debra, 77, 78, 88
Battley, Jackie, 245
Begala, Paul, 257–58
Bell, Chris, 13–14
Bennett, Bob, 79, 81
Bennett, William, 162
Blackard, Pamela, 77, 78, 87, 88, 100
Blood Sport, 202–3
Blue Room Christmas tree ornaments, 183, 185, 187
Bonior, David, 212
Boston Globe, 251
Bowen, Bill, 22
Bradley, Ed, 75, 95–96, 98
Brady, John, 118–19
Breaking the News: How the Media Undermine Democracy, 127,

131–32, 274
Brock, David, 30–31, 57, 58, 73, 108–9, 130, 183, 185, 186–87, 188–89, 203–9, 238, 271–73
Broder, David, 253
Brown, Charlotte, 95–98, 104
Brown, L.D., 273
Brown, Mark, 71
Brown, Ron, 120, 162
Bruce W. Eberle and Associates, Inc. See Eberle, Bruce W. and Associates
Bryan, Willie, 230
Bryant, John, 243–44
Buchanan, Bay, 206
Buchanan, Pat, 221
Buckley, William F., Jr., 117
Burden of Proof, broadcast, 83
Burr, Aaron, 10
Bush, George, 118, 221, 227
Butler, Jon, 133

C

Callender, James, 8, 136–37, 249
Cammarata, Joseph, 75, 79–80, 81, 82–83, 94–95, 104
Campbell, Donovan, Jr., 84, 104
Capital Gang, 232–33, 253
broadcasts, 247
Carlson, Margaret, 244–45
Carpenter-McMillan, Susan, 81, 83, 92, 103–6
and Jones, Paula, 82–84
Carson, H.R. "Kit", 225, 228, 240
Carter, L.H. "Kip," 245–46
Carville, James, 154
Cato Institute, 124, 206
CBS Evening News, broadcast, 189
Center for Media and Public Affairs, 253
Central Intelligence Agency, 177–78
Chicago Tribune, 104–6, 252, 256
Christian American magazine, 175
Christian Broadcasting Network, 171, 173
Christian Coalition, 166, 174, 244
Circle of Power, videotape, 23
Citizens for a Sound Economy, 125
Citizens for Honest Government, 155, 169
Citizens United, 29
Clark, Cara, 37, 39–40
Clark, Roy, 26, 28, 33, 34
Clift, Eleanor, 232
Clinton, Bill, 121
accused, 156–62, 167–68, 200
Contra support, 22–23
drug and gun smuggling, 22–23
illicit romances, 22–23, 27, 182–83
misuse of state employees, 23, 26–27
misuse of state vehicles, 23, 26–27

presidential campaign slush fund, 27
and Arkansas Development Finance Agency, 18–19
"distinguishing characteristics," 82, 88, 92–95
and Flowers, Gennifer, 18–19, 27–30, 35–36, 41, 63–65
tape recordings of, 14, 28–30, 42–48, 52–56
and Foster, Vince, 147
interview with 60 Minutes, 63–66
and Jones, Paula, 11–12, 72, 73, 75–76, 78, 79, 87–88, 89, 109
and LA Airport haircut, 251
and Nichols, Larry, 21, 22, 23
and Republicans, 52, 56
and Willey, Kathleen, 101–2
Clinton, Chelsea, 211–14
Clinton, Hillary, 124, 204–6, 268, 271
and Foster, Vince, 182–83
interview with 60 Minutes, 63–66
and Limbaugh, Rush, 236–39
Clinton Chronicles, videotape, 23, 77, 85, 154–62, 166–70, 197, 199–200, 240
Clinton health-care plan, 124–27, 237
CNBC, 167, 226, 273
CNN, 77, 83, 166, 188–89, 191, 232–33, 247
broadcasts, 73–74
Colford, Paul, 230–32
Collins, Mary Ann, 26
Columbia Journalism Review, 138
Competitive Enterprise Institute, 125
Conason, Joe, 83, 203
Concepts Plus, 56
Conservative Political Action Conference, 75
Contract with America, 127, 175
Contras, 14, 16
Cook, George, 74
Cossack, Roger, 83
Coughlin, Father Charles E., 163–64
Crane, Ed, 124
Crocker, Harry, 186–87
Crossfire, 77, 166–67, 271
Crosswell, Harry, 136–37
Crowe, David, 223
C-SPAN, 85–86, 189, 207

D

Dallas Morning News, 251
D'Amato, Alfonse, 142–43, 196
Dateline NBC, 192, 194–95
Davidson, James Dale, 153
Davis, Gilbert, 75, 79–80, 81, 94–95, 104
Davis, L.J., 158–59, 214–15
DeGeneres, Ellen, 238